RURAL SOCIOLOGY

RURAL SOCIOLOGY

Dr. Gajanafar Alam

CENTRUM PRESS
NEW DELHI-110002 (INDIA)

CENTRUM PRESS
H.O.: 4360/4, Ansari Road, Daryaganj,
New Delhi-110002 (India)
Tel: 23278000, 23261597, 23255577, 23286875
B.O.: No. 1015, Ist Main Road, BSK IIIrd Stage,
IIIrd Phase, IIIrd Block, Bangalore-560085 (INDIA)
Tel: 080-41723429
Email: centrumpress@gmail.com
Visit us at: www.centrumpress.com

Rural Sociology

First Edition, 2011

ISBN 978-93-80921-56-3

PRINTED IN INDIA

Printed at Tarun Offset Printers, Delhi-110053

Contents

Preface

Rural life is the principal pivot around which whole Indian social life revolves. India is a land of agriculture. Its history, customs and traditions, complex social organization and unity in diversity etc. can be understood by the study of rural life. Rural sociology is the scientific study of rural society. It involves a systematic study of rural society, its institutions, activities, interactions and social change. It not only deals with the social relationships of man in a rural environment but also takes urban surroundings into consideration for a comparative study. According to A.R Desai rural sociology should be to make a systematic, scientific and comprehensive study of the rural social organization of its structure, function and objective tendencies of development and on the basis of such a study to discover the laws of its development.

T.L Smith says that some investigators study social phenomena that are present only in or largely confined to the rural environment to persons engaged in agricultural occupation. Such sociological aspects and principles as one derived from the study of rural social relationships may be referred to as rural sociology. Bertrand has observed that in the broadest definition rural sociology is the study of human relationships in rural environment. Rural sociology is a holistic study of rural social setting. It provides us with valuable knowledge about the rural social phenomena and social problems which helps us in understanding rural society and making prescriptions for its all round progress and prosperity.

In India the importance of rural sociology gained recognition after independence. The agrarian context occupies special status both in the social scientific literature on India and in the literature on agrarian societies in general. However unlike studies on caste, kinship, village community, gender, study of agrarian relations did not occupy a central position in Indian sociology. The first systematic study of rural India was done by D.N Majumdar followed by N.K Bose, S.C Dubey, M.N Shrinivas. However it was with the publication of Andre 'Be'teille's Studies in Agrarian Social Structure in 1974 that agrarian sociology gained professional respectability within the two disciplines. Peasant studies in a way arrived in India with village studies. The collection of essays, Village India, edited by Marriot with its emphasis on little communities and great communities was brought out under the direct supervision of Robert Redfield. By defining little communities not in relation to land but through other social institutions such as kinship, religion and the social organization of caste there was a shift away from looking at the rural population in relation to agriculture and land. Caste hierarchy came to be defined in terms of ritual or social interaction over institutions of commensality and marriage.

According to Nelson up to the comparatively recent times the story of man is largely the story of rural man. So rural society is the basic foundation of human life, the keystone of the developmental process and the basic unit of social structure. Villages have been in existence since time immemorial unlike cities which are of more recent origin. In the Indian context rural sociology is of greater significance of the following reasons. According to S.C Dubey from time immemorial village has been a basic and important unit in the organization of Indian social life. Unique nature of transformation of Indian society where elements of traditional and modern cultures have been juxtaposed. For rural development and solution of rural problems according to A.R Desai this systematic study of rural organization of its structure; function and evolution has not only become necessary but also urgent after the advent of independence. Growing influence of industrialization and urbanization. Village as the basic unit of study. Scientific study of village community is a prerequisite for democratic decentralization. In modern India, the need of rural sociology is very urgent and it is progressive social science gaining importance.

The aim of the book is to put researchers engaged in different areas of research on a common platform so as to be benefited by the current state of knowledge in the field of this subject.

1

Introduction

Rural sociology is a field of sociology associated with the study of social life in non-metropolitan areas. It is the scientific study of social arrangements and behaviour amongst people distanced from points of concentrated population or economic activity. Like any sociological discipline, rural sociology involves the examination of statistical data, interviews, social theory, observation, survey research, and many other techniques.

In contrast to rural sociology, urban sociology is the study of urban social life.

Agribusiness is one focus of rural sociology and much of the field is dedicated to the economics of farm production. Other areas of study include rural migration and other demographic patterns, environmental sociology, amenity-led development, public lands policies, so-called "boomtown" development, social disruption, rural health care and education polices, etc.

Rural sociology became prominent during the late industrial revolution in France, Ireland, Prussia, Scandinavia, and the US. As urban incomes and quality of life rose, a social gap appeared between urban and rural dwellers.

Early works of Max Weber in the late 19th century has been concerned with rural sociology. It was first coined in USA.

Origin and Development of Rural Sociology

Rural sociology is a new branch of sociology with studies being carried out from 19th century. The prominent scholars engaged in rural sociology during this period were-Sir Henry

Maine, Etton, Stemann, Baden Powell, Slater and Pallock etc. The period of 1890-1920 in America saw the rural societies facing many socio-economic problems which attracted the attention of the intelligentsia thus establishing study of rural society as an academic discipline. The appointment of Country life Commission by Theodore Roosevelt was an important landmark in the history of rural sociology. In 1916 the first text book on sociology was published by J.N Gillettee.

It was first originated in the United States of America. It has taken more than half a century to become established as a distinct academic field or professional study. The main contributors to the development of rural sociology are-Charles Sanderson, Burtherfield, Ernast Burnholme, John Morris Gillin, Franklin H. Giddings and Thomas Nixon Carver. It was President Roosevelt who, through the appointment of 'Country Life Commission' gave a good encouragement to the development to the rural sociology in 1908. The report of this Commission encouraged the studies of rural society.

In 1917 the Department of Rural Sociology was set up by the American Sociological Society. In 1919, a 'Rural Sociology Department' was established under the chairmanship of Dr. C. J. Galpin. The Great Depression of 1930 provided another stimulus to the growth of rural sociology.

In 1937, 'Rural Sociological Society' was formed. It started publishing a professional journal 'Rural Sociology' containing results of rural sociological research. C. J. Galpin of University of Wisconsin developed techniques for defining and delimiting the rural community. His approach is still popular today.

The Great Second World War gave yet another fillip to the growth of rural sociology. The destruction caused by the war demanded reconstruction. The reconstruction work brought further encouragement to the science. By 1958 there were about 1000 professional rural sociologists in America. Rural sociology crossed the boundaries of America and became popular in Europe. A European Society for Rural Sociology was formed in 1957, and a similar organisation was started in Japan also. In developing countries, the role of the rural sociologists is primarily in the applied field of more effective planning and operation of rural community development programmes.

The Second World War caused heavy destruction and damage to human society which needed reconstruction. As a result rural sociology got an impetus in USA. The main concern of rural sociology came to be the understanding and diagnosing of the social and economic problems of farmers. More emphasis was placed on issues such as the internal structures of community life and the changing composition of rural populations than on their relationships with land or the social aspects of agricultural production.

Theoretically rural sociology remained caught up in bipolar notions of social change whereas rural often got defined as the opposite of urban. Rurality was conceptualized as an autonomous sociological reality. The identification of rural sociology with rural society has also raised questions about its relevance in the western context where no rural areas were left anymore and almost the entire population had become urbanized.

In response to these critiques of rural sociology a new sub-discipline of sociology emerged that operated largely within the functionalist paradigm and was preoccupied with the study of the community life of rural people. This sub-discipline known as sociology of agriculture focused its attention on understanding and analysing the social framework of agricultural production and the structures of relations centered on land. It raised questions about how and on what terms the agrarian sector was being integrated into the system of commodity production and about the unequal distribution of agricultural incomes and food among the different social categories of people.

The sociology of agriculture also distinguished itself from peasant studies on the grounds that its focus was on capitalist farming where the production was primarily for the market, not on peasants producing for their own consumption by using family labour. Thus it claimed more kinship with the tradition of the political economy of agriculture or agrarian studies. At the methodological level, historical inquiries became as relevant as ethnographic/empirical studies. This conceptual shift during the early 1970s also helped in bringing sociologists working on agrarian issues in the western countries closer to those concerned with agrarian transformations in the third world.

Scope of Rural Sociology

The scope or subject-matter of rural sociology is basically the study of rural society with all its complexities. According to Lawry and Nelson, 'The subject-matter of rural sociology is the description and analysis of the progress of various groups as they exist in the rural environment.' The main tasks of rural sociology can be mentioned here. They are as follows,

1. Rural Community and Rural Problems.

   This includes the characteristics and nature of rural community and its problems.

2. Rural Social Life.

   This includes various aspects of the rural people.

3. Rural Social Organization.

   This includes the study of various rural social organizations and institutions including family and marriage.

4. Rural Social Institutions and Structure.

   This includes the study of dogmas, customs, traditions, morals, conventions, practices and various political, economic, religious and cultural institutions

5. Rural Planning and Reconstruction.

   Rural sociology has great practical applications. Hence rural planning and reconstruction are also the main tasks of rural sociology to be dealt with.

6. Social Change and Social Control in Rural Social Setup: It is here we study the impact of city on rural life. The mechanisms of social control of the rural society are also examined here.

7. Religion and Culture in Rural Society.

   Religion plays an important role in the rural set up. Culture of rural society exhibits striking peculiarities. These come within the domain of rural sociology.

8. Rural Social Processes.

   Different social processes such as cooperation, competition, integration, differentiation, isolation etc., that take place in rural society are also studied in rural sociology.

9. Differences between Urban and Rural Society.

   The study of rural society includes the differences between urban and rural society also.

Importance of Rural Sociology

The practical value of the study of rural sociology is widely recognised today. As long as the villages and the rural society assume importance, the rural sociology shall continue to acquire importance. The value of rural sociology can be understood by the following points:

1. Rural Population is in Majority: The world's is more rural than urban. More than two-third of people of the world live in villages. It is the village that forms the basis of society. Rural sociology is inevitable for the study of the majority of the population.
2. Intimate Relationship between the Land and Man: Man is born out of land and his entire culture depends on it. Land has been the part of and parcel of human life. Progress starts from the village. The type of land partially conditions the type of society and the opportunities for human development. This close relationship between man and land has also been recognised by economists and political scientists.
3. Villages and Rural Life from the Source of Population: Cities normally grow out of towns and villages. No city can come into existence all of a sudden without having a rural background. A village, when improved and thickly populated, becomes a town or city. Thus it is the village population that forms the source of urban life.
4. Psychological Approach to the Rural Life: Rural progress, rural reconstruction or improvement of rural societies is possible only when the people have correct idea about the rural way of life and problems. Rural sociology touches upon the rural psychology and provides a good understanding of the rural people and their society.

"All of us know," for example, that people prefer to live in cities because there are more opportunities, services, and great personal fulfillment. "Everyone knows" that successful business and economic development must stay focused on metropolitan locations to maximize transportation and labor costs. "Everyone knows" that many of our small towns and villages are in distress and that even though the *unsettling* of the countryside may be a national tragedy, it amounts to no more than a natural process that will continue to occur over the next century.

Defining Rural

There are many ways to define areas that are "rural." Although the general idea of specifically conceptualizing "rural" areas came into use in the 1920s with its basis in sociology, many, if not most, of the current explanatory frameworks evolved to provide guidance for the distribution of government monies or to perform a census of places and people. As a corollary to these classification systems, there persists the traditional assumptions that tend to go along with the word "rural," assumptions that are often ungrounded and at best belie the diversity inherent in areas typically grouped together as "rural" or "nonmetropolitan." For instance, it is a commonly held belief that farming is a mainstay of most rural economies. In fact, fewer than one-fifth of rural counties in North America now have a significant economic dependence on farming, and the 20% of nonmetro counties that have farming as their principal economic base contain less than 10% of the nonmetro population (Deavers, 1992). Moreover, the geopolitical boundaries that usually serve as the basis for these classifications often are not optimal.

The Urban-Rural Imbalance

Since 1950 it should be clear that metropolitan settlement structure leading to urban conglomerations is the dominant growth form of the world. Metropolitan areas will account for 70 percent of the net growth in world population during the 1990s-an additional 67 million people every year. Other than natural increase, the prime engine of metropolitan growth is rural-to-urban migration. It is, however, important to note that rural-to-metropolitan trends have changed directions several times in the latter part of the 20 Century. It would appear that change, rather than stability, is the typical demographic and economic situation for most of the world's rural and nonmetropolitan areas at the end of the 20th Century.

The United Nations reports that 43 percent of the world's population lived in urban areas in 1990; a 34 percent increase since 1960. In the next several years (2005), the world will pass a historic milestone: more than half of its population — or more than three billion people — will live in cities. At the turn of the century, only 14 percent of the Earth's population called cities home — and just 11 centres on the planet had more than one million inhabitants.

Now there are 400 cities with populations of at least one million, and 20 megacities with populations exceeding 10 million, with a half dozen of them approaching or exceeding the 20 million level. While the developing world still flocks to core cities, much of Europe, North America, the Russian Federation, and Australia are reversing the process: emptiness at the center and growth on the edges-or the new "Edge City" metropolitan areas.

At the halfway mark of the 21st Century, more than 70 percent of the world's population will live within the metropolitan framework (an area now loosely defined up to 40-100 kilometres from the older urban cores). In most more developed nations, especially in North America and Europe, the urban-rural distribution now stands at 75-80 percent metropolitan to 20-25 percent rural.

The most common factor contributing to rural-to-urban migration is rural unemployment resulting in part from rural areas having higher fertility levels than urban areas, according to Lori S. Ashford, a senior policy analyst with the Population Reference Bureau (PRB). A shortage of basic technology in rural areas also promotes out-migration and environmental degradation; it has led to a serious shortage of arable land in many communities throughout the developing world. While the growth of cities can contribute to economic progress, the study notes that problems arise when urbanization "occurs so rapidly that it strains the ability of urban governments to provide housing, sanitation, public safety, and other necessary services—and when there are not enough jobs."

The New Paradigm

The relationship between government and economic development began to change marked during the late 1970's and early 1980's. The beginning of the 1980's saw many less developed countries heavily borrowed and unable to service their debt. The physical plant and infrastructure fashioned in the 1950s and 1960s-often of exceptionally poor quality-created high levels of service costs that even the most developed nations could not bear. Hardest hit were the rural economies and regional settlement patterns resulting in a virtually unabated flow of resources to the metropolitan areas. The final result was the beginning of the demise of the centrally-planned economy and the ushering of the "Age of Austerity." The concept of integrated population and development planning had to be adjusted in light of the changes brought about by this austerity.

Many planners and development analysts regarded the goals of development under austerity as self-evident and non-problematic, seeing the only problems as concerning how to attain them. The new paradigm recognized that both the environment and human settlement where *open* systems and regulated by things happening beyond local and national boundaries-*the Global Economy*-and greatly affected by natural and human imbalances. In short, the *urbancentric* view of the world was called into question, especially the prevalent notion that the purpose of rural areas was to provide food, fuel, and cheap workers. The new paradigm not only recognizes the connectivity of the urban-rural spheres, but also addresses the issue of rural vitality. For, unless rural areas are revitalized, the metropolitan centres must ultimately provide the rescue funds and resources to support the countryside. The solution is what we typically call *economic development.* In principle, the new paradigm called for self-sustaining economic growth and social policy designed to provide the requisites of existence and citizenship. While the former can help provide the fuel for the latter, we must be under no illusion that growth itself will fulfil basic needs.

The New Century Approach to Rural Planning

The most important question to be asked is "are rural areas and country towns sustainable as working and living communities?" Many rural areas have proven to be *persistent*-they have sustained while both inner city and suburban area have declined in the face of metropolitan spread. The only reasonable conclusion that can be reached concerning this persistence is their *diversity*. Less than a century ago the rural economy depended almost entirely on resource extraction, agriculture (and support service to agriculture), and fishing.

Economic Diversity

The rural areas that show the most favorable growth and economic strength have their economies based on recreation and tourism. Throughout most of North and South America, Western Europe, Australia, and New Zealand the lure of the natural environment and tourism (place and historicity) are significant parts of their economies. Firms and industries built around the exploitation of amenities show exceptionally strong growth and are a world leader in providing new jobs.

Are rural economies built around tourism and amenities sustainable? Thought on this question is decidedly mixed and generally negative. Tourism, in one form or another is the world's second largest industry. As a whole, this activity *mines* and *extracts* wealth in the form of money and exports the final resources to metropolitan areas where the corporations and trusts reside. Tourism is dependent on wealth and increasing affluence-it is not an activity within reach of the world's poor. Thus, there is a closed cycle of events whereby tourism and amenity based economies demand ever increasing affluence and affluence itself is associated with migration to metropolitan areas. Tourism and amenity jobs are among the lowest paying service industries in the world-or what is termed minimum or subsistence wage in most countries. The firms that service the local industries are labor intensive and built around employment in food service, lodging and accommodation, information assistance, maintenance, and service sales to the travelling public. Since most tourism is seasonal, the industry depends on high migration rates based on *boom and bust* seasons that in turn demand the cheapest labor available. Factors such as poor seasonal weather, higher transportation costs due to both profit taking and increasing costs for fuels can send a local economy into shambles within a short period of time-causing some of the highest unemployment rates in any industry. Finally, there is the long term (and often conflicting) goal of greater economic sustainability in local areas based on tourism and amenities. The goal is to extend visiting seasons by creating greater opportunity to capture market share of tourism monies. Since 1980 the most popular methods in the western world are gaming or gambling, conventions/meetings, and multiple use recreation (golfing, theme parks, and similar facilities). The controversy over gaming/gambling as a supplement to economic diversity continues in a worldwide debate. Regardless, it has achieved phenomenal rates of return and now appears to be reaching saturation as larger scale enterprises are developed. Wage and salary incomes paid to industry employees are among the highest in rural areas.

Remoteness

Remoteness is the one characteristic that all true rural areas share in common. It is viewed as both an asset and a major liability. Many development specialists and rural sociologists take the stance that remoteness and isolation is an asset. They argue that small structure, vertical leadership, and cooperation are important strengths that contribute to ethic and social identity. Although they acknowledge that interlocal cooperation with regional towns is important, they also counter that individual community ties are the most important process in local development. They imply that to dismiss the importance of local pride, concern, and problem solving capabilities would ignore much of the community's true resource base. On the other hand, current economic development practice now strongly encouraged in rural areas promotes inter-community cooperation, assimilation with other communities, and common work towards development. This is based on the theory that small size and remoteness is *the* major inhibitor of development efforts. Thus, the other side of the problem is how to overcome distance factors in rural areas. In general, remoteness factors are related to four major policy choices in central planning: transportation, critical service deliver, communications, and jobs skills/training.

Communications, more specifically telecommunications amounting to both advanced systems of current technologies, and emerging forms of real time delivery, are predicted by many to be the total planning solution for rural areas. Unlike transportation outcomes, which must overcome *place to place* remoteness, telecommunications offers the hope of *in-place* service and need delivery. It is attractive, if for no other reason, because it offers quick and incremental *upgrade paths*-often at a decreasing marginal costs-rather than enormous sunk costs experienced in transportation and regional development.

The final factor to be discussed, because it serves to impact the cost of remoteness, is job skills/training. No society or societal sector in the global world can afford to concentrate its educational and development resources solely in metropolitan areas. Yet, decentralization of educational resources and development ranks exceptionally high on the list of major expenditures of any nation aspiring to greater sustainability and vitality. Both public and private systems have responded throughout this century to deliver education, jobs skills, and general training to remote areas-both in-place and through regional centres coordinating with outlying communities. But, it would appear that, even with local self-help and capacity building programs, the delivery of these vital services is reaching maximum effort under present funding and technology.

Lack of Resources

A lack of basic resources to meet rural residences' needs is repeatedly shown as a major factor in a community's inability to sustain and maintain community identity and commitment. Resources are understood to mean both fiscal (material) and human and therefore most planning solutions employ a two-pronged set of policies designed to increase resource capacity.

Efforts to redirect material resources to rural areas have been ongoing throughout the 20th Century and far out number programs targeted towards urban areas. Worldwide, major efforts include wide-ranging programs such as education (extension), farm and price supports, direct grants-in-aid, revenue sharing, new towns, and health care-to mentioned but a few. No comprehensive assessment of the effectiveness of these programs exists, but few will venture to say that trillions of dollars poured into rural development has not made a difference in the shape of the nonmetropolitan sectors of our countries. Many rural sociologists argue that it is the scarceness of resources, the need for austerity, and the concomitant appreciation for the assets that do exist that creates the unique blend of community and sustainability thought to be prevalent in the world's nonmetropolitan areas. On the other hand, it is also widely argued that it is the dependence of small communities on others for aid that creates a limited perspective or community vision and a clearly articulated path into the future. Whatever blend of perspective, it is abundantly clear that the request for resources is an all-consuming factor in the life of small communities.

Work Diversity and New Rural Industries

Much of the local economic development (L.E.D.) literature promotes the development of new rural industries (RIs) as one path to a sustainable countryside. There is little argument that one of the keys to attaining a vital, living countryside is increased job opportunity and quality employment. Although RIs lag behind new service enterprises as the fastest growing component of the rural economy, nevertheless, they play a critically important role in rural economic diversification. However, a minority of rural researchers point to the rise of RIs, specifically in developing regions, as a sign of distress rather than positive rural development.

Tambunan [1995] and others argue that there are two quite different conditions under which rural labor might shift from traditional agriculture, fishing, forestry and extractive pursuits: (a) when labor is pulled or "attracted" out of agriculture into better non-agricultural opportunities; or, (2) when labor is "pushed" or forced out of agriculture by declining employment opportunities into relatively worse RIs (marginal occupations) whose capacity to absorb large quantities is achieved at the cost of extremely low, and possibly declining incomes.

The first type of RIs (attracted) are typically run on a more or less stable basis with a business goal of surplus generation and growth using hired labor and a certain degree of technical sophistication. This is in contrast to the second type of RIs which are often seasonal, run with the help of unpaid family labor, using rather primitive technology catering mainly to local markets.

The argument against sustainability and a total planning solution is that a heavy presence of the second type of RIs denotes increasing poverty in the region. Some researchers note, therefore, that the presence of the second type of RIs can only be justified on the basis of their labor intensity and not productivity or income gains.

Building Local Capacity as a Route to Sustainability

Throughout North America, much of Western Europe, Australia, and New Zealand, community generated rural revitalization (generally termed Local Economic Development-or LED) is currently a matter of considerable profile. A prominent feature of this activity is what is termed the *process related dimensions* of rural LED-meaning that the capacity of individual communities to bring about a better future for themselves depends in no small measure on how well they are equipped in terms of leadership and team related skills. The root challenge of all rural communities must be the shaping of new strategies responsive to the enduring realities of rural economies and cultural life-high unemployment; persistent poverty; deteriorated social well-being; lower earnings; and diminished health care-as well as changing national and global circumstances. Revitalizing "rural" must include the participation of small communities in search of positive change, whereby local people are encouraged to think more about their futures and to put into practice their ideas for securing those futures. Capacity building, therefore, deals mostly with the ability of local people to solve problems. These *process dimension programs* seek to bring about change by forging new skills within rural communities related to leadership, mediation and conflict resolution, group processes, understanding the business of government, and the articulation of a shared vision. In the simplest terms, capacity building can be defined as increasing the ability of people and institutions to do what is required of them [Newlands, 1981].

Counterurbanizing the Countryside-Evidence of Change?

Throughout this century migration flows worldwide follow a recognizable pattern: from rural to urban, from mountains to plains, from undeveloped countries to developed countries. These population flows are marked by diversity, complexity, and change leaving many of the small, remote rural areas in a final stage of disintegration. Thus, population reversal (*counterurbanization*) has become one of the hallmarks of a sustainable, living rural countryside.

On a worldwide scale, recent literature assesses counterurbanism as occurring throughout much of the world-albeit at very diverse rates. In truth, the evidence for urban population dispersal is strong while the proof for rural rejuvenation is weak. As noted, the reasons for this phenomena are diverse and complex, and should not be confused with temporary labor migration, but from an overall standpoint there are three controlling factors.

First, it is important to understand that the predominant growth form in the world today-metropolitanism-is undergoing considerable change. Traditional rural communities lying within 65 to 120 kilometres of the metropolitan fringe show a strong propensity to expand in population size and economic diversity. This large sphere of distance influencing surrounding fringe areas, sometimes called *penturbia* or the *component economic area*, is quite possible the final wave of spatial development of large urban centres before urban agglomeration occurs. Forces associated with this change are many, but predictable. In the U.S., it is often associated with the quest for more affordable housing, less computing to work, educational opportunities for children, lifestyle and amenities. Since most-if not nearly all-of the communities within the 65-120 k growth ring are classified as rural or small town (ranging from 15,000 to 5,000 and under), it is not surprising that demographers report new rural growth and counterurbanism.

Second, not all of the more remote rural areas have experienced depopulation. Fully 25-30 percent of communities in the more developed countries report that small towns have gained in population during the past 30 years. Again, the factors associated with this growth are complex, but can be said to center around several major causes. The presence of tertiary (university) education systems is important, as is the location near major transportation links. The main factor, however, at least in North America and Western Europe, are amenity rich areas attracting lifestyles, tourism, recreation, elderly retirement, and land investment opportunities.

Third, although the most remote rural communities show considerable aggregate population loss, some (but not many) seem to have beat the odds and sustained or even exhibit growth while their neighboring communities have perished. The evidence for this counterurbanism is sketchy at best and relies mainly on individual case studies rather than aggregate data, and for every success story there appears to be dozens of declining towns.

There is solid evidence that renewed local leadership from in migrant entrepreneurs (especially retirements) plays a role in some counter-urbanization. Governmental and private economic development programs must surely account for a portion of this reversal-although the evidence is not clear. The economic phenomena of *clustering of related economic activities* may, in fact, play a greater role. Governmental direction of capital expenditures, often using triage concepts, seems to have an impact in larger remote rural communities when prisons, hospitals, and related facilities are constructed.

Regional Country Towns and Rural Stabilization

Certainly one of the bright spots among rural researchers is the role played by the Country Towns in remote, rural areas. Called *"growth poles"* or *"regional centres"* in the 1960s, these large towns-or small cities, as some prefer-appear to provide a major stabilizing force in all nonmetropolitan areas.

Regional country towns display a wide population variance, depending on the degree of remoteness and economic function. In North America, regional towns rarely display a population base less than 10,000 persons, but the median size is 25,000 and will range upwards to 50,000 persons.

Diverse dependency will typically begin to appear around the 10,000 person level and becomes statistically significant at 25,000 persons. Diverse dependency is a term coined by the United States Bureau of Economic Research and rests on the concept of local economic function.

Economic Dependency Types include:

1. Farming-dependent—Farming contributes a weighted annual average of 35 percent or more of total labor and proprietor income.
2. Mining-dependent—Mining contributes a weighted annual average of 25 percent or more of total labor and proprietor income.
3. Manufacturing-dependent—Manufacturing contributes a weighted annual average of 35percent or more of total labor and proprietor income.
4. Government-dependent—Government contributes a weighted annual average of 25 percent or more of total labor and proprietor income.
5. Services-dependent—Service activities (private and personal services, agricultural services, wholesale and retail trade, finance and insurance, transportation and public utilities) contribute a weighted annual average of 50 percent or more of total labor and proprietor income.
6. Non-specialized— Not classified as a specialized economic type.

There is worldwide evidence that the larger regional country towns are rapidly approaching non-specialized economies, although employment tends to be heavily weighted in favor of services and manufacturing, as they assume the leading provider roles in their spheres of influence. It also appears that they have or will soon gain the necessary concentration of capital, population mass, and economies of scale to provide the essential development functions, health care services, manufacturing and employment opportunities, and cultural assets to sustain large and remote rural hinterlands.

The concept of rural *triage* is especially important for centralized decision makers considering policies on regional towns.

Triage is, of course, an emergency medical technique for concentrating on those patients that show the best promise of recovery rather than those in critical condition or those that will probably stabilize. Given the assumption that small, remote rural centres have little hope of a sustainable future unless they are linked to unique resources, and that rural communities tied to metropolitan influence will be sustainable in the future, the best policy may be to concentrate on all but the most critical resources on those communities which, given immediate attention, demonstrate great promise.

Regional country towns fit this classification nicely. First, they are survivors in their spheres of influence-they have managed to gain supremacy over their economic hinterlands. Second, they are sustainable from the standpoint that they have the capacity to provide both employment, food, and shelter at some of the most reasonable costs in the world today, Third, they can provide a partial solution to the *exit roads syndrome* from smaller rural areas by providing retirement opportunities for the elderly and educational chances for youth who would otherwise naturally migrate to metropolitan areas.

Finally, they provide an excellent occasion for government to decentralize their social and service functions in the more remote areas of a nation. If the concept of local economic redevelopment holds promise, then it must decentralized empowerment to the local place.

The Impact of Telecommunications

"While we weren't looking, the future arrived"! Since the middle 1980s, futurists such as Alvin Toffler [Toffler, 1985] have said that "it is certainly no secret that our society is moving away from a manufacturing focus and becoming an information driven machine... The nascent markets of the next century are based on value-added service which are typically the result of adept information management.". The heart of this new information *Third Wave* technology is the digital network and digital communications via the computer modem, faxes, and wireless telephones.

The true, large scale impact of telecommunications on rural areas lies some distance in the future; some would say between the year 2030 and 2050 before global wireless is a truly dependable and integrated source of doing business. Even now in 1997, digital communications through the *Internet* are reforming some selected market relationships between rural and metro locations. Without a doubt, telecommunications will have a marked impact on the two overriding factors that affect non-metropolitan performance: remoteness and labor pools.

Reliable, real time telecommunications cannot solve, but will certainly diminish the impact of distance between more remote rural locations and their major markets and suppliers in metro areas. The bourgeoning service sector worldwide that is essentially responsible for the assimilation, interpretation, and management of information will no longer be place bound-location will be irrelevant assuming that global communications will be the same everywhere.

Telecommunications will be a major factor in transforming, rather than reforming, the way rural communities do business and live their lives. No amount of digital information can reform the basic distinction between the urbanized and the small place given the massive imbalance of resources. It cannot be *a total planning solution*, but it can help to create a greater competitiveness in the way rural people receive their education, medical and social care, market their goods, acquire their supplies, and conduct their affairs. It is assumed that rural areas already showing signs of great vitality will be best positioned to benefit from the new technologies and more remote centres already in decline the least. There is, however, a counter hypothesis to this argument. Telecommuting may contribute to further suburbanization and urban sprawl by releasing households from location constraints related to maximum acceptable commute time and distance. Because the practical use of modern digital telecommunications is such a relatively new activity, no studies have been able to confirm or deny this hypothesis (Handy, 1994). If this indeed occurs, the environmental costs of further sprawl could far outweigh benefits received by reduced automobile and office use. It is difficult to estimate the likelihood of this scenario because there are so many factors contributing to housing location decisions.

The second overriding factor related to rural-metro imbalance likely to be impacted by telecommunications is the labor pool itself. Remote, rural areas may (at least according to some studies and many common perceptions in local economic development) be good places to start both services and new start-up firms, but they cannot sustain the need for increased capital and labor due to lack of available resources and worker pools. The concept of *telecommuting*-large groups of workers who are place bound throughout a nation, but who work for a remote and centralized firm via digital communications-will diminish the need for regional labor. The argument that telecommunications can never supplant the need for specific site, skilled labor in manufacturing and fabrication will always remain valid, however it is necessary to realize that most now agree that the distinction between value-added activities and services is becoming less important.

Conclusions-Century's End and a New Millennium

Change is the price of the rejuvenation of the countryside and the survival of small towns. In most cases, adequate levels of employment and income cannot be expected from traditional sectors-especially if rural areas are expected to decouple from metros. The real choice, as Galston suggests, will be between decline and forms of innovation that will leave neither individual lives nor the structure of social relations unchanged. Some, perhaps many, rural residents will both resent and regret these changes, but they cannot be avoided. Every way of life requires some economic basis, but a commitment to preserving a *total way of life* in the face of profound economic and social change cannot hope to succeed. Individuals who are devoted to continuity of place, who want a sustainable base for the generations who follow, must therefore accept some degree of discontinuities of economic and social life.

"To be successful, efforts to rejuvenate the rural countryside must rest on genuine local preferences. Underlying these preferences is some understanding of what rural individuals, considered simply as citizens of a country, are thought to deserve. Since the 1940s many countries have made the political determination that all citizens, regardless of place, were entitled to electricity, decent roads, schools, and adequate water/ wastewater facilities. The question in the next century is whether access to information management through digitalization and fiber optics will be similarly defined as elements of social citizenship. The question is on the table, and the viability of most of our rural areas hangs in the balance."

Rural Sociology in Europe

Rural sociology as it is understood in the United States came into being in Europe only after World War II. On the surface, this seems somewhat surprising. An important part of the population of Europe is still rural. During the last few decades in most European countries the percentage of the active population engaged in agriculture was higher than in the United States, in several countries much higher. Sociology as a science originated from Europe. So why no rural sociology at an earlier date?

There are several reasons which help to explain this phenomenon. First of all, one has to bear in mind that rural sociology as we know it now is not just *the* sociology of rural life. One could imagine a rural sociology in many respects quite different from the present. Rural sociology as we know it in America and elsewhere has strong roots in practice. Even if it would not be right to call rural sociology just an applied science, it would be equally wrong to deny its strong interest in the problems of daily life and its striving for applicability. Rural sociology never would have developed in the way it did if it had not shown its importance for the betterment of rural life. But before World War II, sociology in Europe was hardly seen by nonprofessionals as a science which had a practical value. This conclusion was right. Sociology as it was taught and studied in Europe before the war was, for the greater part, highly theoretical and often even philosophical in character. Thus, there was no place for a rural sociology with a strong orientation to applicability.

Many sociologists even sought generalizations at such a high level that differences between rural and nonrural society hardly came into consideration, so that on a more abstract level there were not many chances for a special study of rural life either. At any rate, one can state that the kind of rural sociology which has been developed in America did not fit into the dominating concept of sociology in Europe before 1940.

You may reply that more or less the same was true for America. Rural sociology was not conceived as a welcome child of general sociology m your country either. As you know, rural sociology originated here in fact from the Land Grant Colleges, that means from institutes for applied higher education, and not from the general universities. I know that it took some time before it was accepted as a legitimate daughter of general sociology. Even in 1951, when I visited your country, I had the feeling that at some of your institutes of higher learning there was still some tension between rural sociology and general sociology. Not all general sociologists seemed to be convinced that rural sociology was a respectable kind of sociology. But I have the impression, nevertheless, that already during the thirties the chances for the acceptance of rural sociology as a branch of sociology in general were much better in America than in Europe.

The climate for the acceptance of rural sociology in Europe would have been better, perhaps, if the communication between scholars in the field of sociology in Europe and America before the war had been as good as it was after the war. In fact, the contacts between scientists in Europe and America in general, and between the sociologists in particular, before the war were rather few. It would not be right to say that American sociology was unknown in Europe, but the European sociologists, in general, were not quite aware of what was going on in America.

Of the fathers of sociology in the United States, one could find some publications on their bookshelves, but one could not say that they had an influence of importance on sociological thinking in Europe. Only a few in Europe were conscious of the fact that already at the end of the twenties American sociologists were beginning to write a new page in the history of sociology.

With few exceptions, the European sociologists did not know that by careful gathering of data by means of fieldwork and by an equally careful processing of these data by statistical methods, the Americans were introducing a new type of research which would change the face of sociology drastically. Only at the end of the thirties did they become gradually aware that in this respect something of great importance was developing, but this had hardly any effect before the end of the war.

The fact that in Europe there was no rural sociology in the modern sense did not mean, of course, that more or less systematic knowledge about rural life was totally lacking. In several countries other disciplines showed an interest in rural life. In France, for example, human geographers of the group of *Vidal de la Blache* were strongly interested in the study of the socio-economic way of life—*genre de vie—oi* rural regions. In Germany elements of the study of social life of the countryside were incorporated in the so-called *Agrarpolitik* (agricultural policy), which was taught to the students in agriculture at the German universities and colleges.

The many problems which tried to be solved during the years of reconstruction after the war and the growing consciousness of rapid social change led to the increasing awareness that, for the foundation of a well-balanced policy, systematic scientific knowledge of the conditions and processes in social life is indispensable. That Was true also with regard to agriculture and rural life. Both experienced extremely rapid changes in Europe after the war, which created problems for the ministries of agriculture and other agencies. In almost all European countries sociologists were called to help these countries solve their difficulties. People in charge o£ the extension services gradually began to see that the economie problems of the farmer could not be solved by purely technical and economie approaches. They began to see that advisory work is not just a thing to be learned by trial and error only, but that the extension worker can find a sound basis for his work in scientific knowledge provided by sociology and psychology. Today it has become clear that the countryside needs a drastic physical reconstruction to adjust it to modern social, economie, and technical conditions; and physical planners £eel that they cannot do the job without the help o£ sociology. Churches, village communities, farmers unions, and other voluntary associations in the countryside, including cooperatives, all feel a need for change or at least for a reconsideration of their own position. Often they ask the advice of sociologists. Rural family life, including problems of retirement, demands much more attention than it got formerly; and it is again the sociologist who has to find out the real character of the problems and of their causes.

Thus, in almost all countries in Western Europe sociological research in rural areas started. Even in some countries behind the Iron Curtam there is an interest in rural sociology. Poland

and Yugoslavia have to be mentioned especially, but in Czechoslovakia there seems to be some interest also.

Does this mean that rural sociology in Europe is in a satisfactory state at the moment and that we can expect that it will show a continuous growth in the near future? Let me try to give you a picture of its present state so you can form your own judgment.

It seems that in Europe not much is to be expected for rural sociology from the general universities, at least as far as they do not have agricultural faculties. In the survey of rural sociology in Europe which was published by Mendras in the first issue of *Sociologia Ruralis,* he mentions only one university (the University of Stockholm) where rural sociology was taught as a separate part of a course in general sociology. I can only add that in my own country students in general sociology from other universities are permitted to come to my university, the Agricultural University of Wageningen, to take rural sociology as a part of the study for their final degree, and a number of them do so. The universities of the European continent have, in general, a strong urban background and show—much more than in America—a great resistance to the introduction of anything which could be considered as appüed science.

Thus, almost the only hope in academie life for rural sociology Hes with agricultural universities and colleges and faculties of agriculture in general universities. That hope certainly is not vain. In almost all Western European countries, at one or more institutes for higher education in agriculture, rural sociology is taught. But it would be a mistake to suppose that means an education of rural sociologists.

Methods of Study

Sociological research methods may be divided into two broad categories:

Quantitative Designs

In the social sciences, quantitative research refers to the systematic empirical investigation of quantitative properties and phenomena and their relationships. The objective of quantitative research is to develop and employ mathematical models, theories and/or hypotheses pertaining to phenomena. The process of measurement is central to quantitative research because it provides the fundamental connection between empirical observation and mathematical expression of quantitative relationships.

Quantitative research is used widely in social sciences such as psychology, sociology, anthropology, and political science. Research in mathematical sciences such as physics is also 'quantitative' by definition, though this use of the term differs in context. In the social sciences, the term relates to empirical methods, originating in both philosophical positivism and the history of statistics, which contrast qualitative research methods.

Qualitative methods produce information only on the particular cases studied, and any more general conclusions are only hypotheses. Quantitative methods can be used to verify, which of such hypotheses are true.

A comprehensive analysis of 1274 articles published in the top two American sociology journals between 1935 and 2005 found that roughly two thirds of these articles used quantitative methods.

Overview

Quantitative research is generally made using scientific methods, which can include:

- The generation of models, theories and hypotheses
- The development of instruments and methods for measurement
- Experimental control and manipulation of variables
- Collection of empirical data
- Modeling and analysis of data
- Evaluation of results.

In the social sciences particularly, quantitative research is often contrasted with qualitative research which is the examination, analysis and interpretation of observations for the purpose of discovering underlying meanings and patterns of relationships, including classifications of types of phenomena and entities, in a manner that does not involve mathematical models. Approaches to quantitative psychology were first modelled on quantitative approaches in the physical sciences by Gustav Fechner in his work on psychophysics, which built on the work of Ernst Heinrich Weber. Although a distinction is commonly drawn between qualitative and quantitative aspects of scientific investigation, it has been argued that the two go hand in hand. For example, based on analysis of the history of science, Kuhn (1961) concludes that "large amounts of qualitative work have usually been prerequisite to fruitful quantification in the physical sciences". Qualitative research is often used to gain a general sense of phenomena and to form theories that can be tested using further quantitative research. For instance, in the social sciences qualitative research methods are often used to gain better understanding of such things as intentionality (from the speech response of the researchee) and meaning (why did this person/group say something and what did it mean to them?)(Kieron Yeoman).

Although quantitative investigation of the world has existed since people first began to record events or objects that had been counted, the modern idea of quantitative processes have their roots in Auguste Comte's positivist framework.

Use of Statistics

Statistics is the most widely used branch of mathematics in quantitative research outside of the physical sciences, and also finds applications within the physical sciences, such as in statistical mechanics. Statistical methods are used extensively within fields such as economics, social sciences and biology. Quantitative research using statistical methods starts with the collection of data, based on the hypothesis or theory. Usually a big sample of data is collected-this would require verification, validation and recording before the analysis can take place. Software packages such as SPSS and R are typically used for this purpose. Causal relationships are studied by manipulating factors thought to influence the phenomena of interest while controlling other variables relevant to the experimental outcomes. In the field of health, for example, researchers might measure and study the relationship between dietary intake and measurable physiological effects such as weight loss, controlling for other key variables such as exercise. Quantitatively based opinion surveys are widely used in the media, with statistics such as the proportion of respondents in favor of a position commonly reported. In opinion surveys, respondents are asked a set of structured questions and their responses are tabulated. In the field of climate science, researchers compile and compare statistics such as temperature or atmospheric concentrations of carbon dioxide.

Empirical relationships and associations are also frequently studied by using some form of General linear model, non-linear model, or by using factor analysis. A fundamental principle in quantitative research is that correlation does not imply causation. This principle follows from the fact that it is always possible a spurious relationship exists for variables between which covariance is found in some degree. Associations may be examined between any combination of continuous and categorical variables using methods of statistics.

Measurement

Views regarding the role of measurement in quantitative research are somewhat divergent. Measurement is often regarded as being only a means by which observations are expressed numerically in order to investigate causal relations or associations. However, it has been argued that measurement often plays a more important role in quantitative research. For example, Kuhn argued that within quantitative research, the results that are shown can prove to be strange. This is because accepting a theory based on results of quantitative data could prove to be a natural phenomenon.

When measurement the parts from theory, it is likely to yield mere numbers, and their v ry neutrality makes them particularly sterile as a source of remedial suggestions. But numbers register the departure from theory with an authority and finesse that no qualitative technique can duplicate, and that departure is often enough to start a search (Kuhn, 1961).

In classical physics, the theory and definitions which underpin measurement are generally deterministic in nature. In contrast, probabilistic measurement models known as the Rasch model and Item response theory models are generally employed in the social sciences. Psychometrics is the field of study concerned with the theory and technique for measuring social and psychological attributes and phenomena. This field is central to much quantitative research that is undertaken within the social sciences.

Quantitative research may involve the use of *proxies* as stand-ins for other quantities that cannot be directly measured. Tree-ring width, for example, is considered a reliable proxy of ambient environmental conditions such as the warmth of growing seasons or amount of rainfall. Although scientists cannot directly measure the temperature of past years, tree-ring width and other climate proxies have been used to provide a semi-quantitative record of average temperature in the Northern Hemisphere back to 1000 A.D. When used in this way, the proxy record (tree ring width, say) only reconstructs a certain amount of the variance of the original record. The proxy may be calibrated (for example, during the period of the instrumental record) to determine how much variation is captured, including whether both short and long term variation is revealed. In the case of tree-ring width, different species in different places may show more or less sensitivity to, say, rainfall or temperature: when reconstructing a temperature record there is considerable skill in selecting proxies that are well correlated with the desired variable.

Quantitative Methods

Quantitative methods are research techniques that are used to gather quantitative data-information dealing with numbers and anything that is measurable. Statistics, tables and graphs, are often used to present the results of these methods. They are therefore to be distinguished from qualitative methods.

In most physical and biological sciences, the use of either quantitative or qualitative methods is uncontroversial, and each is used when appropriate. In the social sciences, particularly in sociology, social anthropology and psychology, the use of one or other type of method has become a matter of controversy and even ideology, with particular schools of thought within each discipline favouring one type of method and pouring scorn on to the other. Advocates of quantitative methods argue that only by using such methods can the social sciences become truly scientific; advocates of qualitative methods argue that quantitative methods tend to obscure the reality of the social phenomena under study because they underestimate or neglect the non-measurable factors, which may be the most important. The modern tendency (and in reality the majority tendency throughout the history of social science) is to use eclectic approaches. Quantitative methods might be used with a global qualitative frame. Qualitative methods might be used to understand the meaning of the numbers produced by quantitative methods. Using quantitative methods, it is possible to give precise and testable expression to qualitative ideas. This combination of quantitative and qualitative data gathering is often referred to as mixed-methods research.

Examples

- Research that consists of the percentage amounts of all the elements that make up Earth's atmosphere.
- Survey that concludes that the average patient has to wait two hours in the waiting room of a certain doctor before being selected.
- An experiment in which group x was given two tablets of Aspirin a day and Group y was given two tablets of a placebo a day where each participant is randomly assigned to one or other of the groups. The numerical factors such as two tablets, percent of elements and the time of waiting make the situations and results quantitative.

Qualitative Designs

Qualitative research is a method of inquiry appropriated in many different academic disciplines, traditionally in the social sciences, but also in market research and further contexts. Qualitative researchers aim to gather an in-depth understanding of human behaviour and the reasons that govern such behaviour. The qualitative method investigates the *why* and *how* of decision making, not just *what*, *where*, *when*. Hence, smaller but focused samples are more often needed, rather than large samples. Qualitative methods produce information only on the particular cases studied, and any more general conclusions are only hypotheses (informative guesses). Quantitative methods can be used to verify which of such hypotheses are true.

History

Until the 1970s, the phrase 'qualitative research' was used only to refer to a discipline of anthropology or sociology. During the 1970s and 1980s qualitative research began to be used in other disciplines, and became a significant type of research in the fields of education studies, social work studies, women's studies, disability studies, information studies, management studies, nursing service studies, political science, psychology, communication studies, and many other fields. Qualitative research occurred in the consumer products industry during this period, with researchers investigating new consumer products and product positioning/advertising opportunities. The earliest consumer research pioneers including Gene Reilly of The Gene Reilly Group in Darien, CT, Jerry Schoenfeld of Gerald Schoenfeld & Partners in Tarrytown, NY and Martin Calle of Calle & Company, Greenwich, CT, also Peter Cooper in London, England, and Hugh Mackay in Mission, Australia. There continued to be disagreement about the proper place of qualitative versus quantitative research. In the late 1980s and 1990s after a spate of criticisms from the quantitative side, new methods of qualitative research evolved, to address the perceived problems with reliability and imprecise modes of data analysis. During this same decade, there was a slowdown in traditional media advertising spending, so there was heightened interest in making research related to advertising more effective.

In the last thirty years the acceptance of qualitative research by journal publishers and editors has been growing. Prior to that time many mainstream journals were prone to publish research articles based upon the natural sciences and which featured quantitative analysis.

Distinctions from quantitative research (In simplified terms- Qualitative means a non-numerical data collection or explanation based on the attributes of the graph or source of data. For example, if you are asked to explain in qualitative terms a thermal image displayed in multiple colours, then you would explain the colour differences rather than the heat's numerical value.)

First, in qualitative research, cases can be selected purposefully, according to whether or not they typify certain characteristics or contextual locations.

Second, the researcher's role receives greater critical attention. This is because in qualitative research the possibility of the researcher taking a 'neutral' or transcendental position is seen as more problematic in practical and/or philosophical terms. Hence qualitative researchers are often exhorted to reflect on their role in the research process and make this clear in the analysis.

Third, while qualitative data analysis can take a wide variety of forms, it differs from quantitative research in its focus on language, signs and meaning. In addition, qualitative research approaches analysis holistically and contextually, rather than being reductionistic and isolationist. Nevertheless, systematic and transparent approaches to analysis are almost always regarded as essential for rigor. For example, many qualitative methods require researchers to carefully code data and discern and document themes consistently and reliably.

Perhaps the most traditional division between the uses of qualitative and quantitative research in the social sciences is that qualitative methods are used for exploration (i.e., hypothesis-generating) or for explaining puzzling quantitative results. Quantitative methods, by contrast, are used to test hypotheses. This is because establishing content validity-do measures measure what a researcher thinks they measure?- is seen as one of the strengths of qualitative research. Some consider quantitative methods to provide more representative, reliable and precise measures through focused hypotheses, measurement tools and applied mathematics. By contrast, qualitative data is usually difficult to graph or display in mathematical terms.

Qualitative research is often used for policy and program evaluation research since it can answer certain important questions more efficiently and effectively than quantitative approaches. This is particularly the case for understanding how and why certain outcomes were achieved (not just what was achieved) but also for answering important questions about relevance, unintended effects and impact of programs such as:

Were expectations reasonable? Did processes operate as expected? Were key players able to carry out their duties? Did the program cause any unintended effects? Qualitative approaches have the advantage of allowing for more diversity in responses as well as the capacity to adapt to new developments or issues during the research process itself. While qualitative research can be expensive and time-consuming to conduct, many fields of research employ qualitative techniques that have been specifically developed to provide more succinct, cost-efficient and timely results. Rapid Rural Appraisal is one formalised example of these adaptations but there are many others.

Data Collection

Qualitative researchers may use different approaches in collecting data, such as the grounded theory practice, narratology, storytelling, classical ethnography, or shadowing. Qualitative methods are also loosely present in other methodological approaches, such as action research or actor-network theory. Forms of the data collected can include interviews and group discussions, observation and reflection field notes, various texts, pictures, and other materials.

Qualitative research often categorizes data into patterns as the primary basis for organizing and reporting results. Qualitative researchers typically rely on the following methods for gathering information: *Participant Observation, Non-participant Observation, Field Notes, Reflexive Journals, Structured Interview, Semi-structured Interview, Unstructured Interview, and Analysis of documents and materials.*

The ways of participating and observing can vary widely from setting to setting. Participant observation is a strategy of reflexive learning, not a single method of observing In participant observation researchers typically become members of a culture, group, or setting, and adopt roles to conform to that setting. In doing so, the aim is for the researcher to gain a closer insight into the culture's practices, motivations and emotions. It is argued that the researchers' ability to understand the experiences of the culture may be inhibited if they observe without participating.

Some distinctive qualitative methods are the use of focus groups and key informant interviews. The focus group technique involves a moderator facilitating a small group discussion between selected individuals on a particular topic. This is a particularly popular method in market research and testing new initiatives with users/workers.

One traditional and specialized form of qualitative research is called cognitive testing or pilot testing which is used in the development of quantitative survey items. Survey items are piloted on study participants to test the reliability and validity of the items.

In the academic social sciences the most frequently used qualitative research approaches include the following:

1. Ethnographic Research, used for investigating cultures by collecting and describing data that is intended to help in the development of a theory. This method is also called "ethnomethodology" or "methodology of the people". An example of applied ethnographic research, is the study of a particular culture and their understanding of the role of a particular disease in their cultural framework.
2. Critical Social Research, used by a researcher to understand how people communicate and develop symbolic meanings.
3. Ethical Inquiry, an intellectual analysis of ethical problems. It includes the study of ethics as related to obligation, rights, duty, right and wrong, choice etc.
4. Foundational Research, examines the foundations for a science, analyses the beliefs and develops ways to specify how a knowledge base should change in light of new information.
5. Historical Research, allows one to discuss past and present events in the context of the present condition, and allows one to reflect and provide possible answers to current issues and problems. Historical research helps us in answering questions such as: Where have we come from, where are we, who are we now and where are we going?

6. Grounded Theory, is an inductive type of research, based or "grounded" in the observations or data from which it was developed; it uses a variety of data sources, including quantitative data, review of records, interviews, observation and surveys.
7. Phenomenology, describes the "subjective reality" of an event, as perceived by the study population; it is the study of a phenomenon.
8. Philosophical Research, is conducted by field experts within the boundaries of a specific field of study or profession, the best qualified individual in any field of study to use an intellectual analyses, in order to clarify definitions, identify ethics, or make a value judgment concerning an issue in their field of study.

Data Analysis

Interpretive Techniques

The most common analysis of qualitative data is observer impression. That is, expert or bystander observers examine the data, interpret it via forming an impression and report their impression in a structured and sometimes quantitative form.

Coding

Coding is an interpretive technique that both organizes the data and provides a means to introduce the interpretations of it into certain quantitative methods. Most coding requires the analyst to read the data and demarcate segments within it. Each segment is labeled with a "code" – usually a word or short phrase that suggests how the associated data segments inform the research objectives. When coding is complete, the analyst prepares reports via a mix of: summarizing the prevalence of codes, discussing similarities and differences in related codes across distinct original sources/contexts, or comparing the relationship between one or more codes.

Some qualitative data that is highly structured (e.g., open-end responses from surveys or tightly defined interview questions) is typically coded without additional segmenting of the content. In these cases, codes are often applied as a layer on top of the data. Quantitative analysis of these codes is typically the capstone analytical step for this type of qualitative data.

Contemporary qualitative data analyses are sometimes supported by computer programs. These programs do not supplant the interpretive nature of coding but rather are aimed at enhancing the analyst's efficiency at data storage/retrieval and at applying the codes to the data. Many programs offer efficiencies in editing and revising coding, which allow for work sharing, peer review, and recursive examination of data.

A frequent criticism of coding method is that it seeks to transform qualitative data into quantitative data, thereby draining the data of its variety, richness, and individual character. Analysts respond to this criticism by thoroughly expositing their definitions of codes and linking those codes soundly to the underlying data, therein bringing back some of the richness that might be absent from a mere list of codes.

Recursive Abstraction

Some qualitative datasets are analysed without coding. A common method here is recursive abstraction, where datasets are summarized, those summaries are then further summarized, and so on. The end result is a more compact summary that would have been difficult to accurately discern without the preceding steps of distillation.

A frequent criticism of recursive abstraction is that the final conclusions are several times removed from the underlying data. While it is true that poor initial summaries will certainly yield an inaccurate final report, qualitative analysts can respond to this criticism. They do so, like those using coding method, by documenting the reasoning behind each summary step, citing examples from the data where statements were included and where statements were excluded from the intermediate summary.

Mechanical Techniques

Some techniques rely on leveraging computers to scan and sort large sets of qualitative data. At their most basic level, mechanical techniques rely on counting words, phrases, or coincidences of tokens within the data. Often referred to as content analysis, the output from these techniques is amenable to many advanced statistical analyses.

Mechanical techniques are particularly well-suited for a few scenarios. One such scenario is for datasets that are simply too large for a human to effectively analyze, or where analysis of them would be cost prohibitive relative to the value of information they contain. Another scenario is when the chief value of a dataset is the extent to which it contains "red flags" (e.g., searching for reports of certain adverse events within a lengthy journal dataset from patients in a clinical trial) or "green flags" (e.g., searching for mentions of your brand in positive reviews of marketplace products).

A frequent criticism of mechanical techniques is the absence of a human interpreter. And while masters of these methods are able to write sophisticated software to mimic some human decisions, the bulk of the "analysis" is nonhuman. Analysts respond by proving the value of their methods relative to either a) hiring and training a human team to analyze the data or b) letting the data go untouched, leaving any actionable nuggets undiscovered.

Paradigmatic Differences

Contemporary qualitative research has been conducted from a large number of various paradigms that influence conceptual and metatheoretical concerns of legitimacy, control, data analysis, ontology, and epistemology, among others. Research conducted in the last 10 years has been characterized by a distinct turn toward more interpretive, postmodern, and critical practices. Guba and Lincoln (2005) identify five main paradigms of contemporary qualitative research: positivism, postpositivism, critical theories, constructivism, and participatory/cooperative paradigms. Each of the paradigms listed by Guba and Lincoln are characterized by axiomatic differences in axiology, intended action of research, control of research process/outcomes, relationship to foundations of truth and knowledge, validity, textual representation and voice of the researcher/participants, and commensurability with other paradigms. In particular, commensurability involves the extent to which paradigmatic concerns "can be retrofitted to each other in ways that make the simultaneous practice of both possible". Positivist and postpositivist paradigms share commensurable assumptions but are largely incommensurable with critical, constructivist, and participatory paradigms. Likewise, critical, constructivist, and participatory paradigms are commensurable on certain issues (e.g., intended action and textual representation).

Validation

A central issue in qualitative research is validity (also known as credibility and/or dependability). There are many different ways of establishing validity, including: member check, interviewer corroboration, peer debriefing, prolonged engagement, negative case analysis, auditability, confirmability, bracketing, and balance. Most of these methods were coined, or at least extensively described by Lincoln and Guba (1985)

Academic Research

By the end of the 1970s many leading journals began to publish qualitative research articles and several new journals emerged which published only qualitative research studies and articles about qualitative research methods.

In the 1980s and 1990s, the new qualitative research journals became more multidisciplinary in focus moving beyond qualitative research's traditional disciplinary roots of anthropology, sociology, and philosophy.

The new millennium saw a dramatic increase in the number of journals specializing in qualitative research with at least one new qualitative research journal being launched each year.

Sociologists are divided into camps of support for particular research techniques. These disputes relate to the epistemological debates at the historical core of social theory. While very different in many aspects, both qualitative and quantitative approaches involve a systematic interaction between theory and data. Quantitative methodologies hold the dominant position in sociology, especially in the United States. In the discipline's two most cited journals, quantitative articles have historically outnumbered qualitative ones by a factor of two. (Most articles published in the largest British journal, on the other hand, are qualitative.) Most textbooks on the methodology of social research are written from the quantitative perspective, and the very term "methodology" is often used synonymously with "statistics." Practically all sociology PhD program in the United States require training in statistical methods. The work produced by quantitative researchers is also deemed more 'trustworthy' and 'unbiased' by the greater public, though this judgment is continues to be challenged by antipositivists.

The choice of method often depends largely on what the researcher intends to investigate. For example, a researcher concerned with drawing a statistical generalization across an entire population may administer a survey questionnaire to a representitive sample population. By contrast, a researcher who seeks full contextual understanding of an individuals' social actions may choose ethnographic participant observation or open-ended interviews. Studies will commonly combine, or 'triangulate', quantitative *and* qualitative methods as part of a 'multi-strategy' design. For instance, a quantitative study may be performed to gain statistical patterns or a target sample, and then combined with a qualitative interview to determine the play of agency.

Sampling

Quantitative methods are often used to ask questions about a population that is very large, making a census or a complete enumeration of all the members in that population infeasible. A 'sample' then forms a manageable subset of a population. In quantitative research, statistics are used to draw inferences from this sample regarding the population as a whole. The process of selecting a sample is referred to as 'sampling'. While it is usually best to sample randomly, concern with differences between specific subpopulations sometimes calls for stratified sampling. Conversely, the impossibility of random sampling sometimes necessitates nonprobability sampling, such as convenience sampling or snowball sampling.

Methods

The following list of research methods is neither exclusive nor exhaustive:

- Archival research or the Historical method: draws upon the secondary data located in historical archives and records, such as biographies, memoirs, journals, and so on.

- Content analysis: The content of interviews and other texts is systematically analysed. Often data is 'coded' as a part of the 'grounded theory' approach using qualitative data analysis (QDA) software, such as NVivo.
- Experimental research: The researcher isolates a single social process and reproduces it in a laboratory (for example, by creating a situation where unconscious sexist judgments are possible), seeking to determine whether or not certain social variables can cause, or depend upon, other variables (for instance, seeing if people's feelings about traditional gender roles can be manipulated by the activation of contrasting gender stereotypes). Participants are randomly assigned to different groups which either serve as controls—acting as reference points because they are tested with regard to the dependent variable, albeit without having been exposed to any independent variables of interest—or receive one or more treatments. Randomization allows the researcher to be sure that any resulting differences between groups are the result of the treatment.
- Survey research: The researcher produces data using interviews, questionnaires, or similar feedback from a set of people sampled from a particular population of interest. Survey items from an interview or questionnaire may be open-ended or closed-ended. Data from surveys is usually analysed statistically on a computer.
- Longitudinal study: An extensive examination of a specific person or group over a long period of time.
- Observation: Using data from the senses, the researcher records information about social phenomenon or behaviour. Observation techniques may or may not feature participation. In participant observation, the researcher goes into the field (such as a community or a place of work), and participates in the activities of the field for a prolonged period of time in order acquire a deep understanding of it. Data acquired through these

techniques may be analysed either quantitatively or qualitatively.

Computational Sociology

Sociologists increasingly draw upon computationally intensive methods to analyze and model social phenomena. Using computer simulations, artificial intelligence, complex statistical methods, and new analytic approaches like social network analysis, computational sociology develops and tests theories of complex social processes through bottom-up modeling of social interactions. Although the subject matter and methodologies in social science differ from those in natural science or computer science, several of the approaches used in contemporary social simulation originated from fields such as physics and artificial intelligence. By the same token, some of the approaches that originated in computational sociology have been imported into the natural sciences, such as measures of network centrality from the fields of social network analysis and network science. In relevant literature, computational sociology is often related to the study of social complexity. Social complexity concepts such as complex systems, non-linear interconnection among macro and micro process, and emergence, have entered the vocabulary of computational sociology. A practical and well-known example is the construction of a computational model in the form of an "artificial society", by which researchers can analyze the structure of a social system.

Practical Applications of Social Research

Social research informs politicians and policy makers, educators, planners, lawmakers, administrators, developers, business magnates, managers, social workers, non-governmental organizations, non-profit organizations, and people interested in resolving social issues in general. There is often a great deal of crossover between social research, market research, and other statistical fields.

2

Village through History

A village is a clustered human settlement or community, larger than a hamlet with the population ranging from a few hundred to a few thousands (sometimes tens of thousands), Though often located in rural areas, the term urban village is also applied to certain urban neighbourhoods, such as the West Village in Manhattan, New York City and the Saifi Village in Beirut, Lebanon, as well as Hampstead Village in the London conurbation. Villages are normally permanent, with fixed dwellings; however, transient villages can occur. Further, the dwellings of a village are fairly close to one another, not scattered broadly over the landscape, as a dispersed settlement.

Historically, villages were the usual form of community for societies that practise subsistence agriculture, and also for some non-agricultural societies. In Great Britain, a hamlet earned the right to be called a village when it built a church.

In many cultures, towns and cities were few, with only a small proportion of the population living in them. The Industrial Revolution attracted people in larger numbers to work in mills and factories; the concentration of people caused many villages to grow into towns and cities. This also enabled specialization of labor and crafts, and development of many trades. The trend of urbanisation continues, though not always in connection with industrialisation. Villages have been eclipsed in importance as units of human society and settlement.

Traditional Villages

Although many patterns of village life have existed, the typical village was small, consisting of perhaps 5 to 30 families.

Homes were situated together for sociability and defence, and land surrounding the living quarters was farmed. Traditional fishing villages were based on artisan fishing and located adjacent to fishing grounds.

South Asia

India

"The soul of India lives in its villages", declared M. K. Gandhi at the beginning of 20th century. According to the 2001 Indian census, 74% of Indians live in 638,365 different villages. The size of these villages varies considerably. 236,004 Indian villages have a population less than 500, while 3,976 villages have a population of 10,000+. Most villages have their own temple, mosque or church depending on the local religious following.

Southeast Asia

Brunei, Indonesia and Malaysia

The term kampung (sometimes spelling *kampong*) in the English language has been defined specifically as "a Malay hamlet or village in a Malay-speaking country" In other words, a *kampung* is defined today as a village in Brunei, Indonesia or Malaysia. In Malaysia, a *kampung* is determined as a locality with 10,000 or fewer people. Since historical times, every Malay village came under the leadership of a *penghulu* (village chief), who has the power to hear civil matters in his village. A Malay village typically contains a *"masjid"* (mosque) or *"surau"* (Muslim chapel), paddy fields and Malay houses on stilts. Malay and Indonesian villagers practice the culture of helping one another as a community, which is better known as "joint bearing of burdens" (*gotong royong*), as well as being family-oriented (especially the concept of respecting one's family [particularly the parents and elders]), courtesy and believing in God (*"Tuhan"*) as paramount to everything else. It is common to see a cemetery near the mosque, as all Muslims in the Malay or Indonesian village want to be prayed for, and to receive Allah's blessings in the afterlife. In Indonesia, the terms differ, villages are called *desa / kelurahan*, and village heads *kepala desa* but the same general concept applies, there is some variation among the vast numbers of Austronesian ethnic groups. In some areas such as Tanah Toraja, elders take turns watching over the village at a command post.

Philippines

In urban areas of the Philippines, the term "village" most commonly refers to private subdivisions, especially gated communities. These villages emerged in the mid-20th century and were initially the domain of elite urban dwellers. Now they are now common in Metro Manila and other major cities in the country and their residents have a wide range of income levels. Such villages may or may not correspond to administrative units (usually barangays) and/or be privately administered. Well-known villages in Metro Manila include Forbes Park and Dasmariñas Village. Barangays more correspond to the villages of old times, and the chairman (formerly a village datu) now settles intrapersonal matters or polices the village, though with much less authority and respect than in Indonesia or Malaysia.

Central and Eastern Europe

Slavic Countries

Selo is a Slavic word meaning "village" in Bosnia and Herzegovina, Bulgaria, Croatia, Macedonia, Russia, Serbia, and Ukraine. For example there are numerous *sela* (plural of *selo)* called Novo Selo in Bulgaria, Croatia, Montenegro and others in Serbia, and Macedonia. In Slovenia, the word *selo* is used for very small villages (less than a thousand people) and in dialects; the Slovene word *vas* is used all over Slovenia.

Bulgaria

In Bulgaria the different types of *Sela* vary from a small selo of 5 to 30 families to one of several thousand people. According to a 2002 census, in that year there were 2,385,000 Bulgarian citizens living in settlements classified as *villages*. A 2004 Human Settlement Profile on Bulgaria conducted by the United Nations Department of Economic and Social Affairs stated that: The most intensive is the migration "city – city". Approximately 46% of all migrated people have changed their residence from one city to another. The share of the migration processes "village – city" is significantly less – 23% and "city – village" – 20%. The migration "village – village" in 2002 is 11%. It also stated that, the state of the environment in the small towns and villages is good apart from the low level of infrastructure.

In Bulgaria it is becoming popular to visit villages for the atmosphere, culture, crafts, hospitality of the people and the surrounding nature. This is called *selski tourism*, meaning "village tourism".

Russia

In Russia, the bulk of the rural population are concentrated in rural localities. Two most common types of rural localities are *derevnya* and *selo*. Historically, the formal indication of status was religious: a city (*gorod*) had a cathedral, a *selo* had a church, while a *derevnya* had neither.

The lowest administrative unit of the Russian Empire, *volost*, or its Soviet or modern Russian successor, *selsoviet*, was usually headquartered in a *selo* and embraced a few neighboring villages.

Between 1926 and 1989, Russia's rural population shrank from 76 million people to 39 million, due to urbanization, collectivization, dekulakization, and the World War II losses, but has nearly stabilized since. During 1930–1937, mass starvation in Russia and other parts of the Soviet Union lead to the death of at least 14.5 million peasants (including 5-7 million in the Holodomor).

Most Russian rural localities have populations of less than 200 people, and the smaller places take the brunt of depopulation: e.g., in 1959, about one half of Russia's rural population lived in villages of fewer than 500 people, while now less than one third does. In the 1960s–1970s, the depopulation of the smaller villages was driven by the central planners' drive to get the farm workers out of smaller, "prospect-less" hamlets and into the collective or state farm's main village, with more amenities.

Most Russian rural residents are involved in agricultural work, and it is very common for villagers to produce their own food. As prosperous urbanites purchase village houses for their second homes, Russian villages sometimes are transformed into dacha settlements, used mostly for seasonal residence.

The historically Cossack regions of Southern Russia and parts of Ukraine, with their fertile soil and absence of serfdom, had a rather different pattern of settlement from central and northern Russia. While peasants of central Russia lived in a village around the lord's manor, a Cossack family often lived on its own farm, called *khutor*. A number of such *khutors* plus a central village made up the administrative unit *stanitsa*. Such a *stanitsa* village, often with a few thousand residents, was usually larger than a *selo* in central Russia.

The term *aul/aal* is used to refer mostly Muslim-populated villages in Caucasus and Idel-Ural, without regard to the number of residents.

Ukraine

In Ukraine *Selo* is the lowest administrative unit. *Khutir* and *Stanytsia* are not part of the administrative division anylonger due to the collectivization. There is a higher level of the rural administrative division, *Selysche*.

Western & Southern Europe

United Kingdom

A village in the UK is a compact settlement of houses, smaller in size than a town, and generally based on agriculture or, in some areas, mining, quarrying or sea fishing.

The major factors in the type of settlement are location of water sources, organization of agriculture and landholding, and likelihood of flooding. For example, in areas such as the Lincolnshire Wolds, the villages are often found along the spring line halfway down the hillsides, and originate as spring line settlements, with the original open field systems around the village. In northern Scotland, most villages are planned to a grid pattern located on or close to major roads, whereas in areas such as the Forest of Arden, woodland clearances produced small hamlets around village greens.

Some villages have disappeared (for example, deserted medieval villages), sometimes leaving behind a church or manor house and sometimes nothing but bumps in the fields. Some show archaeological evidence of settlement at three or four different layers, each distinct from the previous one. Clearances may have been to accommodate sheep or game estates, or enclosure, or may have resulted from depopulation, such as after the Black Death or following a move of the inhabitants to more prosperous districts. Other villages have grown and merged and often form hubs within the general mass of suburbia — such as Hampstead, London and Didsbury in Manchester. Many villages are now predominantly dormitory locations and have suffered the loss of shops, churches and other facilities. For many British people, the village represents an ideal of Great Britain, as with Adlestrop. Seen as being far from the bustle of modern life, it is represented as quiet and harmonious, if a little inward-looking. This concept of an unspoilt Arcadia is present in many popular representations of the village such as the radio serial *The Archers* or the best kept village competitions.

Many villages in South Yorkshire, North Nottinghamshire, North East Derbyshire, County Durham, South Wales and Northumberland are known as pit villages. These (such as Murton, County Durham) grew from hamlets when the sinking of a colliery in the early 20th century resulted in a rapid growth in their population and the colliery owners built new housing, shops, pubs and churches. Some pit villages outgrew nearby towns by area and population; for example, Rossington in South Yorkshire came to have over four times more people than the nearby town of Bawtry. Some pit villages grew to become towns; for example, Maltby in South Yorkshire grew from 500 people in the 19th century to over 17,000 in 2007.

In the UK, the main historical distinction between a hamlet and a village was that the latter had a church, and so usually was the centre of worship for an ecclesiastical parish. However, some civil parishes may contain more than one village. The typical village had a pub or inn, shops, and a blacksmith. But many of these facilities are now gone, and many villages are dormitories for commuters. The population of such settlements ranges from a few hundred people to around five thousand. A village is distinguished from a town in that:

- A village should not have a regular agricultural market, although today such markets are uncommon even in settlements which clearly are towns.
- A village does not have a town hall nor a mayor.
- If a village is the principal settlement of a civil parish, then any administrative body that administers it at parish level should be called a parish council or parish meeting, and not a town council or city council. However, some civil parishes have no functioning parish, town, or city council nor a functioning parish meeting. In Wales, where the equivalent of an English civil parish is called a Community, the body that administers it is called a Community Council. However, larger councils may elect to call themselves town councils. Unlike Wales, Scottish community councils have no statutory powers.
- There should be a clear green belt or open fields surrounding its parish borders. However this may not be applicable to urbanised villages: although these may not considered to be villages, they are often widely referred to as being so; an example of this is Horsforth in Leeds.

France

Same general definition as in the UK.

An independent association named *Les Plus Beaux Villages de France*, was created in 1982 to promote assets of small and picturesque French villages of quality heritage. As of 2008, 152 villages in France have been labelled as "The Most Beautiful Villages of France".

Spain

Spain has plenty of little villages around its territory. Country life is more usual in Castile and Aragón. Every village has a church or hermitage.

Portugal

Same general definition as in Spain.

Netherlands

In the flood prone districts of the Netherlands, villages were traditionally built on low man-made hills called terps before the introduction of regional dyke-systems. In modern days, the term *dorp* (lit. "village") is usually applied to settlements no larger than 20,000, though there's no official law regarding status of settlements in the Netherlands.

Middle East

Lebanon

Like France, villages in Lebanon are usually located in remote mountainous areas. The majority of villages in Lebanon retain their Aramaic names or are derivative of the Aramaic names, and this is because Aramaic was still in use in Mount Lebanon up to the 18th century.

Many of the Lebanese villages are a part of districts, these districts are known as "kadaa" which includes the districts of Baabda (Baabda), Aley (Aley), Matn (Jdeideh), Keserwan (Jounieh), Chouf (Beiteddine), Jbeil (Byblos), Tripoli (Tripoli), Zgharta (Zgharta/Ehden), Bsharri (Bsharri), Batroun (Batroun), Koura (Amioun), Miniyeh-Danniyeh (Minyeh/Sir Ed-Danniyeh), Zahle (Zahle), Rashaya (Rashaya), Western Beqaa (Jebjennine/ Saghbine), Sidon (Sidon), Jezzine (Jezzine), Tyre (Tyre), Nabatiyeh (Nabatiyeh), Marjeyoun (Marjeyoun), Hasbaya (Hasbaya), Bint Jbeil (Bint Jbeil), Baalbek (Baalbek), and Hermel (Hermel).

The district of Danniyeh conists of thirty six small villages, which includes Almrah, Kfirchlan, Kfirhbab, Hakel al Azimah, Siir, Bakhoun, Miryata, Assoun, Sfiiri, Kharnoub, Katteen, Kfirhabou, Zghartegrein, Ein Qibil.

Danniyeh is a region located in Miniyeh-Danniyeh District in the North Governorate of Lebanon. The region lies east of Tripoli, extends north as far as Akkar District, south to Bsharri District and Zgharta District and as far east as Baalbek and Hermel. Dinniyeh has an excellent ecological environment filled with woodlands, orchards and groves. Several villages are located in this mountainous area, the largest town being Sir Al Dinniyeh.

An example of a typical mountainous Lebanese village in Dannieh would be Hakel al Azimah which is a small village that belongs to the district of Danniyeh, situated between Bakhoun and Assoun's boundaries. It is in the centre of the valleys that lie between the Arbeen Mountains and the Khanzouh.

Syria

Syria contains a large number of villages that vary in size and importance, including the ancient, historical and religious villages, such as Ma'loula, Sednaya, and Brad (Mar Maroun's time). The diversity of the Syrian environments creates significant differences between the Syrian villages in terms of the economic activity and the method of adoption. Villages in the south of Syria (Huran, Jabal Al-Arab), the north-east (the Syrian island) and the Orontes River basin depend mostly on agriculture, mainly grain, vegetables and fruits. Villages in the region of Damascus and Aleppo depend on trading. Some other villages, such as Marmarita depend heavily on tourist activity.

Mediterranean cities in Syria, such as Tartus and Latakia have similar types of villages. Mainly, villages were built in very good sites which had the fundamentals of the rural life, like water. An example of a Mediterranean Syrian village in Tartus would be Al-Annaze, which is a small village that belongs to the area of Al Sauda. The area of Al Sauda is called a nahiya, which is a subdistrict.

Sub-Saharan Africa

Australasia & Oceania

Pacific Islands Communities on pacific islands were historically called villages by English speakers who traveled and settled in the area. Some communities such as several Villages of Guam continue to be called villages despite having large populations that can exceed 40,000 residents.

New Zealand

The traditional Mâori village was the pâ, a fortified hill-top settlement. Tree-fern logs and flax were the main building materials.

Australia The term village often is used in reference to small planned communities such as retirement communities or shopping districts, and tourist areas such as ski resorts. Small rural communities are usually known as townships. Larger settlements are known as towns.

South America

Argentina Usually set in remote mountainous areas, some also cater to winter sports and/or tourism, see: Uspallata, La Cumbrecita, Villa Traful and La Cumbre

North America

United States

In the United States, the meaning of "village" varies by geographic area and legal jurisdiction. In many areas, "village" is a term, sometimes informal, for a type of administrative division at the local government level. Since the Tenth Amendment to the United States Constitution makes local government for the most part a matter for the states rather than the federal government, the states are free to have political subdivisions called "villages," or not to do so, and to define the word in many different ways.

Typically, a village is a type of municipality, although it can also be a special district or an unincorporated area. It may or may not be recognized for governmental purposes.

Informal Usage

In informal usage, a U.S. village may be simply a relatively small clustered human settlement without formal legal existence. In colonial New England, a village typically formed around the church meetinghouses that was located in the center of each town. Many of these colonial settlements still exist as town centres. With the advent of the Industrial Revolution, industrial villages also sprang up around water-powered mills, mines, and factories. Because most New England villages were contained within the boundaries of legally established towns, many such villages were never separately incorporated as municipalities. A relatively small unincorporated community, similar to a hamlet in New York state, or even a relatively small community within an incorporated city or town, may be termed a village. This informal usage may be found even in states that have villages as an incorporated municipality and is similar to the usage of the term "unincorporated town" in states having town governments.

Formal Usage

States that formally recognize villages vary widely in the definition of the term. Most commonly, a village is either a special district or a municipality. As municipalities, a village may:

1. differ from a city or town in terms of population;
2. differ from a city in terms of dependence on a township; or
3. be virtually equivalent to a city or town.

Alaska

While municipalities in Alaska are not called villages, Alaska native villages are recognized under the Alaska Native Claims Settlement Act.

Although not officially called villages, the natives and other Alaska residents refer to most small towns as villages.

Delaware

Municipalities in Delaware are called cities, towns, or villages. There are no differences among them that would affect their classification for census purposes.

Florida

Municipalities in Florida are called cities, towns, or villages. They are not differentiated for census purposes.

Idaho

All municipalites in Idaho are called cities, although the terms "town" and "village" are sometimes used in statutes.

Illinois

Municipalities in Illinois are called cities, towns, or villages. A village has up to a few hundred people.

Louisiana

A village in Louisiana is a municipality having a population of 1,000 or fewer.

Maine

In Maine, village corporations or village improvement corporations are special districts established in towns for limited purposes.

Massachusetts

All of the land area in Massachusetts is allocated to incorporated municipalities called either a city or town. Some municipalities (such as Newton, Massachusetts) have villages, and where they exist they are the equivalent of neighborhoods, which usually have no corporate existence and no official boundaries or government recognition. Sometimes villages and neighborhoods are recognized incidentally, through declarative signs, parking districts, or names used by the United States Post Office.

Maryland

In Maryland, a locality designated "Village of..." may be either an incorporated town or a special tax district. An example of the latter is the Village of Friendship Heights.

Michigan

In Michigan, villages differ from cities in that, whereas villages remain part of the townships in which they are formed, thereby reducing their home-rule powers, cities are not part of townships. Because of this, village governments are required to share some of the responsibilities to their residents with the township.

Minnesota

Villages that existed in Minnesota as of January 1, 1974, became statutory cities, as opposed to charter cities. Cities may or may not exist within township areas.

Mississippi

A village in Mississippi is a municipality of 100 to 299 inhabitants. They may no longer be created.

Missouri

The municipalities of Missouri are cities and villages. Unlike cities, villages have no minimum population requirement.

Nebraska

In Nebraska, a village is a municipality of 100 through 800 inhabitants, whereas a city must have at least 800 inhabitants. All villages, but only some cities, are within township areas. A city of the second class (800-4,999 inhabitants) may elect to revert to village status.

New Hampshire

In New Hampshire, a village district or precinct may be organized within a town. Such a village district or precinct is a special district with limited powers. The New Hampshire Association of Village Districts has a website at www.NHAVD.org

New Jersey

A village in the context of New Jersey local government, refers to one of five types and one of eleven forms of municipal government. Villages, like other municipalities, are not part of a township.

New Mexico

The municipalities in New Mexico are cities, towns, and villages. There are no differences among them that would affect their classification for census purposes.

New York

In New York State, a village is an incorporated area that differs from a city in that a village is within the jurisdiction of one or more towns, whereas a city is independent of a town. Villages thus have less autonomy than cities. A village is usually, but not always, within a single town. A village is a clearly defined municipality that provides the services closest to the residents, such as garbage collection, street and highway maintenance, street lighting and building codes. Some villages provide their own police and other optional services. Those municipal services not provided by the village are provided by the town or towns containing the village. As of the 2000 census, there are 553 villages in New York. There is no limit to the population of a village in New York; Hempstead, the largest village in the state, has 55,000 residents, making it more populous than some of the state's cities. However, villages in the state may not exceed five square miles (13 km^2) in area. Present law requires a minimum of 500 residents to incorporate as a village.

North Carolina

The municipalities in North Carolina are cities, towns, and villages. There are no differences among them that would affect their classification for census purposes.

Ohio

In Ohio, a village is an incorporated municipality with fewer than 5,000 inhabitants. The minimum population for incorporation as a village is 1,600 inhabitants, but this was not always the case, resulting in many very small villages. If a village grows to 5,000 residents, it is automatically designated as a city. Cities or villages may be within township areas; however, if a city or village becomes coterminous with a township, the township ceases to exist as a separate government.

Oklahoma

In Oklahoma, unincorporated communities are called villages and are not counted as governments.

Oregon

In Oregon, one county — Clackamas County — permits the organization of unincorporated areas into villages and hamlets. The boards of such entities are advisory to the county.

Pennsylvania

In Pennsylvania, villages are unincorporated areas within townships. Villages are oftentimes census-designated places. The largest village in Pennsylvania is Upper Darby.

Texas

In Texas, villages may be Type B or Type C municipalities, but not Type A municipalities. The types differ in terms of population and in terms of the forms of government that they may adopt.

Vermont

In Vermont, villages are named communities located within the boundaries of a legally established town. Villages may be incorporated or unincorporated.

Washington

In Washington state, there is no legal definition of a village. Local municipalities are classified as first-class cities, second-class cities, and towns (also called fourth-class cities), with successively fewer governing powers, based on population at the time of incorporation. Colloquially, some areas are called villages, such as the Town of Beaux Arts Village.

West Virginia

In West Virginia, towns and villages are Class IV municipalities, i.e., having 2,000 or fewer inhabitants.

Wisconsin

In Wisconsin, cities and villages are both outside the area of any town. Cities and villages differ in terms of the population and population density required for incorporation.

Incorporated Villages

In twenty U.S. states, the term "village" refers to a specific form of incorporated municipal government, similar to a city but with less authority and geographic scope. However, this is a generality; in many states, there are villages that are an order of magnitude larger than the smallest cities in the state. The distinction is not necessarily based on population, but on the relative powers granted to the different types of municipalities and correspondingly, different obligations to provide specific services to residents.

In some states such as New York, Wisconsin, or Michigan, a village is an incorporated municipality, usually, but not always, within a single town or civil township. Residents pay taxes to the village and town or township and may vote in elections for both as well. In some cases, the village may be coterminous with the town or township. There are also many villages which span the boundaries of more than one town or township, and some villages may even straddle county borders.

There is no limit to the population of a village in New York; Hempstead, the largest village in the state, has 55,000 residents, making it more populous than some of the state's cities. However, villages in the state may not exceed five square miles (13 km^2) in area.

In the state of Wisconsin a village is always legally separate from the towns that it has been incorporated from. The largest village is Menomonee Falls, which has over 32,000 residents.

Michigan and Illinois also have no set population limit for villages and there are many villages that are larger than cities in those states.

Villages in Ohio are often legally part of the township from which they were incorporated, although exceptions such as Hiram exist, in which the village is separate from the township. They have no area limitations, but become cities if they grow a population of more than 5,000.

In Maryland, a locality designated "Village of..." may be either an incorporated town or a special tax district. An example of the latter is the Village of Friendship Heights.

In states that have New England towns, a "village" is a center of population or trade, including the town center, in an otherwise sparsely-developed town or city — for instance, the village of Hyannis in the city of the Barnstable, Massachusetts.

Unincorporated Villages

In many states, the term "village" is used to refer to a relatively small unincorporated community, similar to a hamlet in New York state. This informal usage may be found even in states that have villages as an incorporated municipality, although such usage might be considered incorrect and confusing.

Village Life

Medieval villages consisted of a population comprised of mostly of farmers. Houses, barns sheds, and animal pens clustered around the center of the village, which was surrounded by plowed fields and pastures. Medieval society depended on the village for protection and a majority of people during these centuries called a village home. Most were born, toiled, married, had children and later died within the village, rarely venturing beyond its boundaries.

Common enterprise was the key to a village's survival. Some villages were temporary, and the society would move on if the land proved infertile or weather made life too difficult. Other villages continued to exist for centuries. Every village had a lord, even if he didn't make it his permanent residence, and after the 1100's castles often dominated the village landscape. Medieval Europeans may have been unclear of their country's boundaries, but they knew every stone, tree, road and stream of their village. Neighboring villages would parley to set boundaries that would be set out in village charters.

Medieval peasants were either classified as free men or as "villeins," those who owed heavy labor service to a lord, were bound to the land, and subject to feudal dues. Village life was busy for both classes, and for women as well as men. Much of this harsh life was lived outdoors, wearing simple dress and subsisting on a meager diet.

Village life would change from outside influences with market pressures and new landlords. As the centuries passed, more and more found themselves drawn to larger cities. Yet modern Europe owes much to these early medieval villages.

India is an agriculture country and most of its people live in villages. A village is a collection of small huts in the midst of fields on which the village farmers work. Some villages are big while others are comparatively smaller. They are generally cut off from the cities and have a different kind of life.

The villagers live in the midst of natural surroundings. The charm of nature justify the remark of the famous poet Cowper, "God made the country and man made the town", As we rise early in the morning, we can listen to the sweet songs of birds. We can enjoy the beauty of the rising sun and the sweet breeze of the greenery of fields around, are the various pleasures that abound in the countryside.

The villagers pass a healthy, peaceful life. There is no smoke and noise of the city factories. They breathe fresh air which promotes their health. They also get pure ghee and milk. There is no hustle and bustle and no worry as in the modern life. The villagers, therefore, are happy and healthy. They lead a simple life and their desires are few. They are satisfied with what they have and never dream of those luxuries and comforts that modern science has provided us with in such ample measure.

Most of the people who live in villages are farmers. They cultivate their farms situated in the neighbored of the villages. They go to their fields early in the morning where they work till evening, ploughing, sowing or reaping, according to seasons. Spinning and weaving is one of the most important cottage industries of a village. It helps to increase their meager income. Beside this, some people keep shops and provided the necessities of life of the villagers. Other works as potters, carpenters, blacksmith, etc, to fulfil their needs.

The villagers are deeply religious. They worship a number of gods and goddesses. They devote regular time to player and worship. The village priest enjoys great respect. But they are highly orthodox and any change is dislike and opposed. Many kinds of superstitions flourish among them. They live in constant fear of ghost. They believe in a number of omens.

The villagers are socially knit together. Their life is co-operate and interdependent. They depend on each other for the supply of their daily wants. They share in the joys and sorrow of each other. They help each other in time of need. Their social sense is so strong that the guest of one is considered as the guest of all. In a town or city, one does not care to know even one's neighbour. But each villages is familiar with the family history of other villagers. In the evening they assemble in the village "Chopal" with there 'hukkas' and chatting and talking goes on till late the night. This is their simple recreation.

But the village life has also some serious drawbacks. The villagers are extremely poor. They live in one roomed "*kachcha*" mud houses, which often fall to the ground in the rains. In this way, they are put to great hardship. Suitable houses must be constructed for them. At present there are only a few *Pucca* houses in villages. In spite of their hard work, they are not able to earn enough to provide themselves with even two square meals a day. They are ill-clad and ill-fed. As they are not able to save anything, in a need they have to borrow from the village money lender. They are frequently in debt which they are often never able return. Scientific methods of agriculture must be used, and government should provide facilities of this purpose. There is no doubt that much improvement has been made in this respect in recent times but it is not enough.

The villages are illiterate. Most of them do not even know how to write their names. There are no suitable arrangements for their education or for the education of their children. Even when there is a school, it is highly unsatisfactory. The teachers is ill-paid and takes no interest in his work. Their ignorance makes them superstitious and conservative. They are content with their old methods of cultivation and do not like scientific methods.

In villages, there are no suitable arrangement for treatment of the sick. Often there is no qualified doctor. The village Vaids and Hakims are mere quacks who kill more patients than they cure. The villages are highly in sanitary and many infectious disease breakout from time to time. Thousands of people die every year, uncared for an without any medical aid. However, now things are fast changing. Good hospitals have been constructed near each village. Good, qualified doctors are now there in most villages.

Such is the life in an Indian village. In spite of its various drawbacks, it is a better life than that of the city. If I were given the choice, I would prefer to live in the village. The Government has already taken in hand various measures to improve the conditions of the villages. "Jawahar Rozgar Yojana" and "Panchayati Raj" are two of the important steps taken in this direction. Let us hope, in the near feature, their poverty and illiteracy shall be eradicated. A village will then really by a paradise on earth, as God intended it to be.

Indian Village life is a mixture of tranquility, serenity, quietude and innocence. Along with numerous small and big grass fields, several rivers, chirping of birds, swinging of emerald trees, speaking in a low voice the tale of languishment and love to the big and clear blue sky give a mesmerizing, captivating and bewitching effect to the Indian villages. Ever since the country's independence from the British colonial rule in 1947, the economy of the nation has banked upon its agrarian society.

A majority of the persons living in India have involved themselves in agriculture and associated industries, and have thus made the country the quickest developing world economy. The country is hope to people of different castes and creeds which rightly demonstrates the principles of 'Unity in Diversity'. Indian village life is fully relied on agriculture and innate all over the land.

The lifestyle maintained by the people of Indian villages as well as their working styles are as fascinating as the balance offered by the metropolitan city lifestyles.

The primary occupation of the people living in the India villages is agriculture and is therefore reckoned as an unchangeable part of the Indian village culture. Traditionally, village and caste are regarded as similar to each other and the villages in India also follow the same trend. In Indian village life the presence of all the four castes with the hierarchy of the Brahmin is noticed. The caste system which originated long back has however remained unchanged in the village life in India. Although, caste system in its original sense has collapsed yet caste identities are very much present there in the village life in India.

People belonging to different castes in a village deal with each other in kinship terms, which shows the fictive kinship relationships distinguished within each settlement.

Habitually the Indian villagers manifest a deep loyalty to their villages. A rural family which has its root seated deeply in a specific village does not move easily to another. The uniqueness of the village life in India lies in this deep loyalty which is again marked with a rich culture. The mystic charm and the cultural diversities of the village life in India, make the Indian villages that never never land where beauty never fades away, and dream never cease to exist.

The village life in India is idyllic, unchanging with its immense beauty. The villagers of India are normally habituated in sharing and using the common facilities of the village including the village shrines and temples, the village pond, schools, grazing grounds, sitting places, etc.

This interdependence of the village life in India perhaps provides a matchless unity amongst the villagers which supports them in surviving amidst thousands of odds. Village unity is therefore the primary concern of the village life in India.

Characteristically, each of the Indian villages recognizes a particular deity as the protector of the concerned village and the people of that village get together to worship the deity. Religion, which is deeply instilled in the village life in India, further supports the villagers to consider this as an essential part of village prosperity. The uninterrupted village life in India entertain themselves amidst the color of the festivals like Diwali, Holi, Muharram, Dussehra, etc, in the captivating pulse of dance and songs and of course in the emotion of rural theatres.

In the Indian village life, there is a headman who is recognized often to respectfully listen to the village panchayat's decision. The village panchayat comprises of some important men from the major castes of the village. The panchayat in Indian villages are responsible to clarify the disputes within the village boundaries as much as possible, with occasional choices of the interference of police or the court system. In the recent era, the Government supports an elective Panchayat system in the Indian villages.

The Government of India helped the villages with advanced technology for farming implements and presently most of the villages in India have access to modern farming equipments. Now-a-days, the Indian village outskirts boast up with food packaging plants, textile industries, sugar industries and steel plants.

These have created for the village youth suitable employment opportunities. Continuous reform is made by the government in order to fashion the country a 'motor' for the economy of the world. Developments in the agrarian infrastructure, public sector reforms, rural development, righted labor norms, etc have changed the Indian village life. The village life in India blessed with its innocence, purity and uncomplicated saga makes the villages as the quaint, archaic, mystic yet charming places to rediscover nature.

New Trends

Up until recently, large part of the marketing that was done in this country was done, targeting the urban population of the country. Now the marketing potential of the rural part of the country is rapidly growing. Let us get an understanding of the urban and rural break up of the country. 26% of the population lives in the cities or in urban India. The remaining 74% lives in the villages or in rural India. The population of the country is spread over the villages but is very concentrated in the cities. India has six of the largest cities in the world. These are-Calcutta, Bombay, Delhi, Madras, Bangalore and Hyderabad. Besides these cities, there are six other cities that are growing at a very rapid rate and have a huge concentration of the population. These are-Ahmedabad, Kanpur, Pune, Nagpur, Lucknow and Jaipur. In addition to these cities, there are around 4000 towns that have concentrations of the population.

In the cities, there are a lot of jobs available now-a-days due to call centres and BPO's. This has given many more people purchasing power. Items that were luxury items a few years a go are seen in every house in the cities.

Besides the cities 74% of Indian population lives in the villages. As the standard of living in the villages also improves, many modern facilities are available in almost every house hold in the villages too. Now a days the TV is there in most of the houses in the villages too. This has exposed them to a lot of advertising lifestyles and products. The villages have become a huge market that will be of great consequence in the near future. In the future, companies with a strong product distribution system reaching all the villages will have a very strong advantage over the rest.

The country is growing, and is a place where business will thrive in the near future. To understand this better consider the following favorable shifts that have taken place in the consumer patters of buying.

3

History of Rural Community in India

A majority of the total Indian population live in the numerous villages, scattered throughout the country. The rural population in India comprises the core of Indian society and also represents the real India. According to the 2001 Indian census, there are 638,365 villages in India and about 74% of Indian population lives in these villages. The number of people living in each of the Indian villages also varies considerably. It is found that most of the Indian villages have a population of less than 1,000, while there are only a few villages where more than 10,000 people live.

Religion, caste, and language are considered the major determinants of social and political organisation in rural India. More than 80% of the total rural population in India is Hindu and the other major religious communities include the Muslims, Buddhists, Jains, Christians, Sikhs, Parsis, etc. tribals or adivasis are an integral part of the rural population as well. Some of the prominent tribal languages spoken by the tribal population in India include Maithili, Santali, Konkani, Dongri, Meitei (Manipuri), Bodo, etc.

About 70% of the total Muslim population in India speaks Urdu language. However, the languages spoken by the rural population in India largely vary on the native language of the location of these villages. India has one of the densest rural populations in the world. This huge density in the rural population in India puts immense pressure on the natural resources and also adversely affects the quality of life.

The rural population in India comprises several castes and tribes. Introduced in the Vedic period, the caste system still plays a major role in the formation of a village society in India. Traditionally, there are four broad categories of castes (varnas) in Indian villages. These castes include the Brahmins, Kshatriyas, Vaishyas and Sudras. According to Hinduism, the Brahmins are the highest class of the society and all other castes are liable to serve the Brahmins. They comprise a major portion of the entire rural population in India and are also involved in most of the decision making processes in the village. The Brahmins hold important posts in the Village Panchayats as well. Apart from these four castes, there is also a category of outcastes in the Indian villages. The people of this category were earlier called "untouchables" but now commonly referred to as "dalits". While the people of general castes live in the villages of plane lands, the tribes mostly live in the villages located in deep forests or in the hilly regions of India.

The tribal communities comprise a significant portion of rural population in India. Most of the tribal people live in the deep jungles and hilly regions in India and are engaged in agricultural activities. The tribal communities are also known as Adivasis and a majority of tribes in India live in the states of Orissa, Madhya Pradesh, Chattisgarh, Rajasthan, Gujarat, Maharashtra, Andhra Pradesh, Bihar, Jharkhand, West Bengal, Mizoram, Andaman and Nicobar Islands, etc. The tribal communities in India are officially recognised as "Scheduled Tribes" by the Indian government, in the Fifth Schedule of the Constitution of India.

A majority of the rural population in India lives on agriculture and linked occupations in the rural areas. Though, agriculture has been the primary occupation of rural people in India since the ancient period, the scenario is changing day by day. Many Indian villagers have engaged themselves in various non-agricultural occupations in the recent years. There is also a common trend among the Indian villagers to migrate to the urban areas to work as labourers or get into alternate professions. The literacy rate among the rural population in India has also increased significantly in the recent years. The current literacy rate in the Indian rural areas is as high as 65%, which is quite impressive. The rural population in India provides the real picture of the Indian society. However, the Indian villagers face a lot of difficulties like poverty in their daily life. The authorities have taken many initiatives to improve the quality of life of the rural population in India, in the recent years.

Study of Rural Community in India

People in rural areas in India, have many problems such as :-

1) Electricity
2) Education
3) Health
4) Roads
5) Jobs
6) Scope for development
7) Lack of security
8) Illiterate administration
9) No modern facilities
10) No water supply.

The burden of indebtedness in rural India is great, and falls mainly on the households of rural working people. The exploitation of this group in the credit market is one of the most pervasive and persistent features of rural life in India, and despite major structural changes in credit institutions and forms of rural credit in the post-Independence period, Darling's statement (1925), that "the Indian peasant is born in debt, lives in debt and bequeaths debt," still remains true for the great majority of working households in the countryside. Rural households need credit for a variety of reasons.

They need it to meet short-term requirements for working capital and for long-term investment in agriculture and other income-bearing activities. Agricultural and non-agricultural activity in rural areas are typically seasonal, and households need credit to smooth out seasonal fluctuations in earnings and expenditure. Rural households, particularly those vulnerable to what appear to others to be minor shocks with respect to income and expenditure, need credit as an insurance against risk. In a society that has no free, compulsory and universal education or health care, and very few general social security programmes, rural households need credit for different types of consumption. These include expenditure on food, housing, health and education. In the Indian context, another important purpose of borrowing is to meet expenses for a variety of social obligations and rituals.

Introduction

About 75% of the Indian population lives in rural areas and about 80% of this population is dependent on agriculture for its livelihood. Agriculture accounts for about 37% of the national income. The development of the rural areas and of agriculture and its allied activities thus becomes vital for the rapid development of the economy as a whole.In this regard, India has succeeded in developing one of the largest rural banking systems in the world.

Various regulatory measures have been taken enabling the banking system to play an important role in the economic development of the rural areas. The two most prominent measures are rural commercial bank branch expansion, thus moving from class banking to mass banking and secondly, priority sector lending and the formulation of specific development programmes and action plans to facilitate credit flow to the rural sectors. Despite these measures, as per the Debt and Investment Survey, Govt. of India (1992) about 36% of the rural households are found to be outside the fold of institutional credit.

Agricultural Productivity

Even though India occupies the first or second position in the world in several crops in terms of area and production, it's rank in terms of productivity per hectare in the world is 52 for rice, 38 for wheat and much low in several other crops. The productivity of some crops is not only low but also remained stagnant over the years. The yield gap needs to be bridged through an integrated package of technology and agricultural policies to reap the untapped production potential, particularly, in rain-fed and other low productivity areas.

Causes for Backwardness in Villages

Zamindari System, the legacy of the British Rule

India was under British rule for 200 years. British policies were aimed in revenue collection and not rural development. They introduced the zamindari system. The zamindars were deemed the owners of all land and they collected as much revenue as they could from the peasants. The system left the peasants very poor and the zamindars did very little to improve the conditions of the villages. After the country attained independence this system was abolished, but the conditions of the peasants is yet to transform completely.

The Bonded Labour System

It is equivalent to near slavery. Bonded labour is an indebted agricultural worker, who had borrowed from the money lender at usurious rate of interest and had to work in his farm for low wages. The system was used to permanently enslave the worker, as the worker was only able to repay a part of interest and the loan with compounded residual interest went on swelling. The agricultural labour can free himself eventually only by giving his son in bondage as a substitute. Under the 20-point economic programme, the Government India under Prime Minister Mrs.Indira Gandhi abolished bonded labour system and brought legislation to this effect in 1975. Despite the legislation the system is known to persist here and there in select areas.

Other contributory reasons are the total lack of agricultural development under foreign rule, poor communication, roads and other infrastructure development in villages, lack of education and health facilities, and the destruction of the thriving Indian cottage industries on account of competition from the cheap machine made goods imported under British rule

Progress made after the Country attained Independence

1. After Independence the Country adopted planned development. The very first five year plan laid stress on agricultural development. It took a number of measures to bring more land under irrigation. Major

irrigation Dams like Bakra Nangal, Hirakud, Nagarjunasagar, Tungabhadra were constructed which generated power for industrialisation of the country and water for irrigation. A number canals were build to distribute stored water over an extensive area. The Indian farmer, as a result, is now not exclusive depending on the monsoon.

2. Intensive cultivation of land is made possible through farm mechanisation. Tractors are being produced in the country and these are available to the farmers everywhere. Farmers are also using threshing machines, deep boring and irrigation pumps. They get supplies of high yielding improved seeds, fertilisers and other inputs. To enable them to purchase such inputs the rural credit system has been invigorated with Cooperatives, Regional Rural Banks, and Rural Branches of Commercial Banks. The recent boon to the poor Indian peasant is the micro finance system and Self Help Groups that have rendered financial support within the easy reach of all.

3. Land Reform legislation introduced in the country after independence include the abolition of the zamindari system, the abolition of bonded labour system, land ceiling legislation etc.. Legislation was also introduced to relieve rural indebtedness and the money lender could no longer legally collect more than reasonable interest. Untouchability was abolished and special legislation for the upliftment of scheduled cases and scheduled tribes were enacted.

4. Community Development Programmes, Integrated Rural Development Programme, bringing local self-government to the roots of the village through introduction of panchayat raj system ushered a new era of rural development. Development of public health care system, schemes undertaken for promoting literacy and adult education in the country, programmes for development of rural industries are other development programmes that have received the thrust of the Government's development approach.

Future Perspectives

Agriculture, with its large dependent population has to thrive and flourish, in order to secure rural prosperity. To ensure orderly and vigorous growth of agriculture policy and structural issues need to be addressed quickly. Some of the important issues that need to be addressed are-

1. Improving profitability of agriculture, through yield improvements, diversification and reform of agricultural marketing.
2. Strengthening backward linkages and expanding irrigation coverage.
3. Providing forward linkages especially for post harvest management, processing, transport, storage and market infrastructure.
4. Securing a stable long term policy on agricultural commodities trade, including the role of private sector.
5. Encouraging emergence of a market mechanism for agricultural commodities such as a commodities exchange.
6. Streamlining the cooperative credit structure for facilitating hassle free flow of credit.
7. Implementing watershed development projects in the rain-fed and dry-land areas.

Rural Banking Faces Twin Challenges

Banking in rural India is faced with the twin challenges of regulation and distribution. Regulation with respect to banking has been designed for delivery in urban India and distribution required more manpower to be deployed in rural areas. Initiatives like cheque transaction — where the electronic image and not the actual cheque is sent — have in mind the urban customer, he said. "About 500-600 million people in India still do not have bank accounts. For the rural segment, one needs to design no-frills products and deliver hard core value". The other handicap was that while Rs 1-crore business in microfinance required 30 people in terms of manpower, the same volume of business in other portfolios required only one person. Also, contract farming and supply chain integration has not gone the way they should have. Power, telecommunications, banking and transportation had reduced the urban-rural divide, he said. Besides traditional banking services, people in the rural and semi-urban areas are expressing interest in liability and investment products. He said, "Rural India is fast transforming a nation of savers into a nation of investors".

No doubt, villages are in a state of neglect and under-development, with impoverished people, as result of past legacies and defects in our planning process and investment pattern. But the potential in rural India is immense. What if every village in the country is provided with basic amenities, like drinking water, electricity, health care, educational transport, communication and other facilities, with only a smaller population of the village engaged in agriculture and the remaining in other gainful occupations? When this happens India will turn into mighty country.

The purchasing power of the rural population throwing enormous demand for goods and services will boost the national economy tremendously. The day will see the reverse migration of people from the urban slums back to the villages. Rural Development is the subject to come to the forefront after the economic reforms and rural banking will serve the backbone of this development.

The Greatest Problem of Less Population

The Indian government has therefore given rise to some more administrations (but to no avail) to help the people.

Drinking water quality in rural India: Issues and approaches. The rural population of India comprises more than 700 million people residing in about 1.42 million habitations spread over 15 diverse ecological regions. It is true that providing drinking water to such a large population is an enormous challenge. Our country is also characterised by non-uniformity in level of awareness, socio-economic development, education, poverty, practices and rituals which add to the complexity of providing water.

The health burden of poor water quality is enormous. It is estimated that around 37.7 million Indians are affected by waterborne diseases annually, 1.5 million children are estimated to die of diarrhoea alone and 73 million working days are lost due to waterborne disease each year. The resulting economic burden is estimated at $600 million a year. The problems of chemical contamination is also prevalent in India with 1,95,813 habitations in the country are affected by poor water quality. The major chemical parameters of concern are fluoride and arsenic. Iron is also emerging as a major problem with many habitations showing excess iron in the water samples.

Water Crisis in India

The provision of clean drinking water has been given priority in the Constitution of India, with Article 47 conferring the duty of providing clean drinking water and improving public health standards to the State. The government has undertaken various programmes since independence to provide safe drinking water to the rural masses. Till the 10th plan, an estimated total of Rs.1,105 billion spent on providing safe drinking water. One would argue that the expenditure is huge but it is also true that despite such expenditure lack of safe and secure drinking water continues to be a major hurdle and a national economic burden. On one hand the pressures of development is changing the distribution of water in the country, access to adequate water has been cited as the primary factor responsible for limiting development. The average availability of water is reducing steadily with the growing population and it is estimated that by 2020 India will become a water stressed nation. Groundwater is the major source of water in our country with 85% of the population dependent on it.

The 2001 Census reported that 68.2 per cent of households in India have access to safe drinking water. According to latest estimates, 94 per cent of the rural population and 91 per cent of the people living in urban areas have access to safe drinking water. Data available with the Department of Drinking Water Supply shows that of the 1.42 million rural habitations in the country, 1.27 million are fully covered (FC), 0.13 million are partially covered (PC) and 15,917 are not covered (NC).However, coverage refers to installed capacity, and not average actual supply over a sustained period or the quality of water being supplied which is the most essential part.

While accessing drinking water continues to be a problem, assuring that it is safe is a challenge by itself. Water quality problems are caused by pollution and over-exploitation. The rapid pace of industrialisation and greater emphasis on agricultural growth combined with financial and technological constraints and non-enforcement of laws have led to generation of large quantities

Little Community and its Characteristics

In sociology, the concept of community has led to significant debate, and sociologists are yet to reach agreement on a definition of the term. There were ninety-four discrete definitions of the term by the mid-1950s. Traditionally a "community" has been defined as a group of interacting people living in a common location.

The word is often used to refer to a group that is organized around common values and is attributed with social cohesion within a shared geographical location, generally in social units larger than a household. The word can also refer to the national community or global community.

The word "community" is derived from the Old French *communité* which is derived from the Latin *communitas* (*cum*, "with/together" + *munus*, "gift"), a broad term for fellowship or organized society.

Since the advent of the Internet, the concept of community no longer has geographical limitations, as people can now virtually gather in an online community and share common interests regardless of physical location.

Types of Community

A number of ways to categorize types of community have been proposed; one such breakdown is:

1. Geographic communities: range from the local neighbourhood, suburb, village, town or city, region, nation or even the planet as a whole. These refer to communities of *location*.
2. Communities of culture: range from the local clique, sub-culture, ethnic group, religious, multicultural or

pluralistic civilisation, or the global community cultures of today. They may be included as *communities of need* or *identity*, such as disabled persons, or frail aged people.

3. Community organizations: range from informal family or kinship networks, to more formal incorporated associations, political decision making structures, economic enterprises, or professional associations at a small, national or international scale.

Communities are nested; one community can contain another—for example a geographic community may contain a number of ethnic communities.

Location

Possibly the most common usage of the word *"community"* indicates a large group living in close proximity. Examples of local community include:

- A municipality is an administrative local area generally composed of a clearly defined territory and commonly referring to a town or village. Although large cities are also municipalities, they are often thought of as a collection of communities, due to their diversity.
- A neighbourhood is a geographically localized community, often within a larger city or suburb.
- A planned community is one that was designed from scratch and grew up more or less following the plan. Several of the world's capital cities are planned cities, notably Washington, D.C., in the United States, Canberra in Australia, and Brasília in Brazil. It was also common during the European colonization of the Americas to build according to a plan either on fresh ground or on the ruins of earlier Amerindian cities.

Identity

In some contexts, *"community"* indicates a group of people with a common identity other than location. Members often interact regularly. Common examples in everyday usage include:

- A "professional community" is a group of people with the same or related occupations. Some of those members may join a professional society, making a more defined and formalized group. These are also sometimes known as communities of practice.

- A virtual community is a group of people primarily or initially communicating or interacting with each other by means of information technologies, typically over the Internet, rather than in person. These may be either communities of interest, practice or communion. Research interest is evolving in the motivations for contributing to online communities.

Overlaps

Some communities share both location and other attributes. Members choose to live near each other because of one or more common interests.

- A retirement community is designated and at least usually designed for retirees and seniors—often restricted to those over a certain age, such as 56. It differs from a retirement home, which is a single building or small complex, by having a number of autonomous households.
- An intentional community is a deliberate residential community with a much higher degree of social communication than other communities. The members of an intentional community typically hold a common social, political or spiritual vision and share responsibilities and resources. Intentional communities include Amish villages, ashrams, cohousing, communes, ecovillages, housing cooperatives, kibbutzim, and land trusts.

Internet Communities

To a growing part of people the meaning of the word *"community"* indicates a smaller or larger group of internet users signing up to become members of a community page/ system on internet. Examples of internet communities include:

- A business community is often an administrative community with possibilities to add CV's and other business-related information.

- An interest community is a based on specialized areas such as art, golf or bird watching.
- A general community is wider in its range-opening for its users to create areas, pages and groups.

Special Nature of Human Community

Definitions of community as "organisms inhabiting a common environment and interacting with one another," while scientifically accurate, do not convey the richness, diversity and complexity of human communities. Their classification, likewise is almost never precise. Untidy as it may be, community is vital for humans. M. Scott Peck expresses this in the following way: "There can be no vulnerability without risk; there can be no community without vulnerability; there can be no peace, and ultimately no life, without community."

Characteristics of the Rural Landscape

A classification system of eleven characteristics has been developed for reading a rural landscape and for understanding the natural and cultural forces that have shaped it. Landscape characteristics are the tangible evidence of the activities and habits of the people who occupied, developed, used, and shaped the land to serve human needs; they may reflect the beliefs, attitudes, traditions, and values of these people.

The first four characteristics are processes that have been instrumental in shaping the land, such as the response of farmers to fertile soils. The remaining seven are physical components that are evident on the land, such as barns or orchards. Many, but not all, rural properties contain all eleven characteristics. When historic processes are linked to existing components, the rural landscape can be viewed as a unified whole. The section "Documentation of Landscape Characteristics" shows the relationship of the eleven characteristics and the features represented by them.

This classification system is a tool for gathering and organizing information. First of all, it is used to develop historic contexts for rural areas. The processes define specific themes, such as dairy farming or Belgian settlement, that have influenced historic development. The physical components define historic features of the landscape that may be used to describe significant property types and to identify properties eligible for listing in the National Register.

Second, the system is used to identify and evaluate the significant properties of a rural area or to determine the eligibility of a particular rural landscape. Through field survey and historic research, characteristics are associated with specific features, such as field patterns or roadways, and provide an understanding of an area or property's historic land uses and physical evolution.

Third, as information about existing characteristics is related to the historic contexts for a geographical area, assessments of significance, integrity, and boundaries can be made for specific properties. Information is evaluated to determine whether, within a rural area or region, a large historic district or separate properties should be considered for listing in the National Register. A comparison of past and present characteristics within a single property helps determine whether the property retains historic integrity and what the National Register boundaries should be.

Finally, the classification system provides a format for documenting rural properties on National Register forms. It can be used to organize the description and statement of significance for a specific rural property on the registration form. It is also useful for organizing information about rural historic contexts and property types on the multiple property documentation form.

Processes

Land Uses and Activities: Land uses are the major human forces that shape and organize rural communities. Human activities, such as farming, mining, ranching, recreation, social events, commerce, or industry, have left an imprint on the landscape. An examination of changing and continuing land uses may lead to a general understanding of how people have interacted with their environment and provide clues about the kinds of physical features and historic properties that should be present. Topographic variations, availability of transportation, the abundance or scarcity of natural resources (especially water), cultural traditions, and economic factors influenced the ways people use the land. Changing land uses may have resulted from improved technology, exhausted soils or mineral deposits, climatic changes, and new economic conditions, as well as previous successes or failures. Activities visible today may reflect traditional practices or be innovative, yet compatible, adaptations of historic ones.

Patterns of Spatial Organization: The organization of land on a large scale depends on the relationship among major physical components, predominant landforms, and natural features. Politics, economics, and technology, as well as the natural environment, have influenced the organization of communities by determining settlement patterns, proximity to markets, and the availability of transportation.

Organization is reflected in road systems, field patterns, distance between farmsteads, proximity to water sources, and orientation of structures to sun and wind. For example, spatial patterns can be seen in the grid of square mile townships and 160-acre farmsteads in the Midwest established by the land ordinances of 1785 and 1787; the distribution of towns every seven miles along a railroad corridor; and the division of land in Louisiana, by the French long-lot system, to ensure that every parcel has river frontage.

Large-scale patterns characterizing the settlement and early history of a rural area may remain constant, while individual features, such as buildings and vegetation, change over time. Changes in technology, for example, may have altered plowing practices, although the location of plowed fields, and, therefore, the overall historic pattern may remain the same.

Response to the Natural Environment: Major natural features, such as mountains, prairies, rivers, lakes, forests, and grasslands, influenced both the location and organization of rural communities. Climate, similarly, influenced the siting of buildings, construction materials, and the location of clusters of buildings and structures. Traditions in land use, construction methods, and social customs commonly evolved as people responded to the physiography and ecological systems of the area where they settled. Early settlements frequently depended upon available natural resources, such as water for transportation, irrigation, or mechanical power. Mineral or soil deposits, likewise, determined the suitability of a region for particular activities. Available materials, such as stone or wood, commonly influenced the construction of houses, barns, fences, bridges, roads, and community buildings.

Cultural Traditions: Cultural traditions affect the ways that land is used, occupied, and shaped. Religious beliefs, social customs, ethnic identity, and trades and skills may be evident today in both physical features and uses of the land. Ethnic customs, predating the origins of a community, were often transmitted by early settlers and perpetuated by successive generations. Others originated during a community's early development and evolution. Cultural groups have interacted with the natural environment, manipulating and perhaps altering it, and sometimes modifying their traditions in response to it.

Cultural traditions determined the structure of communities by influencing the diversity of buildings, location of roads and village centres, and ways the land was worked. Social customs dictated the crops planted or livestock raised. Traditional building forms, methods of construction, stylistic finishes, and functional solutions evolved in the work of local artisans. For example, rustic saunas appeared among the outbuildings of Finnish farmsteads in northwestern Michigan, while community churches occupied isolated crossroads in the High Plains. Taro, grown as a staple in the Hawaiian daily diet, also assumed an important role in the traditional luau. At the Amana Colonies in Iowa, large expanses of farmland and forest—based upon communal ownership, a village settlement pattern, and religious beliefs—varied from the rectangular grid typical of Midwestern family farms.

Components

Circulation Networks: Circulation networks are systems for transporting people, goods, and raw materials from one point to another. They range in scale from livestock trails and footpaths, to roads, canals, major highways, and even airstrips. Some, such as farm or lumbering roads, internally served a rural community, while others, such as railroads and waterways, connected it to the surrounding region.

Boundary Demarcations: Boundary demarcations delineate areas of ownership and land use, such as an entire farmstead or open range. They also separate smaller areas having special functions, such as a fenced field or enclosed corral. Fences, walls, tree lines, hedge rows, drainage or irrigation ditches, roadways, creeks, and rivers commonly marked historic boundaries.

Vegetation Related to Land Use: Various types of vegetation bear a direct relationship to long-established patterns of land use. Vegetation includes not only crops, trees, or shrubs planted for agricultural and ornamental purposes, but also trees that have grown up incidentally along fence lines, beside roads, or in abandoned fields. Vegetation may include indigenous, naturalized, and introduced species.

While many features change over time, vegetation is, perhaps, the most dynamic. It grows and changes with time, whether or not people care for it. Certain functional or ornamental plantings, such as wheat or peonies, may be evident only during selected seasons. Each species has a unique pattern of growth and life span, making the presence of historic specimens questionable or unlikely in many cases. Current vegetation may differ from historic vegetation, suggesting past uses of the land. For example, Eastern red cedars or aspens indicate the natural succession of abandoned farmland in the Midwest.

Buildings, Structures, and Objects: Various types of buildings, structures, and objects serve human needs related to the occupation and use of the land. Their function, materials, date, condition, construction methods, and location reflect the historic activities, customs, tastes, and skills of the people who built and used them.

Buildings—designed to shelter human activity—include residences, schools, churches, outbuildings, barns, stores, community halls, and train depots. Structures—designed for functions other than shelter—include dams, canals, systems of fencing, systems of irrigation, tunnels, mining shafts, grain elevators, silos, bridges, earthworks, ships, and highways. Objects—relatively small but important stationary or movable constructions—include markers and monuments, small boats, machinery, and equipment. Rural buildings and structures often exhibit patterns of vernacular design that may be common in their region or unique to their community. Residences may suggest family size and relationships, population densities, and economic fluctuations. The repeated use of methods, forms, and materials of construction may indicate successful solutions to building needs or demonstrate the unique skills, workmanship, or talent of a local artisan.

Clusters: Groupings of buildings, fences, and other features, as seen in a farmstead, ranch, or mining complex, result from function, social tradition, climate, or other influences, cultural or natural. The arrangement of clusters may reveal information about historical and continuing activities, as well as the impact of varying technologies and the preferences of particular generations. The repetition of similar clusters throughout a landscape may indicate vernacular patterns of siting, spatial organization, and land use. Also, the location of clusters, such as the market towns that emerged at the crossroads of early highways, may reflect broad patterns of a region's cultural geography.

Archeological Sites: The sites of prehistoric or historic activities or occupation, may be marked by foundations, ruins, changes in vegetation, and surface remains. They may provide valuable information about the ways the land has been used, patterns of social history, or the methods and extent of activities such as shipping, milling, lumbering, or quarrying. The ruins of mills, charcoal kilns, canals, outbuildings, piers, quarries, and mines commonly indicate previous uses of the land. Changes in vegetation may indicate abandoned roadways, homesites, and fields. The spatial distribution of features, surface disturbances, subsurface remains, patterns of soil erosion and deposition, and soil composition may also yield information about the evolution and past uses of the land.

Small-scale elements: Small-scale elements, such as a foot bridge or road sign, add to the historic setting of a rural landscape. These features may be characteristic of a region and occur repeatedly throughout an area, such as limestone fence posts in Kansas or cattle gates in the Buffalo River Valley of Arkansas. While most small-scale elements are long-lasting, some, such as bales of hay, are temporal or seasonal. Collectively, they often form larger components, such as circulation networks or boundary demarcations. Small-scale elements also include minor remnants—such as canal stones, road traces, mill stones, individual fruit trees, abandoned machinery, or fence posts—that mark the location of historic activities, but lack significance or integrity as archeological sites.

Peasant Society and its Features

A peasant is an agricultural worker who generally owns or rents only a small plot of ground. The word is derived from 15th century French *païsant* meaning one from the *pays*, or countryside, ultimately from the Latin *pagus*, or outlying administrative district (when the Roman Empire became Christian, these outlying districts were the last to Christianise, and this gave rise to "pagan" as a religious term). The term peasant today is sometimes used in a pejorative sense for impoverished farmers.

Peasants typically make up the majority of the agricultural labour force in a Pre-industrial society, dependent on the cultivation of their land: without stockpiles of provisions they thrive or starve according to the most recent harvest. The majority of the people in the Middle Ages were peasants. Pre-industrial societies have diminished with the advent of globalization and as such there are considerably fewer peasants to be found in rural areas throughout the world (as a proportion of the total world population).

Though "peasant" is a word of loose application, once a market economy has taken root the term *peasant proprietors* is frequently used to describe the traditional rural population in countries where the land is chiefly held by smallholders. It is sometimes used by people who consider themselves of higher class as *slang* to refer pejoratively to those of poorer education who come from a lower income background.

In many pre-industrial societies, peasants comprised the bulk of the population. Peasant societies often had well developed social support networks. Especially in harder climates, members of the community who had a poor harvest or suffered other hardships were taken care of by the rest of the community. Peasants usually only had one set of clothing, two at most. Also, a peasant usually owed their lord 20% of their earnings. They also owed the priest or bishop 10% of their ownings. Of course, knights could, and would usually demand tributes for keeping them alive. Overall, the peasant usually retained only 10-20% of their total work and earnings.

Peasant societies can often have very stratified social hierarchies within them. Rural people often have very different values and economic behaviour from urbanites, and tend to be more conservative. Peasants are often very loyal to inherited power structures that define their rights and privileges and protect them from interlopers, despite their low status within those power structures.

Fernand Braudel devoted the first volume–called *The Structures of Everyday Life*–of his major work, *Civilization and Capitalism 15th–18th Century* to the largely silent and invisible world that existed below the market economy.

Since it was the literate classes who left the most records, and these tended to dismiss peasants as figures of coarse appetite and rustic comedy, the term "peasant" may have a pejorative rather than descriptive connotation in historical memory. Society was theorized as being organized into three "estates": those who work, those who pray, and those who fight.

Medieval European Peasants

The relative position of peasants in Western Europe improved greatly after the Black Death unsettled the demography of medieval Europe.

In the wake of this disruption to the established order, later centuries saw the invention of the printing press, the development of widespread literacy and the enormous social and intellectual changes of the Enlightenment.

This evolution of ideas in an environment of relatively widespread literacy laid the groundwork for the Industrial Revolution, which enabled mechanically-and chemically-augmented agricultural production while simultaneously increasing the demand for factory workers in cities. Urban factory-workers, with their low skill and large numbers, quickly came to occupy the socio-economic stratum formerly the preserve of the medieval peasants.

This process happened in an especially pronounced and truncated way in Eastern Europe. Lacking any catalysts for change in the 14th century, Eastern European peasants largely continued upon the original medieval path until the 18th and 19th centuries. The Tsars then began to notice that though the West had made enormous strides, they had not; they responded by forcing the largely illiterate peasant populations under their control to embark upon a course of Westernization and industrialization.

Peasant Revolution and Peasant Studies

The field of peasant studies as such was rooted in the early work of scholars such as Florian Znaniecki and Fei Xiaotong, and post-war studies of the Great Tradition and Little Tradition in work of lRobert Redfield. In the 1960s, anthropologists and historians began to rethink the role of peasant revolt in world history and their own disciplines. This rethinking was partly in response to American involvement in the Vietnam War, which critics on the left regarded as an attempt to repress a peasant revolution. Peasant Revolution was seen as a Third World response to capitalism and imperialism.

The anthropologist Eric Wolf, for instance, drew on the work of earlier scholars in the Marxist tradition, such as Daniel Thorner, who saw the rural population as a key element in the transition from feudalism to capitalism. Wolf and a group of scholars criticized both Marx and the field of modernization theorists for treating peasants as lacking the ability to take action. James C. Scott's field observation in Malaysia convinced him that villagers were active participants in their local politics even though they were forced to use indirect methods. Many of these activist scholars looked back to the Peasant Movement in India and the theories of revolution in China led by Mao Zedong starting in the 1920s. The anthropologist Myron Cohen, however, asked why the rural population in China were called "peasants" rather than "farmers," a distinction he called political rather than scientific. One important outlet for their scholarly work and theory was the Journal of Peasant Studies.

Peasant Society and the Image of Limited Good

The members of every society share a common cognitive orientation which is, in effect, an unverbalized, implicit expression of their understanding of the "rules of the game" of living imposed upon them by their social, natural, and supernatural universes. A cognitive orientation provides the members of the society it characterizes with basic premises and sets of assumptions normally neither recognized nor questioned which structure and guide behaviour in much the same way grammatical rules unrecognized by most people structure and guide their linguistic forms. All normative behaviour of the members of a group is a function of their particular way of looking at their total environment, their unconscious acceptance of the "rules of the game" implicit in their cognitive orientation.

A particular cognitive orientation cannot be thought of as world view in a Redneldian sense, i.e., as something existing largely at a conscious level in the minds of the members of the group.' The average man of any society cannot describe the underlying premises of which his behaviour is a logical function any more than he can outline a phonemic statement which expresses the patterned regularities in his speech. As Kluckhohn has pointed out, cognitive orientations (he speaks of "configurations") are recognized by most members of a society only 3n the sense that they make choices "with the configurations as unconscious but determinative backgrounds" (1943:218),

In speaking of a cognitive orientation—the terms "cognitive view," "world view' "world view perspective," "basic assumptions," "implicit premises' and perhaps "ethos" may be used as synonyms—I am as an anthropologist concerned with two levels of problems: (1) the nature of the cognitive orientation itself which I see as something "psychologically real," and the ways in which and the degree to which it can be known; and (2) the economical representation of this cognitive orientation by means of models or integrating principles which account for observed behaviour, and which permit prediction of behaviour yet unnoted or unperformed. Such a model or principle is, as Kluckhohn has often pointed out, an inferential construct or an analytic, abstraction derived from observed behaviour, A model or integrating principle is not the cognitive orientation itself, but for purposes of analysis the two cannot be separated, A well-constructed model is, of course, nut really descriptive of behaviour at all (as is, for example, the term "ethos as used by Gillin. [1955] to describe contemporary Latin American culture). A good model is heuristic and explanatory, not descriptive, and it has predictive value. It encourages an analyst to search for behaviour patterns, and relationships between patterns, which he may not yet have recognised, simply because logically—if the model is sound—it is reasonable to expect to find them. By the same token, a sound model should make it pos-. Bible to predict how people are going to behave when faced with certain, alternatives-A model therefore has at least two important functions: it is conducive to better Held work, and it has practical utility as a guide to policy and action in developmental programs.

A perfect model or integrating principle of a particular world view should subsume *all* behaviour of the members of a group. In practice il is unreasonable to expect this. But the best model is the one that subsumes the greatest amount of behaviour in such fashion that there are no mutually incompatible parts in the model, i.e., forms of behaviour cast together in what is obviously a logically inconsistent relationship. Kluckhohn speculated about the possibility of a single model, a dominant "master configuration" characterizing an entire society, for which he suggested the terms "integration" (1941:128) and "ethos" (1943:221), but I believe he never attempted the task of describing a complete ethos. Opler, on the other hand, has described Lipan Apache culture in terms of twenty "themes" which are, however, to a considerable extent descriptive, and which in no way approximate a master model (1946).'

How does an anthropologist fathom the cognitive orientation of the group he studies, to find patterns that will permit building a model or stating an integrating principle? Componential analysis and other formal semantic methods have recently been much in vogue, and these techniques unquestionably can tell us a great deal. But the degree of dissention among anthropologists who use these methods suggests that they are not a single royal road to "God's truth" (cf. Burling 1964). I suspect there will always remain a considerable element of ethnological art in the processes whereby we come to have some understanding of a cognitive orientation. However we organize our thought processes, we are engaging in an exercise in structural analysis in which overt behaviour (and the simpler patterns into which this behaviour is readily seen to fall) is viewed somewhat as a reflection or representation of a wider reality which our sensory apparatus can never directly perceive. Or, we can view the search for a cognitive view as an exercise in triangulation. Of each trait and pattern the question is asked, "Of what implicit assumption might this behaviour be a logical function?" When enough questions have been asked, the answers will be found to point in a common direction. The model emerges from the point where the lines of answers intersect. Obviously, an anthropologist well acquainted with a particular culture cannot merely apply simple rules of analysis and automatically produce a model for, or even a description oi, a world view. In effect, we are dealing with a pyramidal structure; low-level regularities and coherences relating overt behaviour forms are fitted into higher-level patterns which in turn may be found to fall into place at a still higher level of integration. Thus, a model of a social structure, sound in itself, will be found to be simply one expression of a structural regularity which will have analogues in religion and economic activities.

Since all normative behaviour of the members of a group is a function of its particular cognitive orientation, both in an abstract philosophical sense and in the view of an individual himself, all behaviour is "rational" and sense-making. "Irrational" behaviour can be spoken of only in the context of a cognitive view which did not give rise to that behaviour. Thus, in a rapidly changing world, in which peasant and primitive peoples are pulled into the social and economic Context of whole nations, some of their behaviour may appear irrational to others because the social, economic, and natural universe that in fact controls the conditions of their life is other than that revealed to them—however subconsciously—by a traditional world view. That is, a peasant's cognitive view provides moral and other precepts that are guides to—in fact, may be said to produce—behaviour that may not be appropriate to the changing conditions of life he has not yet grasped. For this reason when the cognitive orientation of large numbers of a nation's people is out of tune with reality, these people will behave in a way that will appear irrational to those who are more nearly attuned to reality. Such peoples will be seen as constituting a drag (as indeed they may be) on a nation's development, and they will be cutting themselves off from the opportunity to participate in the benefits that economic progress can bring.

In this paper I am concerned with the nature of the cognitive orientation of peasants, and with interpreting and relating peasant behaviour as described by anthropologists to this orientation. I am also concerned with the implications of this orientation-and related behaviour to the problem of the peasant's participation in the economic growth of the country to which he may belong.

Specifically, I will outline what I believe to be the dominant theme in the cognitive orientation of classic peasant societies,* show how characteristic peasant behaviour seems to flow from this orientation, and attempt to show that this behaviour—however incompatible with national economic growth—is not only highly rational in the context of the cognition that determines it, but that for the maintenance of peasant society in its classic form, it is indispensable. The kinds of behaviour that have been suggested as adversely influencing economic growth are, among many, the "luck" syndrome, a "fatalistic" outlook, inter-and intra-familial quarrels, difficulties in cooperation, extraordinary ritual expenses by poor people and the problems these expenses pose for capital accumulation, and the apparent lack of what the psychologist McClelland (1961) has called "need for Achievement." I will suggest that peasant participation in national development can be hastened not by stimulating a psychological process, the need for achievement, but by creating economic and other opportunities that will encourage the peasant to abandon his traditional and increasingly unrealistic cognitive orientation for a new one that reflects the realities of the modern world.

The model of cognitive orientation that seems to me best to account for peasant behaviour is the "Image of Limited Good." By "Image of Limited Good" I mean that broad areas of peasant behaviour are patterned in such fashion as to suggest that peasants view their social, economic, and natural universes—their total environment—as one in which all of the desired things in life such as land, wealth, health, friendship and love, manliness and honor, respect and status, power and influence, security and safety, *exist in finite quantity* and *are always in short supply,* as far as the peasant is concerned. Not only do these and all other "good things" exist in finite and limited quantities, but in addition *there is no way directly within peasant power to increase the available quantities.* It is as if the obvious fact of land shortage in a densely populated area applied to all other desired things: not enough to go around. "Good," like land, is seen as inherent in nature, there to be divided and re-divided, if necessary, but not to be augmented.

For purposes of analysis, and at this stage of the argument, I am considering a peasant community to be a closed system. Except in a special—but extremely important—way, a peasant sees his existence as determined and limited by the natural and social resources of his village and his immediate area. Consequently, there is a primary corollary to The Image of Limited Good: if "Good" exists in limited amounts which cannot be expanded, and if the system is closed, it follows that *an individual or a family can improve a position only at the expense of others.* Hence an apparent relative improvement in someone's position with respect to any "Good" is viewed as a threat to the entire community. Someone is being despoiled, whether he sees it or not. And since there is often uncertainty as to wno is losing—obviously it may be ego—*any* significant improvement is perceived, not as a threat to an individual or a family alone, but as a threat to *all* individuals and families.

This model was first worked out on the basis of a wide variety of field data from Tzintzuntzan, Michoacin, Mexico: family behaviour, exchange patterns, cooperation, religious activities, court claims, disputes, material culture, folklore, language, and many other bits and pieces. At no point has an informant even remotely suggested that this is his vision of his universe. Yet each Tzintzuntzeno organizes his behaviour in a fashion entirely rational when it is viewed as a function of this principle which he cannot enunciate.'

The model of Limited Good, when "fed back" to behaviour in Tzintzuntzan, proved remarkably productive in revealing' hitherto unsuspected structural regularities linking economic behaviour with social relations, friendship, love and jealousy patterns, health beliefs, concepts of honor and masculinity, *egoismo* manifestations—even folklore (Foster 1964a). Not only were structural regularities revealed in Tzintzuntzan, but much peasant behaviour known to me from other field work, and reported in the literature, seemed also to be a function of this cognitive orientation. This has led me to offer the kinds of data I have utilized in formulating this model, and to explain the interpretations that seem to me to follow from it, as characterizing in considerable degree classic peasant societies, in the hope that the model will be tested against other extensive bodies of data. I believe, obviously, that if the Image of Limited Good is examined as a high-level integrating principle characterizing ' peasant communities, we will find within our individual societies unsuspected structural regularities and, on a cross-cultural level, basic patterns that will be most helpful in constructing the typology of peasant society. The data I present in support of this thesis arc illustrative, and arc not based on an exhaustive survey of peasant literature.

In the following pages I will offer evidence under four headings that seems to me to conform to the model I have suggested. I will then discuss the implications of this evidence.

When the peasant views his economic world as one in which Limited Good prevails, and he can progress only at the expense of another, he is usually very near the truth. Peasant economies, as pointed out by many authors, are not productive. In the average village there *is* only a finite amount of wealth produced, and no amount of extra hard work will significantly change the figure. In most of the peasant world land has been limited for a long, long time, and only in a few places have young farmers in a growing community been able to hive off from the parent village to start on a level of equality with their parents and grandparents. Customarily land is not only limited, but it has become increasingly limited, by population expansion and soil; deterioration. Peasant production techniques remained largely; unchanged for hundreds, and even thousands of years; at best, in farming, this means the-Mediterranean plow drawn by oxen, supplemented by human* powered hand tools. Handicraft techniques in weaving, pottery-making, wood-s working and building likewise have changed little over the years.

In fact, it seems accurate to say that the average peasant sees little or no : relationship between work and production techniques on the one hand, and: the acquisition of wealth on the other. Rather, wealth is seen by villagers in the same light as land: present, circumscribed by absolute limits, and having no relationship to work. One works to eat, but not to create wealth. Wealth, like land, is someting that is inherent in nature. It can be divided up and passed around in various ways, but, within the framework of the villagers' traditional world, it does not grow. Time and tradition have determined the shares each family and individual hold; these shares are not static, since obviously they do shift. But the reason for the relative position of each villager is known at any given time, and any significant change calls for explanation.

The evidence that friendship, love, and affection are seen as strictly limited in peasant society is strong. Every anthropologist in a peasant village soon realizes the narrow path he must walk to avoid showing excessive favor or friendship toward some families, thereby alienating others who will feel deprived, and hence reluctant to help him in his work. Once I brought a close friend from Tzintzuntzan, working as a bracero in a nearby town, to my Berkeley home. When safely away from the camp he told me his brother was also there. Why did he not tell me, so I could have invited him? My friend replied, in effect, that he was experiencing a coveted "good" and he did not want to risk diluting the satisfaction by sharing it with another.

Adams reports how a social worker in a Guatemalan village unwittingly prejudiced her work by making more friends in one barrio than in the other, thereby progressively alienating herself from potential friends whose help she needed (1955:442). In much of Latin America the institutionalized best friend, particularly among post-adolescents, variously known as the *amigo carnal,* or the *cucllo* or *camaraderia* (the latter two described by Reina for Guatemala [1959]) constitutes both recognition of the fact that true friendship is a scarce commodity, and serves as insurance against being left without any of it. The jealousies and feelings of deprivation felt by one partner when the other leaves or threatens to leave sometimes lead to violence.

Widespread peasant definitions of sibling rivalry suggest that a mother's ability to love her children is viewed as limited by the amount of love she possesses. In Mexico when a mother again becomes pregnant and weans her nursing child, the child often becomes *chipil.* It fusses, cries, clings to her skirt, and is inconsolable. The child is said to be *celoso,* jealous of its unborn sibling whose presence it recognizes and whom it perceives as a threat, already depriving him of maternal love and affection. Chfpil is known as *chip* or *chipe* in Guatemala, where it is described in a classic article by Paul (1950), as *sipe* in Honduras, and simply as *celos* ("jealousy") in Costa Rica. *Chucaque* in southern Colombia, described as the jealousy of a child weaned because of its mother's pregnancy, appears to be the same thing (communicated by Dr. Virginia Gutierrez de Pineda).

A similar folk etiology is used among the semi-peasant peoples of Buganda to explain the onset of *kwashiorkor* in a child recently weaned. If the mother is again pregnant, the child is said to have *obwosi,* and shows symptoms of pale hair, sweating of hands and feet, fever, diarrhea, and vomiting. "The importance of pregnancy is such that if a woman takes a sick child to a native doctor the first question he asks is 'Are you pregnant?'". The African logic is the reverse of, but complementary to, that of Latii America: it is the *unborn child* that is jealous of its older sibling, whom it tries to poison through the mother's milk, thereby forcing weaning. In both areas, insufficient quantities of love and affection are seen as precipitating the crisis. In Buganda, "In the local culture it is essential that the mother should devote herself to the unborn child or a child recently born, at the expense of any other children; *there does not seem to be an easy acceptance of the idea that there can be enough love for all".*

Similarly, in an Egyptian village, sibling rivalry is recognized at this period in a child's development. As in Latin America, jealousy is one way; it is always the older who is jealous of the younger. "It is also acknowledged that the youngest child becomes jealous immediately his mother's abdomen becomes enlarged on pregnancy and he is usually told of the forthcoming event." This jealousy, in excess, may have ill effects on the child, causing diarrhea, swellings, lack of appetite, temper tantrums, and sleeplessness.'

In parts of Guatemala chipe is a term used to express a husband's jealousy of his pregnant wife, for temporary loss of sexual services and for the attention to be given to the baby. Tepoztlán husbands also suffer from *chipilez,* becoming sleepy and not wanting to work. Oscar Lewis says a husband can be cured by wearing a strip of his wife's skirt around his neck (1951:378). In Tonalá, Jalisco, Mexico, husbands often are jealous of their adolescent sons and angry with their wives because of the affection the latter show their offspring. A wife's love and affection are seen as limited; to the extent the son receives what appears to be an excessive amount, the husband is deprived. In the Egyptian village described by Ammar a new mother-in-law is very affectionate toward her son-in-law, thereby making her own unmarried sons and daughters jealous. By showing affection to the outsider, the woman obviously is seen as depriving her own offspring of something they wish.

It is a truism to peasants that health is a "good" that exists in limited quantities. Peasant folk medicine does not provide the protection that scientific medicine gives those who have access to it, and malnutrition frequently aggravates conditions stemming from lack of sanitation, hygiene, and immunization. In peasant societies preoccupation with health and illness is general, and constitutes a major topic of interest, speculation, and discussion. Perhaps the best objective evidence that health is viewed within the framework of Limited Good is the widespread attitude toward blood which is, to use Adams' expression, seen as "non-regenerative" . For obvious reasons, blood is equated with life, and good blood, and lots of it, means health. Loss of blood—if it is seen as something that cannot be renewed—is thus seen as a threat to health, a permanent loss resulting in weakness for as long as an individual lives. Although best described for Guatemala, the belief that blood is non-regenerative is widespread in Latin America. This belief, frequently unverbalized, may be one of the reasons it is so difficult to persuade Latin Americans to give blood transfusions: by giving blood so that someone can have more, the donor will have less.

Similar beliefs are found in Nigeria (communicated by Dr. Adeniyi-Adeniji Jones) and they are well known in Indian peasant villages. Here the psychological problem is further compounded by the equation of blood with semen: one drop of semen to seven (or forty, depending on area) drops of blood. The exercise of masculine vitality is thus seen as a permanently debilitating act. Only so much sexual pleasure is allotted man, and nothing he can do will increase his measure. Sexual moderation and the avoidance of bloodletting are the course of the prudent man.

In parts of Mexico (e.g., the Michoacán villages of Tzintzuntzan and Erongaricuaro) the limits on health are reflected in views about long hair. A woman's long hair is much admired, but the price is high: a woman with long hair is thought always to be thin and wan, and she cannot expect to have vigor and strength. Sources of vitality are insufficient to grow long hair and still leave an individual with energy and a well-fleshed body.

Oft-noted peasant sensitiveness to real or imagined insults to personal honor, and violent reactions to challenges which cast doubt on a man's masculinity, appear to be a function of the belief that honor and manliness exist in limited quantities, and that consequently not everyone can enjoy a full measure. In rural Mexico, among braceros who have worked in the United States, American ethnologists have often been asked, "In the United States it's the wife who commands, no?" Masculinity and domestic control appear to be viewed much like other desirable things: there is only so much, and the person who has it deprives another. Mexican men find it difficult to believe that a husband and wife can share domestic responsibilities and decision making, without the husband being deprived of his *machismo.* Many believe a wife, however good, must be beaten from time to time, simply so she will not lose sight of a God-decreed familial hierarchy. They are astonished and shocked to learn that an American wife-beater can be jailed; this seems an incredibly unwarranted intrusion of the State into God's plans for the family.

The essence of machismo is valor, and *un hombre muy valienle,* i.e.j-a *macho,* is one who is strong and tough, generally fair, not a bully, but who never dodges a fight, and who always wins. Above all, a macho inspires *respeto* ("respect"). One achieves machismo, it is clear, by depriving others of access to it. In Greece *philotimo,* a "love of honor," equates closely with Mexican machismo. A man who is physically sound, lithe, strong, and agile has philotimo. If he can converse well, show wit, and act in other ways that facilitate sociability and establish ascendency, he enhances his philotimo. One attacks another male through his philotimo, by shaming or ridiculing him, by showing how he lacks the necessary attributes for a man. Consequently, avoiding ridicule becomes a major concern, a primary defence mechanism among rural Greek males. In a culture shot through with envy and competitiveness, there is the ever-present danger of attack, so a man must be prepared to respond to a jeer or insult with a swift retort, an angry challenge, or a knife thrust. "Philotimo can be enhanced at the expense of another. It has a see-saw characteristic; one's own goes up as another's declines... the Greek, in order to maintain and increase his sense of worth, must be prepared each moment to assert his superiority over friend and foe alike. It is an interpersonal combat fraught with anxiety, uncertainty, and aggressive potentials. As one proverb describes it, 'When one Greek meets another, they immediately despise each other".

If, in fact, peasants see their universe as one in which the good things in life are in limited and unexpandable quantities, and hence personal gain must be at the expense of others, we must assume that social institutions, personal behaviour, values, and personality will all display patterns that can be viewed as functions of this cognitive orientation. Preferred behaviour, it may be argued, will be that which is seen by the peasant as maximizing his security, by preserving his relative position in the traditional order of things. People who see themselves in "threatened" circumstances, which the Image of Limited Good implies, react normally in one of two ways: maximum cooperation and sometimes communism, burying individual differences and placing sanctions against individualism; or extreme individualism. Peasant societies seem always to choose the second alternative.

The reasons are not clear, but two factors may bear on the problem. Cooperation requires leadership. This may be delegated democratically by the members of a group itself; it may be assumed by a strong man from within the group; or it may be imposed by forces lying outside the group. Peasant societies—for reasons that should be clear in the following analysis—are unable by their very nature to delegate authority, and assumption of authority by a strong man is, at best, temporary, and not a structural solution to a problem.

The truncated political nature of peasant societies, with real power lying outside the community, seems effectively to discourage local assumption and exercise of power, except as an agent of these outside forces. By the very nature of peasant society, seen as a structural part of a larger society, local development of leadership which might make possible cooperation is effectively prevented by the rulers of the political unit of which a particular peasant community is an element, who see such action as a potential threat to themselves.

Again, economic activities in peasant societies require only limited cooperation. Peasant families typically can, as family units, produce most of their food, farm without extra help, build their houses, weave cloth for their clothes', carry their own produce to market and sell it—in short, take care of themselves with a degree of independence impossible in an industrial society, and difficult in hunting-fishing-gathering societies. Peasants, of course, usually do not live with the degree of independence here suggested, but it is more clearly possible than in any other type of society.

Whatever the reasons, peasants are individualistic, and it logically follows from the Image of Limited Good that each minimal social unit (often the nuclear family and, in many situations, a single individual) sees itself in perpetual, unrelenting struggle with its fellows for possession of or control over what it considers to be its share of scarce values. This is a position that calls for extreme caution and reserve, a reluctance to reveal true strength or position. It encourages suspicion and mutual distrust, since things will not necessarily be what they seem to be, and it also encourages a male self image as a valiant person, one who commands respect, since he will be less attractive as a target than a weakling. A great deal of peasant behaviour, I believe, is exactly what we would predict from these circumstances. The works of Lewis (1951), Banfield (1958), Simmons (1959), Carstairs (1958), Dube (1958), the Weisers (1963), and Blackman (1927) (summarized by Foster 1960-1961) and my others testify to the "mentality of mutual distrust" that is widespread in peasant societies.

Since an individual or family that makes significant economic progress or acquires a disproportionate amount of some other "good" is seen to do so at the expense of others, such a change is viewed as a threat to the stability of the community. Peasant culture is provided with two principal mechanisms with which to maintain the essential stability:

a) an agreed-upon, socially acceptable, preferred norm of behaviour for its people, and
b) a "club" and a "carrot," in the form of sanctions and rewards, to ensure that real behaviour approximates this norm.

The agreed-upon norm that promotes maximum community stability is behaviour that tends to maintain the status quo in relationships. The individual or family that acquires more than its share of a "good," and particularly an economic "good," is, as we have seen, viewed as a threat to the community at large. Individuals and families which are seen to or are thought to progress violate the preferred norm of behaviour, thereby stimulating cultural mechanisms that redress the imbalance. Individuals or families that lose something, that fall behind, are seen as a threat in a different fashion; their envy, jealousy, or anger may result in overt or hidden aggression toward more fortunate people. The self-correcting mechanisms that guard the community balance operate at three levels, viz:

1) Individual and family behaviour. At this level I am concerned with the steps taken by *individuals* to maintain their positions in the system, and the ways in which they try to avoid both sanctions and exploitation by fellow villagers.

2) Informal and usually unorganized group behaviour. At this level I am concerned with the steps taken by the *community,* the sanctions that are invoked when it is felt someone is violating the agreed-upon norm of behaviour. Negative sanctions are the "club."

3) Institutionalized behaviour. At this level I am concerned with the "carrot": major community expressions of cultural forms which neutralize achieved imbalances. Each of these forms will be examined in turn.

3.1) On the individual-family level, two rules give guidance to preferred behaviour. These can be stated as:

a) Do not reveal evidence of material or other improvement in your relative position, lest you invite sanctions; should you display improvement, take action necessary to neutralize the consequences.

b) Do not allow yourself to fall behind your rightful place, lest you and your family suffer.

A family deals with the problem of real or suspected improvement in its relative position by a combination of two devices. First, it attempts to conceal evidence that might lead to this conclusion, and it denies the veracity of suggestions to this effect. Second, it meets the charge head on, admits an improvement in relative position, but shows it has no intention of using this position to the detriment of the village by neutralizing it through ritual expenditures, thereby restoring the status quo. Accounts of peasant communities stress that in traditional villages people do not compete for prestige with material symbols such as dress, housing, or food, nor do they compete for authority by seeking leadership roles. In peasant villages one notes a strong desire to look and act like everyone else, to be inconspicuous in position and behaviour. This theme is well summed up in the Wisers' paragraph on the importance of dilapidated walls suggesting poverty as a part of a family's defence (1963:120).

Also much remarked is the peasant's reluctance to accept leadership roles. He feels—for good reason—that his motives will be suspect and that he will be subject to the criticism of neighbors. By seeking, or even accepting, an authority position, the ideal man ceases to be ideal. A "good" man therefore usually shuns community responsibilities (other than of a ritual nature); by so doing he protects his reputation. Needless to say, this aspect of socially-approved behaviour heavily penalizes a peasant community in the modern world by depriving it of the leadership which is now essential to its development.

The mechanism invoked to minimize the danger of loss of relative position appears to center in the machismo-philotimo complex. A tough, strong man whose fearlessness in the face of danger, and whose skill in protecting himself and his family is recognized, does not invite exploitation. A "valiant" individual can command the "respect" so much sought after in many peasant societies, and he can strive toward security with the goal in mind (however illusory) of being able to live—as is said in Tzintzuntzan—*sin compromises* ("without obligations" to, or dependency on, others). A picture of the ideal peasant begins to emerge: a man who works to feed and clothe his family, who fulfills his community and ceremonial obligations, who minds his own business, who does not seek to be outstanding, but who knows how to protect his rights! Since a macho, a strong man, discourages exploitation, it is clear that personality characteristic has a basic function in peasant society. Not sur- f prisingly, defence of this valuable self-image may, by the standards of other societies, assume pathological proportions, for it is seen as a basic weapon in the struggle for life.

The ideal man must avoid the appearance of presumption, lest this be; interpreted as trying to take something that belongs to another. In tracing' the diffusion of new pottery-making techniques in Tzintzuntzan I found that no one would admit he had learned the technique from a neighbor. The inevitable reply to my question was *Me puse a pensar* ("I dreamed it up all by myself"), accompanied by a knowing look and a tapping of the temple with the; forefinger. Reluctance to give credit to others, common in Mexico, is often; described as due to *egoísmo,* an egotistical conceited quality. Yet if egofsmo, f as exemplified by unwillingness to admit profiting by a neighbour's new pottery knowledge, is seen as a function of an image of Limited Good, it is clear that a potter *must* deny that the idea is other than his own. To confess that he "borrowed" an idea is to confess that he has taken something not rightfully his, that he is consciously upsetting the community balance and the self image he tries so hard to maintain. Similarly, in trying to determine how compa-drazgo (godparenthood) ties are initiated, I found no informant who admitted he had asked a friend to serve; he always was asked by another. Informants | appear to fear that admission of asking may be interpreted as presuming or imposing on another, trying to get something to which they may not be entitled.

A complementary pattern is manifest in the general absence of compliments in peasant communities; rarely is a person heard to admire the performance of another, and when admiration is expressed by, say, an anthropologist, the person admired probably will try to deny there is any reason to compliment him. Reluctance of villagers to compliment each other again looks, at first glance, like egofsmo. But in the context of the Limited Good model, it is seen that such behaviour is proper. The person who compliments is, in fact, guilty of aggression; he is telling someone to his face that he is rising above the dead level that spells security for all, and he is suggesting that he may be confronted with sanctions.

Consider this interpretation as applied to an incident reported in southern Italy: "My attempt, in private, to praise a peasant friend for his large farm and able system of farming brought a prompt and vigorous denial that he did anything special. He said, 'There is no system, you just plant.' This attitude was expressed by others in forced discussions of farming" (Cancian 1961:8). Dr. Cancian offers this as illustrating the peasant's lack of confidence in his own ability to change his environment. Speaking specifically of agriculture, he writes that "All the examples indicate denial of the hope of progress in agriculture and alienation from the land". I believe the peasant viewed Dr. Cancian's praise as threatening, since it reminded him of his vulnerability because of his superior farming methods. His denial is not of hope of progress, but of cause for anyone to envy him.

The ideal man strives for moderation and equality in his behaviour. Should he attempt to better his comparative standing, thereby threatening village stability, the informal and usually unorganized sanctions appear. This is the "club," and it takes the form of gossip, slander, backbiting, character assassination, witchcraft or the threat of witchcraft, and sometimes actual physical aggression. These negative sanctions usually represent no formal community decision, but they are at least as effective as if authorized by law. Concern with public opinion is one of the most striking characteristics of peasant communities.

Negative sanctions, while usually informal, can be institutionalized. In peasant Spain, especially in the north, the charivari *(cencerrada)* represents such an instance. When an older man marries a much younger woman— usually a second marriage for the groom—marriageable youths serenade the couple with cowbells *(cencerros)* and other noisemakers, parade straw-stuffed manikins representing them through the streets, incense the manikins with foul-smelling substances, and shout obscenities. It seems clear that this symbolizes the resentment of youths, who have not yet had even one wife, against the inequalities represented by an older man who has already enjoyed marriage, who takes a young bride from the available pool, thereby further limiting the supply for the youths. By institutionalizing the sanctions the youths are permitted a degree of freedom and abuse not otherwise possible.

Attempted changes in the balance of a peasant village are discouraged by the methods just described; *achieved* imbalance is neutralized, and the balance restored, on an institutional level. A person who improves his position is encouraged—by use of the carrot—to restore the balance through conspicuous consumption in the form of ritual extravagance. In Latin America he is prcssured into sponsoring a costly fiesta by serving as *mayordomo.* His reward is prestige, which is viewed as harmless. Prestige cannot be dangerous since it is traded for dangerous wealth; the mayordomo has, in fact, been "disarmed," shorn of his weapons, and reduced to a state of impotence. There is good reason why peasant fiestas consume so much wealth in fireworks, candles, music, and food; and why, in peasant communities the rites of baptism, marriage, and death may involve relatively huge expenditures. These practices are a redistributive mechanism which permits a person or family that potentially threatens community stability gracefully to restore the status quo, thereby returning itself to a state of acceptability. Wolf, speaking specifically of the "closed" Indian peasant community of Mexico as it emerged after the

Conquest, puts it this way: "the system takes from those who have, in order to make all men have-nots. By liquidating the surpluses, it makes all men rich in sacred experience but poor in earthly goods. Since it levels differences of wealth, it also inhibits the growth of class distinctions based on wealth.... In engineering parlance, it acts as a feedback, returning a system that is beginning to oscillate to its original course" (1959:216).

I have said that in a society ruled by the Image of Limited Good there 'is no way, save at the expense of others, that an individual can get ahead. This is true in a closed system, which peasant communities approximate. But even a traditional peasant village, in another sense, has access to other systems, and an individual can achieve economic success by tapping sources of wealth that are recognized to exist outside the village system. Such success, though envjed, is not seen as a direct threat to community stability, for no one within the community has lost anything. Still, such success must be explained. In today's transitional peasant communities, seasonal emigration for wage labor is the most available way in which one can tap outside wealth. Hundreds of thousands of Mexican peasants have come to the United States as braceros in recent years and many, through their earnings, have pumped significant amounts of capital into their communities. Braceros generally are not criticized or attacked for acquisition of this wealth; it is clear that their good fortune is not at the direct expense of others within the village. Fuller finds a similar realistic appraisal of the wealth situation in a Lebanese community: "they [the peasants] realize... that the only method of increasing their incomes on a large scale is to absent themselves from the village for an extended period of time and to find work in more lucrative areas" (1961:72).

These examples, however, are but modern variants of a much older pattern in which luck and fate—points of contact with an open systen—are viewed as the only socially acceptable ways in which an individual can acquire more "good" than he previously has had. In traditional (not transitional) peasant communities an otherwise inexplicable increase in wealth is often seen as due to the discovery of treasure which may be the result of fate or of such positive action as making a pact with the Devil. Recently I have analysed treasure tales in

Tzintzuntzan and have found without exception they are attached to named individuals who, within living memory, have suddenly begun to live beyond their means. The usual evidence is that they suddenly opened stores, in spite of their known previous poverty (Foster 1964a). Erasmus has recorded this interpretation among Sonora villagers (1961:251), Wagley finds it in an Amazon small town (1964:128), and Friedmann reports it in southern Italy (1958:21). Clearly, the role of treasure tales in communities like these is to account for wealth that can be explained in no other manner.

The common peasant concern with finding wealthy and powerful patrons who can help them is also pertinent in this context. Since such patrons usually are outside the village, they are. not part of the closed system. Their aid, and material help, like bracero earnings or buried treasure, are seen as coming from beyond the village. Hence, although the lucky villager with a helpful patron may be envied, the advantages he receives from his patron are not seen as depriving, other villagers of something rightfully theirs. In Tzintzuntzan a villager who obtains a "good" in this fashion makes it a first order of business to advertise his luck and the source thereof, so there can be no doubt as to his basic morality; this behaviour is just the opposite of usual behaviour, which is to conceal good fortune.

Treasure tales and concern with patrons, in turn, are but one expression of a wider view: that any kind of success and progress is due to fate, the favor of deities, to luck, but not to hard work, energy, and thrift. Banfield notes in a south Italian community, "In the TAT stories, dramatic success came only as a gift of fortune: a rich gentleman gave a poor boy a violin, a rich gentlewoman adopted an abandoned child, and so on" (1958:66). Continuing, "Great success, then, is obtained by the favor of the saints or by luck, certainly not by thrift, work, and enterprise. These may be important if one is already lucky, but not otherwise, and few would invest large amounts of effort—any more than they would invest large amounts of fertilizer—on the rather remote possibility of good fortune". Friedmann also finds that the south Italian peasant "firmly believes that the few who have succeeded in making a career were able to do so for some mysterious reason: one hit upon a hidden treasure;

another was lucky enough to win in the lottery; another was called to America by a successful uncle" (1958:21).

All such illustrations underlie a fundamental truth not always recognized in comparing value systems: in the traditional peasant society hard work and thrift are moral qualities of only the slightest functional value. Given the limitations on land and technology, additional hard work in village productive enterprises simply does not produce a significant increment in income. It is pointless to talk of thrift in a subsistence economy in which most producers are at the economic margin; there is usually nothing to be thrifty about. As Fei and Chang point out, "In a village where the farms are small and wealth is accumulated slowly, there are very few ways for a landless man to become a landowner, or for a petty owner to become a large landowner.... It is not going too far to say that in agriculture there is no way really to get ahead.... To become rich one must leave agriculture" (1945:227). And again, "The basic truth is that enrichment through the exploitation of land, using the traditional technology, is not a practical method for accumulating wealth" (Fei and Chang: 1945:302). And, as Ammar says about Egypt, "It would be very difficult with the fellah's simple tools and the sweat involved in his work, to convince him that his lot could be improved by more work" (1954:36).

It is apparent that a peasant's cognitive orientation, and the forms of behaviour that stem therefrom, are intimately related to the problems of economic growth in developing countries. Heavy ritual expenditures, for example, are essential to the maintenance of the equilibrium that spells safety in the minds of traditional villagers. Capital accumulation, which might be stimulated if costly ritual could be simplified, is just what the villager wants to prevent, since he sees it as a community threat rather than a precondition to economic improvement.

In national developmental programs much community-level action in agriculture, health and education is cast in the form of cooperative undertakings. Yet it is abundantly clear that traditional peasant societies are cooperative only in the sense of honoring reciprocal obligations, rather than in the sense of understanding total community welfare, and that mutual suspicion seriously limits cooperative approaches to village problems.' The image of Limited Good model makes clear the peasant logic underlying reluctance to participate in joint ventures. If the "good" in life is seen as finite and non-expandable, and if apart from luck an individual can progress only at the expense of others, what does one stand to gain from a cooperative project? At best an honorable man lays himself open to the charge—and well-known consequences—of utilizing the venture to exploit friends and neighbors; at worst he risks his own defenses, since someone more skilful or less ethical than he may take advantage of the situation.

The Anglo-Saxon virtues of hard work and thrift seen as leading to economic success are meaningless in peasant society. Horatio Alger not only is not praiseworthy, but he emerges as a positive fool, a clod who not knowing the score labors blindly against hopeless conditions. The gambler, instead, is more properly laudable, worthy of emulation and adulation. If fate is the only way in which success can be obtained, the prudent and thoughtful man is the one who seeks ways in which to maximize his luck-position. He looks for the places in which good fortune is most apt to strike, and. tries to be there. This, I think, explains the interest in lotteries in underdeveloped countries. They offer the only way in which the average man can place himself in a luck-position. The man who goes without lunch, and fails to buy shoes for his children in order to buy a weekly ticket, is not a ne'er-do-well; he is the Horatio Alger of his society who is doing what he feels is most likely to advance his position. He is, in modern parlance, buying a "growth stock." The odds are against him, but it is the *only* way he knows in which to work toward success.

Modern lotteries are very much functional equivalents of buried treasure tales in peasant societies, and at least in Tzintzuntzan the correlation is clearly understood. One elderly informant, when asked why no one had found buried treasure in recent years, remarked that this was indeed true but that "Today we Mexicans have the lottery instead." Hence, the "luck" syndrome in underdeveloped countries is not primarily a deterrent to economic progress, as it is sometimes seen from the vantage point of a developed country, but rather it represents a realistic approach to the near-hopeless problem of making significant individual progress. David C. McClelland has argued persuasively that the presence of a human motivation which he calls "the need for Achievement" is a precursor to economic growth, and that it is probably a *causative* factor, that it is "a change in the minds of men which produces economic growth rather than being produced by it". McClelland further finds that in experimental situations children with high *n* Achievement avoid gambling situations because should they win there would be no sense of personal achievement, while children with low *n* Achievement do not perform in a way suggesting they calculate relative risks and behave accordingly. "They [low *n* Achievement children] thus manifest behaviour like that of many people in underdeveloped countries who, while they act very traditionally economically, at the same time love to indulge in lotteries—risking a little to make a great deal on a very long shot". McClelland sees this as showing an absence of a sense of realistic risk calculation.

If the arguments advanced in this paper are sound, it is clear that *n* Achievement is rare in traditional peasant societies, not because of psychological factors, but because display of Achievement is met by sanctions that a traditional villager does not wish to incur. The villager who feels the need for Achievement, and who does something about it, is violating the basic, un-verbalized rules of the society of which he is a member. Parents (or government school programs) that attempt to instill *n* Achievement in children are, in effect, training children to be misfits in their society *as long as it remains a relatively static system.*

As indicated above, I would argue in opposition to McClelland that the villager who buys a lottery ticket *is not* behaving in an inconsistent fashion— that is, rationally in traditional economic matters, irrationally in his pursuit of luck— but in the most consistent fashion possible. He *has* calculated the chances and risks, and in a most realistic manner *in the context of the way in which he sees his traditional environment.* The man who buys a lottery ticket in a peasant society, far from displaying lack of « Achievement, is in fact showing a maximum degree of it. It simply happens that this is about the only display of initiative that is permitted him by his society, since it is the only form not viewed as a threat to the community by his colleagues.

Banfield, and Fei and Chang, appear to see the economic factors in the presence or absence of initiative in much the same light. The former writes about the Italian peasant, "The idea that one's welfare depends crucially upon conditions beyond one's control—upon luck or the caprice of a saint—and that one can at best only improve upon good fortune, not create it—this idea must certainly be a check on initiative". The latter sec, in the Chinese data, evidence that a particular economic attitude is a function of a particular view of life. The traditional economic attitude among Chinese peasants is that of "contentment... an acceptance of a low standard of material comfort", which is contrasted to "acquisitiveness" characteristic of "modern industry and commerce in an expanding universe". "Both attitudes—contentment and acquisitiveness—have their own social context. Contentment is adopted in a closed economy; acquisitiveness in an expanding economy. *Without economic opportunities the striving for material gain is a disturbance to the existing order, since it means plunder of wealth from others....* Therefore, to accept and be satisfied with the social role and material rewards given by the society is essential. But when economic opportunity develops through the development of technology and when wealth can be acquired through the exploitation of nature instead of through the exploitation of man, the doctrine of contentment becomes reactionary because it restricts individual initiative". In other words, change the economic rules of the game and change the cognitive orientation of a peasant society, and a fertile field for the propagation of *n* Achievement is created.

For the above-reasons, I believe most strongly that the primary task in development is not to attempt to create *n* Achievement at the mother's knee but to try to change the peasants' view of his social and economic universe, away from an Image of Limited Good toward that of expanding opportunity in an open system, *so that he can feel safe* in displaying initiative. The brakes on change are less psychological than social. Show the peasant that initiative is profitable, and that it will not be met by negative sanctions, and he acquires it in short order.

This is, of course, what is happening in the world today. Those who have known peasant villages over a period of years have seen how the old sanctions begin to lose their power. Local entrepreneurs arise in response to the increasing opportunities of expanding national economies, and emulative urges, with the city as the model, appear among these people. The successful small entrepreneurs begin to see that the ideal of equality is inimical to their personal interests, and presently they neither seek to conceal their well being nor to distribute their wealth through traditional patterns of ritual extravagance. *N* Achievement bursts forth in full vitality in a few new leaders, and others see the rewards and try to follow suit. The problem of the new countries is to create economic and social conditions in which this latent energy and talent is not quickly brought up against absolute limits, so that it is nipped in the bud. This is, of course, the danger of new expectations—released latent *n* Achievement—outrunning the creation of opportunities.

Viewed in the light of Limited Good peasant societies are not conservative and backward, brakes on national economic progress, because of economic irrationality nor because of the absence of psychological characteristics in adequate quantities. They are conservative because individual progress is seen as—and in the context of the traditional society in fact is—the supreme threat to community stability, and all cultural forms *must* conspire to discourage changes in the status quo. Only by being conservative can peasant societies continue to exist as peasant societies. But change cognitive orientation through changing access to opportunity, and the peasant will do very well indeed; and his *n* Achievement will take care of itself.

4

Folk Society

Folk society, an ideal type or concept of society that is completely cohesive—morally, religiously, politically, and socially—because of the small numbers and isolated state of the people, because of the relatively unmediated personal quality of social interaction, and because the entire world of experience is permeated with religious meaning, the understanding and expression of which are shared by all members. The folk society is generally assumed to be the model of preliterate or so-called primitive societies that anthropologists have traditionally studied.

The most important and enduring modern effort to make the concept of folk culture relevant to anthropology remains the work of the U.S. anthropologist Robert Redfield, who saw folk society as including not only primitive groups but also peasant peoples whose operations entailed some degree of dependence on the city. Although criticized for this interpretation of peasant life, as well as for underrating the impersonal and economic values and relations that may obtain in folk societies, Redfield's construction of the ideal folk culture continues to be the authoritative ideal type. Especially significant characteristics of folk society, as Redfield saw it, are its self-conception as the vessel of the sacred (this conception endowing the moral order with absolute authority and rendering the life-styles rigidly conventionalized) and its quality of being the whole of social and spiritual reality, with functions satisfying all the needs of an individual from birth, through all his life crises and transitions, to death.

Banjara

The Banjara are a class of usually ascribed as nomadic people from the Indian state of Rajasthan, North-West Gujarat, and Western Madhya Pradesh and Eastern Sindh province of pre-independence Pakistan. They claim to belong to the clan of Agnivanshi Rajputs, and are also known as *Banjari, Pindari, Bangala, Banjori, Banjuri, Brinjari, Lamani, Lamadi, Lambani, Labhani, Lambara, Lavani, Lemadi, Lumadale, Labhani Muka, Goola, Gurmarti, Gormati, Kora, Sugali, Sukali, Tanda, Vanjari, Vanzara,and Wanji* Together with the Domba, they are sometimes called the "Gypsies of India". They are divided in three tribes, Maturia, Labana, Charan.]

The Banjara have spread to Andhra Pradesh, Karnataka, Maharashtra, Madhya Pradesh, Rajasthan, Uttar Pradesh and other states of India. About half their number speak Lambadi, one of the Rajasthani dialects of Hindustani, while others are native speakers of Hindi, Telugu and other languages dominant in their respective areas of settlement. Rathore, Parmar, Pawar, Chauhan, castes belong to Vanjara community in Rajasthan and Gujarat now are in General Seats after the communal rights taken place in Rajasthan for Reservation in 2008 as they were landlords in Amarkot, Fathaykot and Sialkot before Partition of India and Pakistan While they are a in OBC in Andhra Pradesh (where they are listed as Sugali) and Orissa, a Scheduled Caste in Karnataka, Haryana, Punjab, and Himachal Pradesh. The word *Banjara* is a deprecated, colloquial form of the word of Sanskrit origin. The sanskit bi-word *Vana chara* transliterated as "Forest wanderers," presumably because of their primitive role in the Indian society as forest wood collectors and distributors.

Culture

Food

The traditional food of Lambadis is Bati which is Roti. Daliya is a dish cooked using many cereal [wheat, jawar]. Banjara people are very much fascinated about non-vegetarian food. SALOI (made from goat blood and other parts of goat) is a non-vegetarian dish made exclusively by Banjara people. They prefer eating spicy food.

Dress

Women are known to wear colorful and beautiful costumes like PHETIYA [as Ghagra] and KANCHALLI [as top] and have tattoos on their hands. The dress is considered fancy and attractive by Western cultures. They use mirror chips and often coins to decorate it. Women put on thick bangles on their arms [PATLI]. Their ornaments are made up of silver rings, coins, chain and hair pleats are tied together at the end by CHOTLA.

Men wear Dhoti and Kurta [short with many folds]. These clothes were designed specially for the protection from harsh climate in deserts and to distinguish them from others.

These are the original inhabitants of Indus Valley Civilization who had to migrate to desert due to Islamic invasions from Himalayas and Hindu Kush.

Arts, Literature and Entertainment

Their customs, language and dress indicate they originated from Rajasthan. They live in settlements called thandas. They lived in zupada [hut]. Now many of them live in cities. They have a unique culture and dance form. On many occasions they gather, sing and dance.

Their traditional occupation is agriculture and trade. Banjaras are also a group of nomadic cattle herders.

The accurate history of Lambanis or Lambadis or Banjaras is not known but the general opinion among them is that they fought for Prithvi Raj against Muhammad of Ghor. The trail of the Lambadi/Banjara can be verified from their language, Lambadi borrows words from Rajasthani, Gujarati, Marathi and the local language of the area they belong to.

Banjaras originally belong to Rajasthan and they were Rajputs who migrated to southern parts of India for trade and agriculture. They settled down in the southern or central area of the country and slowly loosened contacts with Rajasthan, and their original community. Over a period of time both the communities separated and they adopted the local culture. The language spoken by Banjaras settled in Yavatmal district of Vidarbha, Maharashtra is an admixture of Hindi, Rajasthani and Marathi. The word "Banjara" must have evolved from Prakrit and Hindi and Rajasthani words "Bana/Ban or Vana/ Van" meaning Forest or Moorlands and "Chara" meaning 'Movers'. The Banjara are (together with the Domba) sometimes called the "Gypsies of India".

Dance, Lambadi is a special kind of dance of Andhra Pradesh. In this form of dance, mainly the female dancers dance in tune with the male drummers to offer homage to their Lord for a good harvest. At Anupu Village near Nagarjunakonda, Lambadi dance originated. They are actually semi-nomadic tribes who are gradually moving towards civilization. This dance is mainly restricted among the females and rarely the males participate in Lambadi Dance. Lambadi is a special kind of Folk Dance which involves participation by tribal women who bedeck themselves in colorful costumes and jewelry.

Related Communities

In Uttar Pradesh and Gujarat, there are several communities of Muslim Banjaras, who simply Muslim converts from the Banjara caste. The Muker, another Muslim community also traces its ancestry from the Banjara. Two other castes that claim kinship with the Banjara are the Labana of Punjab and Lavana of Rajasthan.

Indian Folk Music

Indian folk music is diverse because of India's vast cultural diversity. It has many forms including bhangra, lavani, dandiya and Rajasthani. The arrival of movies and pop music weakened folk music's popularity, but cheaply recordable music has made it easier to find and helped revive the traditions. Folk music (*desi*) has been influential on classical music, which is viewed as a higher art form. Instruments and styles have influenced classical ragas. It is also not uncommon for major writers, saints and poets to have large musical libraries and traditions to their name, often sung in *thumri* (semi-classical) style. Most of the folk music of India is dance-oriented.

Bhavageete

Bhavageete (literally 'emotion poetry') is a form of expressionist poetry and light music. Most of the poetry sung in this genre pertain to subjects like love, nature, philosophy etc, and the genre itself is not much different from Ghazals, though ghazals are bound to a peculiar metre. This genre is quite popular in many parts of India, notably in Karnataka. This genre may be called by different names in other languages. Kannada Bhavageete draws from the poetry of modern, including Kuvempu, D.R. Bendre, Gopalakrishna Adiga, K.S. Narasimhaswamy, G.S. Shivarudrappa, K. S. Nissar Ahmed, N S Lakshminarayana Bhatta etc. Notable Bhavageete performers include P. Kalinga Rao, Mysore Ananthaswamy, C. Aswath, Shimoga Subbanna, Archana Udupa, Raju Ananthaswamy etc.

Bhangra

Bhangra is a form of dance-oriented folk music that has become a pop sensation in the United Kingdom. The present musical style is derived from the traditional musical accompaniment to the folk dance of Punjab called by the same name, *bhangra* the female dance of punjab is known as gidda.

Bhangra is a form of dance and music that originated in the Punjab region. *Bhangra* dance began as a folk dance conducted by Punjabi Sikh farmers to celebrate the coming of the harvest season. The specific moves of *Bhangra* reflect the manner in which villagers farmed their land. This dance art further became synthesized after the partition of India, when refugees from different parts of the Punjab shared their folk dances with individuals who resided in the regions they settled in. This hybrid dance became *Bhangra*. The folk dance has been popularised in the western world by Punjabi Sikhs and is seen in the West as an expression of South Asian culture as a whole. Today, *Bhangra* dance survives in different forms and styles all over the globe – including pop music, film soundtracks, collegiate competitions and even talent shows.

History

Bhangra dance is based on a Punjabi folk dhol beat called 'bhangra' singing and the beat of the dhol drum, a single-stringed instrument called the iktar (ektara), the tumbi and the chimta. Bhangra music however, is a form of music that originated in 1980s in Britain. The accompanying songs are small couplets written in the Punjabi language called *bolis.* They relate to current issues faced by the singers and (dil di gal) what they truly want to say. In Punjabi folk music, the dhol's smaller cousin, the dholki, was nearly always used to provide the main beat. Nowadays the dhol is used more frequently in folk music however in bhangra dholki is still preferred, with and without the dholki. Additional percussion, including tabla, is less frequently used in bhangra as a solo instrument but is sometimes used to accompany the dhol and dholki. The dholki drum patterns in Bhangra music bear an intimate similarity to the rhythms in Reggae music. This rhythm serves as a common thread which allows for easy commingling between Punjabi folk and Reggae as demonstrated by such artists as the UK's Apache Indian.

In the late 1960s and 1970s, several Punjabi Sikh bands from the United Kingdom set the stage for Bhangra to become a form of music instead of being just a dance. The success of many Punjabi artists based in the United Kingdom, created a fanbase, inspired new artists, and found large amounts of support in both East and West Punjab. These artists, some of whom are still active today, include, Heera Group, Alaap band, A.S. Kang and Apna Sangeet.

In the 1980s

Major migrations of the Sikh Punjabis to the UK brought with them the Bhangra music, which became popular in Britain during the 1980s, although heavily influenced in Britain by the infusion of rock sounds and a need to move away from the simple and repetitive punjabi folk music. It signaled the development of a self-conscious and distinctively British Asian youth culture centred on an experiential sense of self i.e. language, gesture, bodily signification, desires, etc... in a situation in which tensions with British culture and racist elements in British society had resulted in alienation in many minority ethnic groups and fostered a sense of need for an affirmation of a positive identity and culture, and provided a platform for British Asian males to assert their masculinity.

Bhangra dancing was originally perceived as a male dance, a "man's song", with strong, intense movements. However, "Second-generation South Asian American women are increasingly turning to bhangra as a way of defining cultural identity."

In the 1980s Bhangra artists were selling over 30,000 cassettes a week in the UK, but not one artist made their way into the Top 40 UK Chart, despite these artists outselling popular British ones, as most sales were not through the large UK record stores whose sales were recorded by the Official UK Charts Company.

The 1980s is also what is commonly known as the golden age or what the "bhangraheads" refer to as the age of bhangra music which lasted roughly from 1985 to 1993. The primary emphasis during these times was on the melody/riff (played out usually on a synthesizer/harmonium/accordion or a guitar); the musician/composer received as much fanfare if not more, than the vocalist. The folk instruments were rarely used because it was agreed that the music was independent of the instruments being used.

This era saw the very first boy band called the Sahotas, a band made up of five brothers from Wolverhampton, UK. Their music is a fusion: Bhangra, rock and dance fused with their very own distinctive sound.

One of the biggest Bhangra stars of the last several decades is Malkit Singh — known as "the golden voice of the Punjab" — and his group, Golden Star. Malkit was born in June 1963, in the village of Hussainpur in Punjab. He attended the Khalsa College, Jalandhar, in Punjab, in 1980 to study for a bachelor of arts degree. There he met his mentor, Professor Inderjit Singh, who nurtured his skills in Punjabi folk singing and Bhangra dancing. Due to Singh's tutelage, Malkit entered and won many song contests during this time. In 1983 he won a gold medal at the Guru Nanak Dev University, in Amritsar, Punjab, for performing his hit song "Gurh Naloo Ishq Mitha", which later featured on his first album, *Nach Gidhe Wich*, released in 1984. The album was a strong hit among South Asians worldwide, and after its release Malkit and his band moved to the United Kingdom to continue their work. Malkit has now produced 16 albums and has toured 27 countries in his Bhangra career. Malkit has been awarded the prestigious MBE by the British Queen for his services to Bhangra music.

The group Alaap, fronted by Channi Singh, the man made famous by his white scarf, hails from Southall, a Punjabi area in London. Their album *Teri Chunni De Sitaray*, released in 1982 by Multitone, created quite a stir at a time when Bhangra was still in its early days in the UK. This album played a critical role in creating an interest in Bhangra among Asian university students in Britain. Alaap were unique with a live-set that was the best ever to play on the Bhangra stage. Their music oozed perfection, especially within the melody section. The music produced for Alaap included the pioneering scunds by Deepak Khazanchi.

Heera, formed by Bhupinder Bhindi and fronted by Kumar and Dhami, was one of the most popular bands of the 1980s. Fans were known to gate-crash weddings where they played. The group established itself with the albums *Jag Wala Mela*, produced by music maestro of the time Kuljit Bhamra and *Diamonds from Heera*, produced by Deepak Khazanchi, the man behind the new sound of UK Bhangra, on Arishma records. These albums are notable for being amongst the first Bhangra albums to successfully create mix Western drums and synthesizers with traditional Punjabi instruments.

Bands such as "Alaap" and "Heera" incorporated rock-influenced beats into Bhangra because it enabled "Asian youth to affirm their identities positively" within the broader environment of alternative Rock as an alternative way of expression. However, some believe that the progression of Bhangra music created an "intermezzo culture" post-India's Partition, within the unitary definitions of Southeast Asians within the diaspora, thus "establishing a brand new community in their home away from home".

Several other influential groups appeared around the same time, including The Saathies, Bhujungy Group, and Apna Sangeet. Apna Sangeet, most famously known for their hit "Mera Yaar Vajavey Dhol", re-formed in May 2009 after a break-up for charity. They are known as one of the best live acts in Bhangra.

When bhangra and Indian sounds and lyrics were brought together, British-Asian artists began incorporating them in their music. Certain Asian artists, such as Bally Sagoo, Talvin

Singh, Badmarsh, Black Star Liner, and State of Bengal are creating their own form of British hip-hop.

Even more well established groups like Cornershop, Fun-Da-Mental, and Asian Dub Foundation are finding different means and methods to create new sounds that other Asian groups have never formed. By mixing the sounds of bhangra with the popular sounds of hard rock and heavy metal, Asians are able to stay true to their own culture, while being open to a world of change. British Asians have to be conscious of both cultures in their everyday life and now are doing so in their music as well.

In the 1990s

Bhangra took large steps toward mainstream credibility in the 1990s, especially among youths. At the beginning of the nineties, many artists returned to the original, folk beats away from bhangra music, often incorporating more dhol drum beats and tumbi. This time also saw the rise of several young Punjabi singers.

Beginning around 1994, there was a trend towards the use of samples (often sampled from mainstream hip hop) mixed with traditional folk rhythm instruments such as tumbi and dhol. Using folk instruments, hip hop samples, along with relatively inexpensive folk vocals imported from Punjab, Punjabi folk music was able to abolish Bhangra music.

An influential singer was the "Canadian folkster", Jazzy B. Originally from Namasher in Punjab, "Jaswinder Bains", as he is commonly referred to, his debut was in 1992. Having sold over 55,000 copies of his third album, *Folk and Funky*, he is now one of the best-selling Punjabi folk artist in the world, with a vocal style likened to that of Kuldip Manak. Although much of his music has a traditional Punjabi folk beat, he is known for having songs that incorporate a hip hop style such as "Romeo". Jazzy Bains gives wide recognition to the success of his many hits to Sukshinder Shinda, who has produced his music.

In the late 1990s Benjie Shah emerged as the heir to the Bhangra throne. His acoustic sound and his silky smooth voice made him an international sensation. He introduced many people to bhangra and his songs are still on the lips of his many fans. His UK #1 hit song "Short-handed" still holds many retail sales records.

Other influential folk artists include Surinder Shinda-famous for his "Putt Jattan De"-Harbhajan Mann, Manmohan Waris, Meshi Eshara, Sarbjit Cheema, Hans Raj Hans, Sardool Sikander, Sahotas, Geet the MegaBand, Anakhi, Sat Rang, XLNC, B21, Shaktee, Intermix, Sahara, Paaras, PDM, Amar Group, Sangeet Group, and Bombay Talkie. A dj to rise to stardom with many successful hits was Panjabi MC.

In 2010, the story of how Bhangra arrived and developed in the UK was told in the critically acclaimed stage musical *Britain's Got Bhangra*. Produced by Rifco Arts, and starring Shin (a genuine Bhangra star from band DCS), the show's story starts in Punjab in 1977 when a teenager (Twinkle) comes to the UK and, after finding success singing at Temples and weddings, charts the rise and fall of his career and Bhangra music right up to the present day. The show was the first ever Bhangra musical, with much of the show in Punjabi, making use of the live dhol, dholak and tabla throughout, and has traditional folk melodies as well as an original score by Sumeet Chopra with crossovers into pop, rap and R&B. The production had its world premiere at Theatre Royal Stratford East in May 2010 and went on a UK Tour. Another major tour is expected in 2011.

Dances

Bhangra has developed as a combination of dances from different parts of the Punjab region. The term "Bhangra" now refers to several kinds of dances and arts, including Jhumar, Luddi, Giddha, Julli, Daankara, Dhamal, Saami, Kikli, and Gatka.

- Jhumar, originally from Sandalbar, Punjab, comprises an important part of Punjab folk heritage. It is a graceful dance, based on a specific Jhumar rhythm. Dancers circle around a drum player while singing a soft chorus.
- A person performing the Luddi dance places one hand behind his head and the other in front of his face, while swaying his head and arms. He typically wears a plain

loose shirt and sways in a snake-like manner. Like a Jhumar dancer, the Luddi dancer moves around a dhol player.

- Women have a different and much milder dance called Giddha. The dancers enact verses called bolis, representing a wide variety of subjects — everything from arguments with a sister-in-law to political affairs. The rhythm of the dance depends on the drums and the handclaps of the dancers.
- Daankara is a dance of celebration, typically performed at weddings. Two men, each holding colorful staves, dance around each other in a circle while tapping their sticks together in rhythm with the drums.
- Dancers also form a circle while performing Dhamal. They also hold their arms high, shake their shoulders and heads, and yell and scream. Dhamal is a true folk-dance, representing the heart of Bhangra.
- Women of the Sandalbar region traditionally are known for the Saami. The dancers dress in brightly colored kurtas and full flowing skirts called lehengas.
- Like Daankara, Kikli features pairs of dancers, this time women. The dancers cross their arms, hold each other's hands, and whirl around singing folk songs. Occasionally four girls join hands to perform this dance.
- Gatka is a Punjabi Sikh martial art in which people use swords, sticks, or daggers. Historians believe that the sixth Sikh guru started the art of Gatka after the martyrdom of fifth guru, Guru Arjan Dev. Wherever there is a large Punjabi Sikh population, there will be Gatka participants, often including small children and adults. These participants usually perform Gatka on special Punjabi holidays.

In addition to these different dances, a Bhangra performance typically contains many energetic stunts. The most popular stunt is called the moor, or peacock, in which a dancer sits on someone's shoulders, while another person hangs from his torso by his legs. Two-person towers, pyramids, and various spinning stunts are also popular.

Outfits

Traditional men wear a chaadra while doing Bhangra. A chaadra is a piece of cloth wrapped around the waist. Men also wear a kurta, which is a long Indian-style shirt. In addition, men wear pagadi (also known as turbans) to cover their heads.

In modern times, men also wear turla, the fan attached to the pagadi. Colorful vests are worn above the kurta. Fumans (small balls attached to ropes) are worn on each arm.

Women wear a traditional Punjabi dress known as a salwar kameez, long baggy pants tight at the ankle (salwar) and a long colorful shirt (kameez). Women also wear chunnis, colorful pieces of cloth wrapped around the neck.

These items are all very colorful and vibrant, representing the rich rural colors of Punjab. Besides the above, the Bhangra dress has different parts that are listed below in detail:

- Turla or Torla, which is a fan like adornment on the turban
- Pag (turban, a sign of pride/honor in Punjab). This is tied differently than the traditional turban one sees Sikhs wearing in the street. This turban has to be tied before each show
- Kurta-Similar to a silk shirt, with about 4 buttons, very loose with embroidered patterns.
- Lungi or Chadar, A loose loincloth tied around the dancer's waist, which is usually very decorated.
- Jugi: A waistcoat, with no buttons.
- Rumâl: Small 'scarves' worn on the fingers. They look very elegant and are effective when the hands move during the course of bhangra performance.

And you can see a photo of a bhangra dhol drummer, costumed and in full swing.

According to Sanjay Sharma, in her article, she explains/ points out the fact that Bhangra represents Asians and is referred to today as Asian music which accounts for the vast existence of Asian wear and not to mention symbols as part of their traditional dress/costumes.

Lyrics

Bhangra lyrics, always sung in the Punjabi language, generally cover social issues such as love, relationships, money, dancing, getting drunk and marriage. Additionally, there are countless Bhangra songs devoted to Punjabi pride themes and Punjabi heroes. The lyrics are tributes to the rich cultural traditions of the Punjabis. In particular, many Bhangra tracks have been written about Udham Singh and Bhagat Singh. Less serious topics include beautiful ladies with their colorful duppattas, and dancing and drinking in the fields of the Punjab.

Bhangra singers do not sing in the same tone of voice as their Southeast Asian counterparts. Rather, they employ a high, energetic tone of voice. Singing fiercely, and with great pride, they typically add nonsensical, random noises to their singing. Likewise, often people dancing to Bhangra will yell phrases such as *hoi, hoi, hoi*; *balle balle*; *chak de*; *oye hoi*; *bruah* (for an extended length of about 2–5 seconds); *haripa* or *ch-ch* (mostly used as slow beats called Chummer/Jhoomer) to the music.

Some of the more famous Bhangra or Punjabi lyricists include Harbans Jandu (Jandu Littranwala) who has written famous songs like "*Giddhian Di Rani*".

Instruments

Many different Punjabi instruments contribute to the sound of Bhangra. Although the most important instrument is the keyboard, Bhangra also features a variety of string and other drum instruments.

The primary and most important instrument that defines Bhangra is the dhol. The dhol is a large, high-bass drum, played by beating it with two sticks-known as *daggah* (bass end) and *tilli* (treble end). The width of a dhol skin is about fifteen inches in general, and the dhol player holds his instrument with a strap around his neck.

The string instruments include the guitar (both acoustic and electrical), bass, sitar, tumbi, violin and sarangi. The snare, toms, dhad, dafli, dholki, and damru are the other drums. The tumbi, originally played by folk artists such as Lalchand Yamla Jatt and Kuldip Manak in true folk recordings and then famously mastered by chamkila, a famous Punjabi folk singer (not bhangra singer), is a high-tone, single-string instrument. It has only one string, however it is difficult to master. The sarangi is a multi-stringed instrument, somewhat similar to the violin and is played using meends. The sapera produces a beautiful, high-pitched stringy beat, while the supp and chimta add an extra, light sound to Bhangra music. Finally, the dhad, dafli, dholki, and damru are instruments that produce more drum beats, but with much less bass than the dhol drum.

The keyboard and guitar are the most important melodic instruments used in bhangra with even the sitar being used on certain albums.

Percussion

With skilled keyboard, tumbi, guitar & dhol players, Bhangra today has evolved into a largely beat-based music genre, unlike until 1994 when it was slightly more mellow & classical. Pandit Dinesh and Kuljit Bhamra were trained exponents of Indian percussion and helped create the current UK sound, albeit mainly with tabla and dholki for bands like Alaap and Heera. The generation that followed became overly dependent on folk music.

A talented 15 year old percussionist called Bhupinder Singh Kullar, aka 'Tubsy' of Handsworth, Birmingham created a more contemporary style and groove that seemed to fuse more naturally with western music. Songs such as Dhola veh Dhola (Satrang) and albums such as Bomb the Tumbi (Safri Boyz) contained this new style and were very successful.

Then came Sunil Kalyan of Southall, London who also sessioned on many songs and albums. He added a smoothness and sweetness never heard before on the tabla, hailing him as one of the best tabla players in UK Bhangra.

Sukhshinder Shinda later introduced his unique style of dhol playing with the album 'Dhol Beat.' He added a very clean style of dhol playing and helped create the sound for artists such as Jaswinder Singh Bains and Bhinda Jatt. He was regarded at the time as the best Dhol player in UK.

Another influential percussionist was Parvinder Bharat (Parv) of Wolverhampton, who for many years had been percussionist for DCS, his style, speed and improvisational skills were second to none. Parv also introduced playing the Dholak and tabla top end (dhayan) with great effect into the live bhangra scene, a style that has been adopted by most bhangra percussionists ever since.

Other important percussionists include Juggy Rihal of Coventry, Aman Hayer and Billy Sandher of Gravesend.

Remixes

Punjabi folk remixed with hip hop, known lovingly as folkhop, is most often produced when folk vocals are purchased online to be remixed in a studio. Folk vocals are usually sung out to traditional melodies, that are often repeated with new lyrics. This genre is considered a sub genre of Punjabi folk and not accepted as bhangra music.

Many South Asian DJs, especially in America, have mixed Punjabi folk music with house, reggae, and hip-hop to add a different flavor to Punjabi folk. These remixes continued to gain popularity as the nineties came to an end.

Of particular note among remix artists is Bally Sagoo, a Punjabi-Sikh, Anglo-Indian raised in Birmingham, England. Sagoo described his music as "a bit of tablas, a bit of the Indian sound. But bring on the bass lines, bring on the funky-drummer beat, bring on the James Brown samples", to *Time* magazine in 1997. He was recently signed by Sony as the flagship artist for a new sound. The most popular of these is Daler Mehndi, a Punjabi singer from India, and his music, known as "folk Pop". Mehndi has become a major name not just in Punjab, but also all over India, with tracks such as "Bolo Ta Ra Ra" and "Ho Jayegee Balle Balle". He has made the sound of Bhangra-pop a craze amongst many non-Punjabis in India, selling many millions of albums. Perhaps his most impressive accomplishment is the selling of 250,000 albums in Kerala, a state in the South of India where Punjabi is not spoken.

Toward the end of the decade, Bhangra continued to die out, with folkhop artists like Bally Sagoo and Apache Indian signing with international recording labels Sony and Island. Moreover, Multitone Records, one of the major recording labels associated with Bhangra in Britain in the eighties and nineties, was bought by BMG. Finally, a recent Pepsi commercial launched in Britain featured South Asian actors and Punjabi folk music. This, perhaps more than anything else, is a true sign of the emergence of Punjabi folk into popular culture.

Post-Bhangra continues to gain popularity in both the UK and US after the death of bhangra in mid 90s. As mentioned above, artists such as Bally Sagoo offer what was referred to as "Bollywood remixes". This is just one result of the fusion the traditional folk beats and South Asian instruments with that of other contemporary music genres. Other lesser popular offshoots include "Bhangramuffin" and Acid Bhangra. Bhangramuffin mixes traditional Bhangra backgrounds are combined with Ragga; one famous band from this genre is Apache Indian. As the title suggests, Acid Bhangra combines acid music with Bhangra. An interesting result of its popularity was that post-Bhangra gave rise to a new wave of club culture (i.e. Hot 'n Spicy at London's Limelight nightclub and Manchester's Shankeys Soap). Although much of the popularity was centered on South Asian participation, post-Bhangra expressed a "process of musical cultural hybridization and syncretism that moved beyond a straightforward juxtaposition of dance music genres."

Although it sounds like a musical form that would follow the original Bhangra, post-Bhangra most specifically refers to a similar musical form with a greater emphasis on inter-dance-genre dialogues. In this way, post-Bhangra has an element of remixing and fusing Black and Asian styles of dance that is not as prevalent in traditional Bhangra. According to Sanjay Sharma, "just as Bhangra has been in constant dialogue with other (black) dance genres, post-Bhangra carries this through more incisively and intentionally." At the same time though, post-Bhangra contains the same components of racial and cultural affirmation that have been seen in Bhangra before it. In fact, with a larger focus on the dance fusion style and post-Bhangra "[operating] musically more in terms of other genres, of Ragga, Rap or Jungle music," it is very easy to see how this music attacks the essentialism that lay at the heart of the British Empire. Indeed, by fusing such starkly contrasting dance genres, post-Bhangra artists subject racial signifiers such as "Asianness" or "Blackness" to immense scrutiny. While these notions of racial and cultural essentialism can produce national pride and a finite sense of identity, they can also be highly detrimental to society at large. Since essentialism claims that people can be categorized according to some definite essence, it often leads to civil disputes and factionalism and places social boundaries between different groups of people, preventing cultural diffusion. On the flip side, post-Bhangra offers these displaced Asians in the UK an avenue for expressing their condemnation of the rigid essentialism which questions their participation in a black-dominated music scene in the first place. Not only this, but Asian artists address the issue that they too have faced social difficulties in the UK and that their music is truly authentic.

Post-bhangra has been described as a tool for strategic identity politics, presenting itself as a medium for protest against colonialism and racism. By raising awareness to problems of racism within Asian contexts, post-bhangra ventures to model movements created by organizations that have engendered a sense of unique identity for their constituents, such as the Nation of Islam and the Black Panthers. Furthermore, it allows for the expression of frustration related to racial tension that has been blanketed by social apathy. Post-bhangra music has created "new ethnicities" that are pertinent to the historical ties of the Indian subcontinent whilst remaining independent of the region itself. The formation of this new sense of Asian identity has been a leading proponent of post-bhangra, providing Asian youth with a feeling of belonging despite having to struggle to identify with a new culture that is not confined to the cultural norms of their roots nor completely assimilated with any existing culture.

Somewhere between mimicry and appropriation, post-Bhangra manages to feed off of mainstream black dance genres and then flourish in a more localized context, giving it the local importance it has to Asian and Black Britons. Rupa Huq says with respect to post-Bhangra's mainstream popularity that "spring 1998 saw the number one hit 'Brimful of Asha' from Cornershop," indicating that post-Bhangra is gaining the global attention it needs. As this musical form finds its way into mainstream styles and media, the British faces behind it hope to endorse the fight against "white racial terror, neo-colonialism/

imperialism and global racial subjugation." Therefore, post-Bhangra is an important musical form both because it defies essentialism by mixing and clashing seemingly incommensurbale sounds and cultures and because it provides Asian youth in the UK with a vehicle for self-expression as part of a musical scene with which they would otherwise be discouraged from associating.

Cultural Impact

The interpretation of Bhangra must exist in the space where Asian, UK and hip hop cultures meet. There is an expressed concerned that oversimplification of the genre by outsiders is detrimental to the music's message, but artists are responsible for how they express their music's content as well. In "Bhangra's Ambassador, Keeping the Party Spinning" from the New York Times, DJ Rekha is conscious of her cultural accountability to her music. She suggests that "because I'm working with my culture, and it's being accessed or consumed by other cultures, then Bhangra followers often feel that the music is an expression of identity.

As the movement gains momentum, Bhangra music has also gained international recognition. "Asian fusion is a melding of the sounds of the sub-continent with hip-hop beats and R&B influences, and it's no longer destined to be tucked away in the World Music section of your record store." (Mehta, Ashta).

In North America

Punjabi immigrants have encouraged the growth of Punjabi folk music/rural music in the western hemisphere instead of bhangra music. The bhangra industry has not grown in North America nearly as much as it has grown in the United Kingdom. Indian Lion, a Canadian folk artist explains why:

The reasons there's a lot of bands in England is because there's a lot of work in England. In England the tradition that's been going on for years now is that there's weddings happening up and down the country every weekend, and it's part of the culture that they have Bhangra bands come and play, who get paid 1800 quid a shot, you know. Most of the bands are booked up for the next two years. And England is a country where you can wake up in the morning and by lunchtime you can be at the other end of the country, it helps. In Canada it takes 3 days to get to the other side of the country, so there's no circuit there. And it isn't a tradition [in Canada] to have live music at weddings. There are a few bands here that play a few gigs, but nothing major. —*Indian Lion*

However, with the emergence of North American (non bhangra) folk artists such as Manmohan Waris, Jazzy Bains, Kamal Heer, Harbhanjan Maan, Sarabjit Cheema, and Debi Makhsoospuri, and the growth of the remix market, the future of Punjabi folk music in North America looks good.

Sanjay Sharma argues in "Noisy Asians or 'Asian Noise'?" that in the case of bhangra, musical exchanges have not been unidirectional but that in fact, a constant dialogue with other musical sources has taken place.

One of those musical sources is North America. More specifically, bhangra and reggae rhythms, stemming from Jamaica, have been easily fused. While black dance music beats have proved to mesh well with the fast-paced tempo of bhangra, Sharma notes reggae music also contains a *bhangara* rhythm related to the dhol drum. According to an article published on *SikhSpectrum.com*, the dhol drum has even been involved in the appropriation of bhangra in North American culture during Britain's neocolonial period. The arrival of bhangra in North America carries not only sonic importance, but also social and anthropological significance as it represents group cooperation and universal exchange between races, nations, and identities.

However, Sharma also notes the difficulty of bhangra's acceptance in the UK. Bhangra has been seen to be an 'otherness' of a British/South Asian experience. It has also been seen that British culture mostly negates and derides this Asian expression.

In 2001, the arch enemy of bhangra, Punjabi folk, and its hip hop form, folkhop began to exert an influence over US R&B music, when Missy Elliott released the folk hop-influenced song "Get Ur Freak On". In 2003, Punjabi MC's "Mundian To Bach Ke" (Beware of the Boys) was covered by the U.S. rapper Jay-Z. The great popularity of these two tracks led to an even greater usage of Punjabi folk in American music. Additionally, American rapper Pras of The Fugees has recorded tracks with

British alternative bhangra band Swami. Because the original Punjabi folk beat is different from the commercialized version we see today, the use of bhangra beats shows the complexity and ingenuity of hip-hop in North America and how artists gain inspiration from all different genres of music. The commercialization of Punjabi folk and the way it has traveled around the world speaks to the versatility and longevity of the musical style.

bhangra, the dance, has also expanded into the world of fitness. Fitness instructors like television host Sarina Jain have developed fitness routines based on bhangra dance moves for their workout programs.

Bhangra Dance Competitions

Bhangra competitions have been held in the Punjab for many decades. However, now universities and other organizations have begun to hold annual Bhangra dance competitions in many of the main cities of the United States, Canada, and England. At these competitions, young Punjabis, other South Asians, and people with no South Asian background compete for money and trophies. For example, Bruin Bhangra in Los Angeles has become one of the biggest bhangra competition in the nation. Teams from all over United States and Canada come together to compete and show their talent. Every year Bruin Bhangra also invites different well known Punjabi singers. SoCal Bhangra's past list of artists includes RDB, Manak-e, Sukhshinder Shinda, Jassi Sidhu, KS Makhan and Malkit Singh. The eastcoast bhangra team of The George Washington University's South Asian Society hosts the biggest and most prestigious bhangra competition in the United States: Bhangra Blowout. With a crowd of many thousands, it serves as the signature culminating event of the year for the best college bhangra teams. Many regard it as a de facto national championship due to its large scale and the fact that it is the last significant bhangra competition of the American school year.

2010 was the first year for Elite 8 Bhangra Invitational, in Washington DC. This event invited 8 of the top teams from North America to showcase their routines and compete for the number one spot.

In the West, unlike the Punjab, there is less emphasis on traditional songs, and more focus on the flow of a mix; an easy example of this is a team such as "Da Real Punjabis", which is notorious for mixing traditional Bhangra music with hip hop or rock songs. This synergy of the Bhangra dance with other cultures` parallels the music's fusion with different genres. University competitions have experienced an explosion in popularity over the last five years and have helped to promote the dance and music in today's mainstream culture.

In the UK, the first ever major Bhangra Competition "The Bhangra Showdown" was organised by students from Imperial College London and held on 1 December 2007. The competition was held at Indigo2 in the O2 in Greenwich, and was attended by over 1000 people. All proceeds from this show were donated to two charities, Wateraid and The Child Welfare Trust, and the show looks to continue on an annual basis. The show was held once again on 31 January 2009 at the Sadler's Wells Theatre, with proceeds going to the MND Association and The Child Welfare Trust and was attended by around 1,500 people. Six universities took part: Imperial, Queen Mary's, Kingston, Brunel, Birmingham and Leicester/DMU. Birmingham came in 3rd place, Imperial came a very close 2nd and Queen Mary's took 1st place.

The largest student-run organization in Pittsburgh was a bhangra competition called Bhangra In The Burgh. Bhangra In The Burgh was organized by students from Carnegie Mellon University, and is held yearly, this year on January 30, 2010 at the Soldiers and Sailors Memorial in Oakland. Over 2100 people attended last year, and the show was sold out. All proceeds go to the Children's Home of Pittsburgh.

Relation to other Indian Dance Forms

Bhangra can be related to Assam's Bihu dance performed during Bihu festival. Magh Bihu is associated with farming; as the traditional Assamese society is predominantly dependent on farming. Parallels between Bhangra Bihu can be drawn from the fact that the merriments for both of these music forms involve characteristic overtones with dances along with the enthralling beats of percussive musical instruments. Moreover, both Bihu and Bhangra involve high energy dance moves and sequences with young dancers in colorful clothing and the folk music played with the dhol. Both music/dance varieties, though having the similar themes, are distinctly different and have their proper origins in the respective regions of Punjab and Assam Valley

Beat & Boom

Unique Radio Show on 104.9 FM Dallas/Ft Worth, TX. is devoted to new style of Bhangra. Show is broadcasted every Sunday from 7pm to 9pm. New artist can submit music on their website to be played on air. 104.9 FM in Dallas is one of the only 24/7 FM station in the USA that targets South Asian community living abroad.

Lavani

Lavani is a popular folk form of Maharashtra. Traditionally, the songs are sung by female artists, but male artists may occasionally sing Lavanis. The dance format associated with Lavani is known as Tamasha.

Dandiya

Dandiya is a form of dance-oriented folk music that has also been adapted for pop music worldwide, popular in Western India, especially during Navaratri. The present musical style is derived from the traditional musical accompaniment to the folk dance of Dandiya called by the same name, dandiya. Raas or Dandiya Raas is the traditional folk dance form of Vrindavan, India, where it is performed depicting scenes of Holi, and lila of Krishna and Radha. Along with Garba, it is the featured dance of Navratri evenings in Western India.

Etymology

The word “Raas” comes from Sanskrit word “Ras”. The origins of Raas can be traced to ancient times. Lord Krishna performed Rasa lila” (Lila means Lord Krishna’s playful dance. The word “Lila” also refers to things that God does that we do not fully understand).

Forms of Raas

There are several forms of Raas, but “Dandiya Raas”, performed during Navaratri in Gujarat is the most popular form. Other forms of Raas include Dang Lila from Rajasthan where only one large stick is used, and "Rasa lila" from North India. Raas Lila and Dandiya Raas are similar. Some even consider "Garba" as a form of Raas, namely "Raas Garba".

In Dandiya Raas men and women dance in two circles, with sticks in their hands. In the old times Raas did not involve much singing, just the beat of Dhol was enough. "Dandiya" or sticks, are about 18" long. Each dancer holds two, although some times when they are short on Dandiya they will use just one in right hand. Generally, in a four beat rhythm, opposite sides hit the sticks at the same time, creating a nice sound. One circle goes clockwise and another counter clockwise. In the west, people don't form full circles, but instead often form rows.

Origin of Dandiya Raas

Originating as devotional Garba dances, which were always performed in Durga's honour, this dance form is actually the staging of a mock-fight between the Goddess and Mahishasura, the mighty demon-king, and is nicknamed "The Sword Dance". During the dance, dancers energetically whirl and move their feet and arms in a complicated, choreographed manner to the tune of the music with various rhythms. The dhol is used as well as complementary percussion instruments such as the dholak, tabla and others.

The sticks (*dandiyas*) of the dance represent the sword of Durga. The women wear traditional dresses such as colorful embroidered choli, ghagra and bandhani dupattas (traditional attire) dazzling with mirror work and heavy jewellery. The men wear special turbans and kedias, but this varies regionally.

Garba is performed before Aarti (worshipping ritual) as devotional performances in the honor of the Goddess, while Dandiya is performed after it, as a part of merriment. Men and women join in for Raas Dandiya, and also for the Garba. The circular movements of Dandiya Raas are much more complex than those of Garba. The origin of these dance performances or Raas is Krishna. Today, Raas is not only an important part of Navratri in Gujarat, but extends itself to other festivals related to harvest and crops as well. The Mers of Saurastra are noted to perform Raas with extreme energy and vigor.

History

The Dandiya Raas dance originated as devotional Garba dances, which were performed in Goddess Durga's honor. This dance form is actually the staging of a mock-fight between Goddess Durga and Mahishasura, the mighty demon-king. This dance is also nicknamed 'The Sword Dance'. The sticks of the dance represent the sword of Goddess Durga.

The origin of these dances can be traced back to the life of Lord Krishna. Today, Raas is not only an important part of Navaratri in Gujarat but extends itself to other festivals related to harvest and crops as well.

Format

Raas is also performed at social functions and on stage. Staged Raas can be very complex with intricate steps and music. Raas is a folk art and it will change with the times. When African slaves and ship workers (who were Muslims) arrived on the coast of Saurashtra, they adopted Raas as their own and used African drums. While it originated from Hindu tradition, it was adopted by the Muslim community as Saurashtra. Singing entered the Raas scene later on. Initially, most songs were about Lord Krishna, but songs about love, praise of warriors who fought gallant wars, and the Goddess Durga, and even Muslim Raas songs were born. It is common to think that Raas has to be fast, but that is not the case. Grace and slow movements are just as important.

With the advent of C-60 cassettes came the pre-recorded "non stop" Raas music. Soon it overtook the individual Raas items which are rarely recorded nowadays. The disco beat and use of western drum became popular, but you can still visit fine arts college in Vadodara during Navaratri where the musicians sit in the centre and play while people dance around them. Gujarati movies entered the scene in late 50's and 60's. Raas took on a different form as it borrowed heavily from the film industry.

There are other unique forms of Raas such as one in the town of Mahuva where men would tie one hand to a rope extending from above and hold a stick in the other hand. This was strictly in praise of Goddess Durga. If you use broader definition, even "Manjira" can be used to do Raas. There are communities that specialize in Raas with "Manjira". Just like the British police, some men dancing at "Tarnetar" used to wear colourful bands of cloth around their legs, resembling socks. The city of Mumbai developed its own style of Dandiya Raas. Now, during Navratri people use Dandiya, but make it more like a free style dance. "Head bobbing" during Raas is popular in USA among youngsters, but that arrived from the Gujarati movies. Head bobbing was for the singers, not for the dancers.

Costumes and Music

The women wear traditional dresses such as colorful embroidered choli, ghagra and bandahni dupattas, which is the traditional attire, dazzling with mirror work and heavy jewellery. The men wear special turbans and kedias, but can range from area to area. The dancers whirl and move their feet and arms in a choreographed manner to the tune of the music with a lot of drum beats. The dhol is used as well as complementary percussion instruments such as the dholak, tabla, etc. the true dance gets extremely complicated and energetic. Both of these dances are associated with the time of harvest.

Difference between Dandiya and Garba

The main difference between the Garba and Dandiya dance performances is that Garba is performed before Aarti (worshipping ritual) as devotional performances in honor of Goddess Durga while Dandiya is performed after it, as a part of merriment. While Garba is performed exclusively by women, men and women join in for Raas Dandiya. Also known as 'The Dance Of Swords' as performers use a pair of colorfully decorated sticks as symbols, the circular movements of Dandiya Raas are much more complex than that of Garba.

Amongst Indian diaspora

A new form of Raas is taking place in the USA. This is mostly a show item where college students of Indian origin mix non-stop Raas music with strong drum beats and stunts along with "themes" such as wedding, Star Wars and Lion King. They freely mix traditional steps with other steps. Raas will always be dynamic as it represents the circle of life, beating of heart. It is a live folk form that has changed with time and will keep changing.

Pandavani

Pandavani is a folk singing style of musical narration of tales from ancient epic Mahabharata with musical accompaniment and Bhima as hero.

This form of folk theatre is popular in the Indian state of Chhattisgarh and in the neighbouring tribal areas of Orissa and Andhra Pradesh

Teejan Bai is most renowned singer to this style, followed by Ritu Verma..

Origins

The origins of this singing style are not known, and according to its foremost singer Teejan Bai, it might be as old as the Mahabharata itself, as few people could read in those times, and that is how perhaps they passed on their stories, generation after generation.

Overview

Pandavani, literally means stories or songs of Pandavas, the legendary brothers of Mahabharat, and involves the lead singer, enacting and singing with an ektara or a *tambura* (stringed musical instrument), decorated with small bells and peacock feathers in one hand and sometimes *kartal* (a pair of cymbals) on another.

It is part of the tradition of the tellers-of-tales present in every culture or tradition (like Baul singers of Bengal and Kathak performers), where ancient epics, anecdotes and stories are recounted, or re-enacted to educated and entertain the masses. Without the use of any stage props or settings, just by the use to mimicry and rousing theatrical movements, and in between the singer-narrator break into an impromptu dance, at the completion of an episode or to celebrate a victory with the story being retold, yet in its truest sense Pandavani remains an accomplished theatre form.

During a performance, as the story builds, the tambura becomes a prop, sometimes it becomes to personify a *gada*, mace of Arjun, or at times his bow or a chariot, while others it becomes the hair of queen Draupadi or Dushshan thus helping the narrator-singer play all the characters of story.

The singer is usually supported by a group of performers on Harmonium, Tabla, Dholka, Majira and two or three singers who sing the refrain and provide backing vocals.

Each singer adds his or her unique style to the singing, sometimes adding local words, improvising and offering critique on current happenings and an insights through the story.

Gradually as the story progresses the performance becomes more intense and experiential with added dance movements, an element of surprise often used.

The lead singer continuously interacts with the accompanying singers, who ask questions, give commetary, interject thus enhancing the dramatic effect of the performance, which can last for several hours on a single episode of Mahabharata.

Eventually what starts out as a simple story narration turns into full-flegded ballad.

Variations (Shaili)

- Vedamati – the sitting style, mainly used by women, basically invented by Jhaduram Devangan.
- Kapalik – the traditional form, the standing style, where the performer depicts scenes from the epic and improvises consistently. (Teejan Bai's style)

Impact on Popular Culture

Influences of Pandanavi can been clearly seen in the plays of Habib Tanvir, who has been using folk singers of Chattisgarh in his plays, creating a free-style story narration format, typical of Pandavani.

Rajasthani

Rajasthani music has a diverse collection of musician castes, including langas, sapera, bhopa, jogi and Manganiar.

Bauls

The Bauls of Bengal were an order of musicians in 18th, 19th and early 20th century India who played a form of music using a khamak, ektara and dotara. The word Baul comes from Sanskrit *batul* meaning *divinely inspired insanity*. They are a group of Hindu mystic minstrels. They are thought to have been influenced greatly by the Hindu tantric sect of the Kartabhajas as well as by Sufi sects. Bauls travel in search of the internal ideal, *Maner Manush* (*Man of the Heart*).

Garba

"Garba (song), the songs sung in honor of Hindu goddesses during Navratri."

Dollu Kunita

This is a group dance that is named after the Dollu-the percussion instrument used in the dance. It is performed by the menfolk of the Kuruba community of the North Karnataka area. The group consists of 16 dancers who wear the drum and beat it to different rhythms while also dancing. The beat is controlled and directed by a leader with cymbals who is positioned in the center. Slow and fast rhythms alternate and group weaves varied patterns.

Kolata

Kolata is the traditional folk dance of the state of Karnataka, located in Southern India on the western coast. Similar to its North Indian counterpart Dandiya Ras, it is performed with coloured sticks and usually involves both men and women dancing together.

Veeragase

Veeragase is a dance folk form prevalent in the state of Karnataka, India. It is a vigorous dance based on Hindu mythology and involves very intense energy-sapping dance movements. Veeragase is one of the dances demonstrated in the Dasara procession held in Mysore. This dance is performed during festivals and mainly in the Hindu months of Shravana and Karthika.

5

The Village Community

Settlement and Structure

Scattered throughout India are approximately 500,000 villages. The Census of India regards most settlements of fewer than 5,000 as a village. These settlements range from tiny hamlets of thatched huts to larger settlements of tile-roofed stone and brick houses (see Structure and Dynamics, ch. 2). Most villages are small; nearly 80 percent have fewer than 1,000 inhabitants, according to the 1991 census. Most are nucleated settlements, while others are more dispersed. It is in villages that India's most basic business—agriculture—takes place. Here, in the face of vicissitudes of all kinds, farmers follow time-tested as well as innovative methods of growing wheat, rice, lentils, vegetables, fruits, and many other crops in order to accomplish the challenging task of feeding themselves and the nation. Here, too, flourish many of India's most valued cultural forms.

Viewed from a distance, an Indian village may appear deceptively simple. A cluster of mud-plastered walls shaded by a few trees, set among a stretch of green or dun-colored fields, with a few people slowly coming or going, oxcarts creaking, cattle lowing, and birds singing—all present an image of harmonious simplicity. Indian city dwellers often refer nostalgically to "simple village life." City artists portray colorfully garbed village women gracefully carrying water pots on their heads, and writers describe isolated rural settlements unsullied by the complexities of modern urban civilization. Social scientists of the past wrote of Indian villages as virtually self-sufficient communities with few ties to the outside world. In actuality, Indian village life is far from simple. Each village is connected through a variety of crucial horizontal linkages with other villages and with urban areas both near and far. Most villages are characterized by a multiplicity of economic, caste, kinship, occupational, and even religious groups linked vertically within each settlement. Factionalism is a typical feature of village politics. In one of the first of the modern anthropological studies of Indian village life, anthropologist Oscar Lewis called this complexity "rural cosmopolitanism."

Throughout most of India, village dwellings are built very close to one another in a nucleated settlement, with small lanes for passage of people and sometimes carts. Village fields surround the settlement and are generally within easy walking distance. In hilly tracts of central, eastern, and far northern India, dwellings are more spread out, reflecting the nature of the topography. In the wet states of West Bengal and Kerala, houses are more dispersed; in some parts of Kerala, they are constructed in continuous lines, with divisions between villages not obvious to visitors.

In northern and central India, neighbourhood boundaries can be vague. The houses of Dalits are generally located in separate neighborhoods or on the outskirts of the nucleated settlement, but there are seldom distinct Dalit hamlets. By contrast, in the south, where socioeconomic contrasts and caste pollution observances tend to be stronger than in the north, Brahman homes may be set apart from those of non-Brahmans, and Dalit hamlets are set at a little distance from the homes of other castes.

The number of castes resident in a single village can vary widely, from one to more than forty. Typically, a village is dominated by one or a very few castes that essentially control the village land and on whose patronage members of weaker groups must rely. In the village of about 1,100 population near Delhi studied by Lewis in the 1950s, the Jat caste (the largest cultivating caste in northwestern India) comprised 60 percent of the residents and owned all of the village land, including the house sites. In Nimkhera, Madhya Pradesh, Hindu Thakurs and Brahmans, and Muslim Pathans own substantial land, while lower-ranking Weaver (Koli) and Barber (Khawas) caste members and others own smaller farms. In many areas of the south, Brahmans are major landowners, along with some other relatively high-ranking castes. Generally, land, prosperity, and power go together.

In some regions, landowners refrain from using plows themselves but hire tenant farmers and laborers to do this work. In other regions, landowners till the soil with the aid of laborers, usually resident in the same village. Fellow villagers typically include representatives of various service and artisan castes to supply the needs of the villagers—priests, carpenters, blacksmiths, barbers, weavers, potters, oilpressers, leatherworkers, sweepers, waterbearers, toddy-tappers, and so on. Artisanry in pottery, wood, cloth, metal, and leather, although diminishing, continues in many contemporary Indian villages as it did in centuries past. Village religious observances and weddings are occasions for members of various castes to provide customary ritual goods and services in order for the events to proceed according to proper tradition.

Aside from caste-associated occupations, villages often include people who practice nontraditional occupations. For example, Brahmans or Thakurs may be shopkeepers, teachers, truckers, or clerks, in addition to their caste-associated occupations of priest and farmer. In villages near urban areas, an increasing number of people commute to the cities to take up jobs, and many migrate. Some migrants leave their families in the village and go to the cities to work for months at a time. Many people from Kerala, as well as other regions, have temporarily migrated to the Persian Gulf states for employment and send remittances back to their village families, to which they will eventually return.

At slack seasons, village life can appear to be sleepy, but usually villages are humming with activity. The work ethic is strong, with little time out for relaxation, except for numerous divinely sanctioned festivals and rite-of-passage celebrations. Residents are quick to judge each other, and improper work or social habits receive strong criticism. Villagers feel a sense of village pride and honor, and the reputation of a village depends upon the behaviour of all of its residents.

Village Unity and Divisiveness

Villagers manifest a deep loyalty to their village, identifying themselves to strangers as residents of a particular village, harking back to family residence in the village that typically extends into the distant past. A family rooted in a particular village does not easily move to another, and even people who have lived in a city for a generation or two refer to their ancestral village as "our village."

Villagers share use of common village facilities—the village pond (known in India as a tank), grazing grounds, temples and shrines, cremation grounds, schools, sitting spaces under large shade trees, wells, and wastelands. Perhaps equally important, fellow villagers share knowledge of their common origin in a locale and of each other's secrets, often going back generations. Interdependence in rural life provides a sense of unity among residents of a village.

A great many observances emphasize village unity. Typically, each village recognizes a deity deemed the village protector or protectress, and villagers unite in regular worship of this deity, considered essential to village prosperity. They may cooperate in constructing temples and shrines important to the village as a whole. Hindu festivals such as Holi, Dipavali (Diwali), and Durga Puja bring villagers together. In the north, even Muslims may join in the friendly splashing of colored water on fellow villagers in Spring Holi revelries, which involve villagewide singing, dancing, and joking. People of all castes within a village address each other by kinship terms, reflecting the fictive kinship relationships recognized within each settlement. In the north, where village exogamy is important, the concept of a village as a significant unit is lear. When the all-male groom's party arrives from another village, residents of the bride's village in North India treat the visitors with the appropriate behaviour due to them as bride-takers—men greet them with ostentatious respect, while women cover their faces and sing bawdy songs at them. A woman born in a village is known as a daughter of the village while an in-married bride is considered a daughter-in-law of the village. In her conjugal home in North India, a bride is often known by the name of her natal village; for example, Sanchiwali (woman from Sanchi).

A man who chooses to live in his wife's natal village—usually for reasons of land inheritance—is known by the name of his birth village, such as Sankheriwala (man from Sankheri).

Traditionally, villages often recognized a headman and listened with respect to the decisions of the *panchayat*, composed of important men from the village's major castes, who had the power to levy fines and exclude transgressors from village social life. Disputes were decided within the village precincts as much as possible, with infrequent recourse to the police or court system. In present-day India, the government supports an elective *panchayat* and headman system, which is distinct from the traditional council and headman, and, in many instances, even includes women and very low-caste members. As older systems of authority are challenged, villagers are less reluctant to take disputes to court.

The solidarity of a village is always riven by conflicts, rivalries, and factionalism. Living together in intensely close relationships over generations, struggling to wrest a livelihood from the same limited area of land and water sources, closely watching some grow fat and powerful while others remain weak and dependent, fellow villagers are prone to disputes, strategic contests, and even violence. Most villages include what villagers call "big fish," prosperous, powerful people, fed and serviced through the labors of the struggling "little fish." Villagers commonly view gains as possible only at the expense of neighbors. Further, the increased involvement of villagers with the wider economic and political world outside the village via travel, work, education, and television; expanding government influence in rural areas; and increased pressure on land and resources as village populations grow seem to have resulted in increased factionalism and competitiveness in many parts of rural India.

Social Inequality and Exclusion

In every society some people have a greater share of valued resources-money, property, education, health and power than others. These social resources can be divided into three forms of capital-economic capital in the form of material assets and income; cultural capital such as educational qualifications and status; and social capital in the form of networks of contacts and social associations. Often these three forms of capital overlap and one can be converted into the other. For example a person from a well-off family can afford expensive higher education and so can acquire cultural or educational capital. Patterns of unequal access to social resources are commonly called social inequality. Social inequality reflects innate differences between individuals for example their varying abilities and efforts. Someone may be endowed with exceptional intelligence or talent or may have worked very hard to achieve their wealth and status. However by and large social inequality is not the outcome of innate or natural differences between people but is produced by the society in which they live.

Sociological Importance of Village in India

"India lives in its villages"-Mahatma Gandhi.

Literally and from the social, economic and political perspectives the statement is valid even today. Around 65% of the State's population is living in rural areas. People in rural areas should have the same quality of life as is enjoyed by people living in sub urban and urban areas. Further there are cascading effects of poverty, unemployment, poor and inadequate infrastructure in rural areas on urban centres causing slums and consequential social and economic tensions manifesting in economic deprivation and urban poverty. Hence Rural Development which is concerned with economic growth and social justice, improvement in the living standard of the rural people by providing adequate and quality social services and minimum basic needs becomes essential.

The present strategy of rural development mainly focuses on poverty alleviation, better livelihood opportunities, provision of basic amenities and infrastructure facilities through innovative programmes of wage and self-employment. The above goals will be achieved by various programme support being implemented creating partnership with communities, non-governmental organizations, community based organizations, institutions, PRIs and industrial establishments, while the Department of Rural Development will provide logistic support both on technical and administrative side for programme implementation. Other aspects that will ultimately lead to transformation of rural life are also being emphasized simultaneously.

Though the percentage of persons below poverty level in Tamil Nadu has come down significantly between 1993-94 (35.03%) and 1999-2000 (21.12%) as a result of the implementation of various Central and State sponsored schemes, the level of poverty both in absolute numbers (130.40 lakh persons) and percentage of population below poverty line (21.12%) in Tamil Nadu is highest among the four southern States. In spite of huge investments on wage and self-employment programmes, the level of unemployment as per the NSSO 55th round (1999-2000) for Tamil Nadu compared to All India is the second highest among major States in 1987-88 and 1993-94 and third highest in 1999-2000.

The Government's policy and programmes have laid emphasis on poverty alleviation, generation of employment and income opportunities and provision of infrastructure and basic facilities to meet the needs of rural poor. For realising these objectives, self-employment and wage employment programmes continued to pervade in one form or other. As a measure to strengthen the grass root level democracy, the Government is constantly endeavouring to empower Panchayat Raj Institutions in terms of functions, powers and finance. Grama sabha, NGOs, Self-Help Groups and PRIs have been accorded adequate role to make participatory democracy meaningful and effective.

In India the importance of rural sociology gained recognition after independence. The agrarian context occupies special status both in the social scientific literature on India and in the literature on agrarian societies in general. However unlike studies on caste, kinship, village community, gender, study of agrarian relations did not occupy a central position in Indian sociology. The first systematic study of rural India was done by D.N Majumdar followed by N.K Bose, S.C Dubey, M.N Shrinivas. However it was with the publication of Andre'Be'teille's Studies in Agrarian Social Structure in 1974 that agrarian sociology gained professional respectability within the two disciplines.

Peasant studies in a way arrived in India with village studies. The collection of essays, Village India, edited by Marriot with its emphasis on little communities and great communities was brought out under the direct supervision of Robert Redfield. By defining little communities not in relation to land but through other social institutions such as kinship, religion and the social organization of caste there was a shift away from looking at the rural population in relation to agriculture and land. Caste hierarchy came to be defined in terms of ritual or social interaction over institutions of commensality and marriage.

According to Nelson up to the comparatively recent times the story of man is largely the story of rural man. So rural society is the basic foundation of human life, the keystone of the developmental process and the basic unit of social structure. Villages have been in existence since time immemorial unlike cities which are of more recent origin. In the Indian context rural sociology is of greater significance of the following reasons.

According to S.C Dubey from time immemorial village has been a basic and important unit in the organization of Indian social life. Unique nature of transformation of Indian society where elements of traditional and modern cultures have been juxtaposed. For rural development and solution of rural problems according to A.R Desai this systematic study of rural organization of its structure; function and evolution has not only become necessary but also urgent after the advent of independence. Growing influence of industrialization and urbanization. Village as the basic unit of study. Scientific study of village community is a prerequisite for democratic decentralization.

In modern India, the need of rural sociology is very urgent and it is progressive social science gaining importance.

Rural Urban Contrast

Many families and individuals find themselves, at least at some point, questioning the advantages of rural versus urban life. Quality of life is one of the central issues to consider in any comparison between rural versus urban living. While a case can be made for either location as being the best place to live, it is worthwhile to consider how these two options, rural versus urban, are similar and different. Important factors such as the capacity to make general choices, diversity, health, and employment concerns all influence both sides of the comparison and although each both rural and urban living offer great benefits, they both have a seemingly equal number of drawbacks. Rural and urban areas are generally similar in terms of terms of human interaction but differ most widely when diversity and choice are issues.

There are a number of positive as well as negative factors that contribute the overall quality of life in urban centres and if there is any general statement to be made about urban living, it is that there is a great deal of diversity and choice. In urban areas, there are many more choices people can make about a number of aspects of their daily lives. For instance, in urban areas, one is more likely to be able to find many different types of food and this could lead to overall greater health since there could be a greater diversity in diet. In addition, those in urban areas enjoy the opportunity to take in any number of cultural or social events as they have a large list to choose from. As a result they have the opportunity to be more cultured and are more likely to encounter those from other class, cultural, and ethnic groups.

Parents have a number of choices available for the education of their children and can often select from a long list of both public and private school districts, which leads to the potential for better education. It is also worth noting that urban areas offer residents the possibility to choose from a range of employment options at any number of companies or organizations. Aside form this, urbanites have better access to choices in healthcare as well and if they suffer from diseases they have a number of specialists to choose from in their area. According to one study conducted in Canada, "rural populations show poorer health than their urban counterparts, both in terms of general health indicators (i.e. standardized mortality, life expectancy at birth, infant mortality) and in terms of factors such as motor vehicle accidents and being overweight" (Pampalon 421). This could be the result of less reliance on vehicles in urban areas as well as greater emphasis on walking. Despite the conclusions from this study, however, there are a number of drawbacks to urban living as well. Although the life expectancy in cities may be higher, pollution (noise and atmospheric) is an issue that could impact the overall quality of life. In addition to this, overpopulation concerns can also contribute to a decrease in the standard of living.

Rural places do not offer the same level of choice and in very isolated areas and one might be forced to commute long distances to find even a remote selection of the diversity found in urban centres. Still, despite this lack of choice, there are a number of positive sides to rural living in terms of quality of life. For instance, living in a rural area allows residents to enjoy the natural world more easily instead of having to go to parks. In addition, people do not have to fight with the daily stresses of urban life such as being stuck in traffic, dealing with higher rates of crime, and in many cases, paying higher taxes. These absences of stressors can have a great effect on the overall quality of life and as one researcher notes, "People living in rural and sparsely populated areas are less likely to have mental health problems than those living in urban areas and may also be less likely to relapse into depression or mental illness once they have recovered from these in more densely populated areas".

The lack of daily stress found in cities from external factors (traffic, long lines, feeling caged, etc) has much to do with this. While there may not be a large number of stores and restaurants to choose from, those in rural areas have the benefit of land upon which to grow their own food, which is much healthier. Although urban populations have large numbers of social networks and networking opportunities, rural communities offer residents the ability to have long-lasting and more personal relationships since they encounter the same people more frequently. While there are not as many schools to choose from and sometimes rural schools are not funded as well as some others, children can grow up knowing their classmates and experience the benefits of smaller classrooms.

One of the drawbacks to living in a rural area, however, is that unlike urban areas, residents do not have the best opportunity to choose from a range of employment options. While they can commute to larger towns, this gets expensive and is not as convenient as working close to their residence.

In general, if there is any statement to be made about the quality of life of rural living, it is that there is a greater ability to connect with people and the landscape. The quality of life in urban areas is similar to that in rural areas in that both involve a high degree of socialization, even if on a cursory level. Where they differ most noticeably is in the availability of choices and diversity, especially when vital factors (healthcare, education, and employment options) are concerned.

Change in Indian Rural Life

In many ways independence from colonial rule in 1947 marked the beginning of a new phase in the history of Indian agriculture. Having evolved out of a long struggle against colonial rule with the participation of the people from various social categories, the Indian state also took over the task of supervising the transformation of its stagnant and backward economy to make sure that the benefits of economic growth were not monopolized entirely by a particular section of society. It is with this background that development emerged as a strategy of economic change and an ideology of the new regime.

However at the micro-level the structures that evolved during colonial rule still continued to exist. The local interests that had emerged over a long period of time continued to be powerful in the Indian countryside even after the political climate had changed. According to Daniel Thorner the earlier structure of land relations and debt dependencies where a small section consisting of few landlords and money lenders were dominant continued to prevail in the Indian countryside. The nature of property relations, the local values that related social prestige negatively to physical labour and the absence of any surplus with the actual cultivator for investment on land ultimately perpetuated stagnation. This complex of legal, economic and social relations typical of Indian countryside served to produce an effect that Thorner described as a built-in depressor.

Rural Religion

Many Indian villages have Brahmanic temples within them, however the religious focus is mainly on the shrines of the village's goddess and god. Rural Indians inhabit a world full of divine and semi-divine beings; tree spirits (yakshas), ghosts (bhootas), puranic, local, personal and ancestral gods who co-exist in a complex hierarchy. As well as public shrines to the gods, every Hindu home has a domestic shrine and a veneration of sacred trees and snakes were both attested to millennia ago and still play a important part in religious practice and belief today. Unlike in orthodox puranic Hinduism villagers have direct access to the local gods and do not require the intercession of a priest. The Goddess also plays a larger role in local religion and rural religion is centred on specific places of perceived spiritual power. The shrines themselves are relatively simple affairs. They are usually covered and often enclosed on three sides by a low wall. Shrines with buildings on them are quite rare. The simplest form of shrine can consist of a pile of stones by a riverbank or in a field, where, at some point in the past a spirit had made its presence known. Villages often have a number of shrines to different deities located at the edge of the village.

In South India the most visually striking shrines are those dedicated to the god Aiyanar. Aiyanar is a Brahmanised pre-Aryan deity and is regarded as a benign being concerned with the welfare of the village community rather than that of the individual. Shrines to Aiyanar are used on special occasions and can therefore sometimes look neglected. Aiyanars power is dependent on three subordinate gods named Karrupu, Muniyan and Maturaiviran who are regarded as impure spirits.

Aiyanars shrines sometimes contain huge brightly painted terracotta statues of these subordinate gods. Throughout India, a part of ritual practice involves making offerings of food, flowers, incense or terracotta figures, mainly of animals, to the deities. Life size terracotta horses are offered to Aiyanar and are believed to serve the god in the spirit world and carry him around the village at night as he protects it. The horses are renewed from time to time but the old ones are kept so the shrines often contain a small herd. Devotional terracottas are made by professional potters of the Kumhars caste and have a long history going back to the Harrapan culture of 2,500 BCE. The skill of a potter is believed to be a gift of the Gods and the potters are understood to possess a kind of magical power.

Another widely worshipped God in South India is Murukan (the Tamil name of Kartikeya). Murukan is invoked for protection and is a god of war associated with the planet Mars. In village shrines, Murukan is represented by a spear. In areas where he is regarded as the offspring of Shiva and Parvati, a trisul (or trident, an emblem of Shiva) can be found next to the spear. Offerings of ghee or fruit are skewered on to the blade tips although human hair is considered to be the most auspicious offering to Murukan. In addition to the type of offerings made to the male gods the village goddesses can require placating with live offerings. Where Goddess shrines contain anthropomorphic images of the deity, they are usually roughly carved in stone or wood, garlanded with flowers and sometimes dressed in clothing.

An unpaid priest and his assistants have the duty to maintain the shrines (at the community's expense) and to propitiate the deity to ward off communal bad luck and disease. Individual villagers, regardless of caste, can approach the village deity directly as and when they have a need. At specific times of year and during crisis a festival is held in honour of the Goddess. The main feature of these festivals is the sacrifice of an animal, at one time buffalo sacrifice was widely practised, nowadays the victim is more likely to be a goat or chicken. In Northern India the blood from such sacrifices is shunned because it is regarded as impure.

In the South the opposite is true, the blood is liberally flecked and smeared over the altar and devotees, as there is a strong belief in the power of the impure. The meaning of the sacrifice appears to be to release the power of the Goddess into the community. As the Goddess is regarded as both destructive and creative it is not considered wise to allow her presence in the village for very long. Spirit possession is also a feature of the Goddess festival as are severe penances such as hook hanging, fire walking and fire swallowing. Brahmins discourage the practice of animal sacrifice and not all villages Goddesses demand it. Examples of 'vegetarian' Goddesses in Tamil Nadu, include Antal and Sapta Kannimar, while in Orissa Ma Ksetrapala prefers cannabis. Widely known Goddesses such as Mariyamman in Tamil Nadu and Sitala in North India are relived differently from one area or village to the nex+ and offering vary according to their perceived character. In parts of South India Goddess shrines are located to the north of the village. This is significant as the north is associated with spiritual knowledge and disease and so emphasises the innate duality of the Goddess. Western scholars have tended to portray village Goddesses as sinister or malicious and venerate or placated through fear, however they are best described as ambivalent and are the objects of intense devotion.

Snake veneration is also an important part of Indian religion. An important festival called the Nagapanchami is held at the start of the rainy season in August and it is a common sight to see Naga worship all over India by those hoping to be blessed with children. The Nagas are a race of serpents whose origins are described in the Mahabharata and the Varaka Purana. As divine beings they are depicted in human, half human and fully serpent form. In rural areas snakes are commonly found near ant hills and termite mounds, both of which are regarded as the entrances to the otherworld. The mounds are frequently marked with ash and offerings of milk or eggs are made to the resident Naga. Particularly impressive mounds can thatched roofs supported by posts placed over the, similar to some Goddess shrines. Like the dragons of European mythology Nagas are seen as guardians of the otherworld and of treasure. There is also an association between snakes and trees, both being symbols of fertility and the roots of trees, like the termite mound, is seen as an entrance to the otherworld. In South India women desiring children erect snake stones under sacred tress. These stones have stylised cobras carved on them represent the Goddess Nakamal (snake virgin) and are immersed in water for several months to empower them then erected under Nim, or Pipal trees, accompanied by prayer and ritual.

In North India Manasa is invoked for protection against snakebite and to cure infertility and is represented by an earthen snake image, the branch of a tree or a water pot. As mentioned above, trees are considered to be symbols of fertility however overlying this aspect of folk religion is the Vedic concept of the tree as the axis of the Cosmos. The Rg Veda relates how sacrificial offerings were tied to a tree so that the energies released would travel upwards to the realm of Gods. Sacred trees can be found in villages, within a temple complex or shrine and in forests. The tree spirits or Yaksha (male) Yakshini (female) was worshipped in very early times, however much of the reverence shown to them has been transferred to the river Goddesses. The Yaksha is still recognised but villagers can make offerings to their ancestors, local Gods and puranic deities through the tree. The Pipal tree, for example, is believed to be the home of the elder sister of Laksmi, a Goddess named Nairrti, who seems to be a Brahmanised village Goddess. Nairrti could be described as Laksmi's dark side, as she represents misfortune. The Pipal is not touched except on Saturday when Nairrti is believed to visit Laksmi. Shrines to Nairrti are found outside villages. The Gond tribe venerates pairs of trees simply as "man" and "woman". The shade of a tree is also considered sacred. The ancient art of mediumship under sacred trees, especially those in the grounds of temples and shrines is still a common occurrence. In forests trees can be found stained and garlanded with beads, representing Bana Durga (Forest Durga) and shrines to forest Kali can be found under pairs of trees. The trees are given a similar reverence and type of offerings as those given to the Gods.

Sacred spaces are created in the home, often an entire room is used as a place of worship. Offerings of food and incense are made to the Gods, who are represented by the statues made from brass, wood or stone. The help of the deity is sought mainly but not exclusively by the women of the house for a range of personal and domestic issues. The custom of making a sacred vow or Vrat to the deity forms the basis for many domestic rituals. The custom of Vrat originates in part from the Artharvaveda, the last of the four great Vedas which contains spells and incantations derived from folk religion. The knowledge of Vrat rituals is said to have been spread throughout India by magician priests who were accompanied by a sacred prostitute and a musician as they toured villages in brightly painted carts.

The success of the ritual relies upon an implicit belief in magic and the focusing of intent, empowered by gesture and incantation to raise energy. The nature of the rituals varies according to the individual, although they do usually involve recitation of mantras and the making of magical drawings. The ritual may also need repeating on a monthly or seasonal basis.

Finally a vow is made to the deity to perform an austerity, usually fasting for a fixed period, for example every Monday for sixteen weeks, or to provide gifts when the outcome is known.

Rural religion and in particular the local Goddess has tended to be ignored or denigrated by both Indian and Western scholars and regarded as a subject not worthy of serious scholarly investigation. This brief article hopes to have shown that rural religion and the day to day worship of local Gods and Goddesses forms the basis of religious activity in India and provides Hinduism with much of its continuity with India's ancient past.......

Rural Festivals (Cultural Aspect)

Indian Villages celebrate some of the unique festivals that reflect the rural charm and simplicity of the Indian people. The villages of the Indian states are special for their distinguished fairs and festivals, however, festivals like Republic Day, Diwali, Gandhi Jayanti, Id-ul-Fitr, Independence Day and Janmastami are celebrated nationwide. Besides the religious festivals cultural ones are also predominant in the Indian villages.

The Indian Village festivals according to the location of the villages are as follows-

North India Village Festivals-North India comprises the villages of Delhi, Jammu and Kashmir, Himachal Pradesh, Punjab, Haryana, Uttarakhand and Uttar Pradesh. The composite culture and the festivals of North India are closely associated with the Himalayas and sacred rivers, passing across the states. Most of the festivals celebrated in these villages are common and similar in their themes. Karva Chauth, Vasant Panchami, Diwali, Lohri, Buddha Purnima, Kheer Bhawani are the commonly celebrated all across northern India.

East India Village Festivals-East Indian states of West Bengal, Bihar, Jharkhand and Orissa comprise the villages in this region. Cuisine plays a vital role in the eastern Indian festivals. An important feature of the festivals here is that these are diverse. While the most popular festivals celebrated in the villages of West Bengal are the Durga Puja and Kali Puja, Ratha Yatra is celebrated with lot of fervour in Orissa.

The typical rural festivals of eastern India are Jatra Festival, Jhoolan, Poush Mela and Vasanta Utsav. Cultural festivals are also an important part of the East Indian village festivals.

North-East India Village Festivals-The northeastern states of India are Sikkim, Nagaland, Meghalaya, Mizoram, Arunachal Pradesh, Assam, Tripura and Manipur. The culture of these northeastern villages vastly depends on the migrated tribal customs and traditions. The villages of Mizoram, Meghalaya and Nagaland celebrate some tribal festivals like Chapchar Kut, Mim Kut, Ningol Chakouba, Heikru Hitongba among many others.

South India Village Festivals-The villages of South India belong to the states of Kerala, Tamil Nadu, Karnataka, Andhra Pradesh, Goa and Maharashtra. The South Indian culture mostly includes festivals that are related to their coconut preparations, religion and water games; their common festivals are Onam, Pongal and numerous festivals on music and dance are quite popular in south Indian villages. The Andaman and Nicobar Islands are into several tribal festivals, due to their major tribal population.

Central India Village Festivals-The Central Indian villages belong to the states of Madhya Pradesh and Chhattisgarh. Arwa Teej, Kajri Navami, Bhojali and Chherta are the common festival of the rural areas in central India. Splendor, traditional songs, dances and colourful dresses are indispensable from these Indian village festivals.

West India Village Festivals-The West Indian states of Rajasthan and Gujarat have some of the most colorful and cultural villages, celebrating the traditional festivals. These festivities date back to the customs of the early raja and maharaja eras. Besides celebrating the popular Hindu festivals, Jain and Buddhist festivals are also integrated in the culture of these villages.

India is a land of unique festivals, retaining its culture and historical significance; the Indian villages are no exception. The rural Indian boasts some of the oldest and exceptional traditions that have grown as distinguished festivals that not only serve entertainment, but also speaks volumes about the Indian heritage and history. The geographic divisions of India definitely divide the language, rituals and festivals. However, the spirit with which the Indian village festivals are celebrated remain, predominantly, similar.

Rural Family

Indian family structure is believed to be the unit that teaches the values and worth of an honest living that have been carried down across generations. Since the Puranic ages, Indian family structure was that of a joint family, indicating every person of the same clan living together. However, this idea of elaborate living disintegrated in smaller family units.

In India, people learn the essential themes of cultural life within the bondings of a family. In ancient days, the basic units of society had been the patrilineal family unit with wider kinship groupings. The most widely preferred residential unit is the joint family, ideally consisting of three or four patrilineally related generations, all living under one roof, working, worshiping, eating, and cooperating together in communally beneficial social and economic activities. Patrilineal joint families include men related through the male line, along with their wives and children. The young married women live with their husband's relatives after marriage, but they retain important bonds with their natal families as well. Despite the continuous and growing impact of urbanization, secularization, and Westernization, the conventional joint household of Indian family structure, both in ideal and in practice, remains the chief social force in the lives of Indians. Loyalty to family is a deeply imbibed in every member of the family. Large families eventually faced difficulties to suit with modern Indian life. The modern style of livinf, modern occupations and beliefs are eventually confronting problems to get adjusted. The joint family is now quite unfamiliar in cities. However, the relative ties are maintained within the kinships, since these very ties can prove to be crucial while any kind of emergency. Numerous prominent Indian families, such as the Tatas, Birlas, and Sarabhais, retain joint family arrangements even today and they work together to control some of the country's largest financial empires.

The Indian joint family structure is an ancient phenomenon, but it has undergone some change in the late twentieth century.

Living arrangements vary widely depending on region, social status, and economic circumstance. With the passing time, nuclear families have evolved that is a couple living with their unmarried children. There are often strong networks of kinship ties through which economic assistance and other benefits are obtained. Often clusters of relatives live near each other, who are easily available and respond to the give and take of kinship obligations. Even when relatives cannot actually live in close proximity, they typically maintain strong bonds of kinship and attempt to provide each other with economic help, emotional support, and other required benefits.

The Indian joint families grew even larger and finally they divide into smaller units, passing through a expected cycle over time. The breakup of a joint family into smaller units does not necessarily symbolize the rejection of the joint family ideal. Rather, it is usually a reaction to a variety of conditions, including the requirement for some members to move from village to city, or from one city to another to obtain the advantage of employment opportunities.

Splitting of the family is often blamed on quarrelling women, the wives of co-resident brothers and so on. Although women's disputes may, in fact, lead to family division, men's disagreements are responsible as well. Despite cultural ideals of brotherly harmony, adult brothers often quarrel over land and other matters, leading them to decide to live under separate roofs and split their property. Frequently, a large joint family divides after the death of elderly parents, when there is no longer a solitary authority figure to hold the family factions together. After division, each new housing unit, in its turn, usually comes together when sons of the family marry and bring their wives to live in the family home. Some Indian family structure bears special mention because of their unique qualities. In the sub-Himalayan region of Uttar Pradesh, polygyny is generally practiced. A polygynous family comprises a man, his two wives, and their unmarried children. Various other Indian family structures occur there, including the supplemented subpolygynous household, where a woman whose husband lives elsewhere, stays with her children and other adult relatives. Among the Buddhist people of the mountainous Ladakh District of Jammu and Kashmir, fraternal polyandry is practiced; a household may include a set of brothers with their common wife or wives. This family type, in which brothers also share land, is almost certainly linked to the extreme scarcity of cultivable land in the Himalayan region, because it discourages disintegration of holdings.

The inhabitants of the northeastern hill areas are known for their matriliny order that distinguish the decent and inheritance of a family in the female line rather than the male line. One of the largest of these groups, the Khasis of Meghalaya is divided into matrilineal clans. Here, the youngest daughter receives almost all of the inheritance including the house. A Khasi husband lives in his wife's house.

Perhaps the strangest Indian family structure form is the traditional Nayar taravad, or great house. The Nayars are a cluster of castes in Kerala who are high-ranking and prosperous. The Nayars maintained matrilineal households in which sisters and brothers and their children remain as the permanent residents. After an official childhood marriage, each woman received a series of visiting husbands in the taravad. Her children were all considered as the legitimate members of the taravad. The eldest brother of the senior woman managed property, matrilineally inherited. This kind of Indian family structure has been eleminated in the twentieth century, and in the 1990s probably fewer than 5 percent of the Nayars still live in matrilineal taravads. Like the Khasis, Nayar women are well educated and powerful within the family.

Malabar rite Chri tians, an ancient community in Kerala, adopted many Indian family structure practices alike their powerful Nayar neighbors, including naming their sons for matrilineal descent. Their relationship system, however, is patrilineal. Thus, Indian family structure has been varied in varied periods of time and in different regions of the nation. The society structure and regulations have the highest influence on such formations of Indian family structures.

Joint Family System

A Hindu Joint Family or Hindu undivided family (HUF) or a Joint Family is an extended family arrangement prevalent among Hindus of the Indian subcontinent, consisting of many generations living under the same roof. All the male members are blood relatives and all the women are either mothers, wives, unmarried daughters, or widowed relatives, all bound by the common sapinda relationship. The joint family status being the result of birth, possession of joint cord that knits the members of the family together is not property but the relationship. The family is headed by a patriarch, usually the oldest male, who makes decisions on economic and social matters on behalf of the entire family. The patriarch's wife generally exerts control over the kitchen, child rearing and minor religious practices. All money goes to the common pool and all property is held jointly.

There are several schools of Hindu Law, such Mitakshara, the Dayabhaga, the Murumakkattayam, the Aliyasanthana etc. Broadly, Mitakshara and Dayabhaga systems of laws are very common. Family ties are given more importance than marital ties. The arrangement provides a kind of social security in a familial atmosphere. Due to the development of Indian Legal System, of late, the female members are also given the right of share to the property in the HUF. In CIT vs Veerappa Chettiar, 76 ITR 467 (SC), Supreme Court had occasion to decide on an issue whether after the death of all the female members in a HUF, the HUF would still exist.

Six key aspects of Joint Family are:-

- head of the family takes all decision
- all members live under one roof
- share the same kitchen
- three generations living together (though often two or more brothers live together, or father and son live together or all the descendants of male live together)
- income and expenditure in a common pool-property held together.
- a common place of worship
- all decisions are made by the male head of the family-patrilineal, patriarchal.

Indians identify themselves with a particular religion but also affiliate themselves with a specific geographical region or state in India. Religion specifies the form of worship and guides their dayto-day behaviour, while the specific region generally identifies the language one speaks, the literature, art, music one prefers, the food one eats, and the clothing one wears (Segal 1991).

Because India is a secular and ethnically diverse society, there are religious, regional, cultural, social, and educational variations in structural and functional patterns of family life. Hence, it is difficult to generalize values, behaviours, attitudes, norms, mores, practices, traditions, and beliefs about family life from one community to all Indian communities. Because the large majority of Indians are Hindus, this chapter will primarily focus attention on family life in the Hindu community.

The Hindus believe in a multitude of gods and goddess that are an integral aspect of Hindu mythology. Hinduism is a major world religion, has approximately 800 million followers, and also has had a profound influence on many other religions during its long history that dates back to 1500 B.C.E. The ideal Hindu lifestyle is influenced by the teachings in the Upanishads, Vedas, Bhavadgita, Ramayana, and Mahabharata. These scriptures stress the importance of work, knowledge, sacrifice, and service to others and finally, the renunciation of worldly goods in later life (Chekki 1996). Hinduism is not an organized religion like Western religions (Nandan and Eames 1980), but rather a way of life. According to the Hindu ideology, a person's life consists of four stages that correspond with the human life-cycle stages. The first stage is the Brahamacharya ashram (apprenticeship)—this is the period of discipline and education. The second stage is the Grihastha ashram (household and family), devoted to marriage, parenthood, family, and establishment of a household. Stage three is the Vanaprastha ashram (gradual retreat) and is characterized by a gradual retreat and loosening of social, emotional, and material bonds. Finally, the goal of the fourth and final stage, the Sanyasa ashram (renouncement), is to seek solitude, indulge in meditation, prepare for death, and strive for salvation and wisdom.

Most Hindu households have a prayer platform or room that is considered the most sacred place in the home. Most devout Hindus are vegetarians. They pray, fast, and worship their deity at least once a day, especially on holy days and days of festivities. As part of the religious activities, Hindus take regular morning baths, recite and chant certain mantras, light incense, prepare specific food items, offer flowers to the deities, and worship ancestors.

Arranged Marriages in India

People of India basically follow the arranged marriage system, and they consider it as something great. Dating is a taboo in that country. However, it has its own merits and demerits. Indian people give much importance to family relationship. The system seems to protect the family. The parents take care of their children, and the children obey their parents. Parents find suitable spouses for their children from appropriate families. So, there is no chance of marrying outside their own religion, caste, social status or economic class. This protects the couple from the problems that usually originate from disparity of religion, caste and class. Through a marriage two families come into mutual relationship, and both families together try to work out the marriage if problems arise in the marriage.

Nevertheless, the arranged marriage system has its flaws. This system originated when child marriage was the custom in India. Children at an early age, even before their puberty, were given in marriage. Such children could not give valid consent to marriage, and so parents were consenting. The purpose of child marriage was to prevent those children from seeking by themselves (when they become adults) somebody from lower caste or lower class for marriage. It was a means of restriction to their children from marrying outside their race and social status. Thus arranged marriage system is a product of caste system. It has developed to promote racism and classism, and it is not based on any spiritual value.

Child marriages are now abolished by law, and the children are free to choose their own partners, according to law. But, you know, racism is in the blood, and the parents, even now, try to control their children by arranging marriages within the limits of race, caste, class and religion. If children find their own mates, parents would threaten them in many ways — threatening not to give them any share of family property or wealth; threatening to drive them out of their own homes. If any children marry according to their own desire, parents would consider it as a threat and shame to the family. So, many men and women just accept what their parents arrange for them. They don't want to lose their share of property, and they don't want to invite any shame to their family. Even if they don't like the spouse they get, they accept what they receive and suffer the consequences silently. According to divine plan marriage should happen through love and the consent of those who marry. In arranged marriages, it is the parents who decide and give consent. Very often there is so much force and fear involved in marriage—force from the parents and fear from the part of children who wish to marry. It doesn't fit into the modern definition of marriage which is the total partnership of the whole of life which happens through mutual consent and love of those who enter into marital union. Marriage should happen through mature decision of those who marry, and not of their parents.

It also should be noted that arranged marriages are prevalent among the high-caste and high-class people. They are the people who want to protect their "status". People of lower strata do not care about this very much. The reason for this is: they have nothing to lose. However, they also try to imitate the way of higher level people, believing that it is something great. Another reason for arranged marriages among the lower class is ethnic rivalry and pride over their own race.

Matrimonial classifieds in newspapers or help of marriage brokers are sought in arranged marriage when the family fails to find "suitable" spouses for their children. All necessary "qualifications" (racial, religious, economic, educational, etc.) of the "candidates" would be stated in the advertisement.

A modern curse connected with arranged marriage is dowry. It is a social evil in India though it is prohibited by law. When they arrange a marriage, the consent of boy and girl who are to enter into marriage is not important; the negotiation is on the amount of dowry which is to be giver by the girl's family. It has become something like a trade in modern Indian culture.

The girls from poor families, and the girls who are orphans are not good commodities in this trade; so they remain unmarried. If the promised dowry is not given by due date, the girl would be persecuted and thrown out by her husband's family; or, she would die in a "domestic accident". Do not think that I am exaggerating; it is happening in India everyday.

Another drawback of arranged marriage is that the partners to marriage do not know their future spouses before marriage. In arranged marriage it is not important at all. In many cases, the boy and girl who get ready to enter into marriage may see each other two or three times before marriage, and that meeting would be in the presence of parents and other family members. Thus, marriage happens without knowing each other. Many people who work in far away places, especially in gulf countries come home for a leave, and marriage is arranged within a week or two. Legally speaking, you do not give valid consent to accept something you do not know. It is consent that brings a marriage; and, if there is no valid consent, there is no marriage according to the law of the Catholic Church. Marriages contracted because of force or fear would be invalid according to Canon Law. If we strictly analyze, many marriages happening in India are invalid.

Good marriages, that are arranged, do occur. Parents who love their children, and who are not vitiated by false family pride, seek the consent of their children when they are given in marriage. "Good" arranged marriages happen when the parents help their children to find their own partners according to their own desires.

The dating that we find in America is a good opportunity for boys and girls to know each other and select their future partners with total freedom and true consent. However, this opportunity is misused by many boys and girls and have brought disaster to their own lives. They totally discard desires of their family. They take dating for total freedom from parents and religion, and total freedom for sex. This has brought much misunderstanding about dating, especially in the circle of people of India.

Arranged marriage system in India is bad in one sense but good in another sense. It is bad when marriage is arranged with such a hatred and prejudice over other religions, castes and races; it is bad when parents over-protect and control their children to the extent of denying every wish, and even every right of their children in choosing their partners. Arranged marriages are wonderful when parents and children love each other sincerely, and total freedom is given to children for final consent to marriage; and, when arrangements are made for the would-be-spouses to meet and to know each other.

Dating system in America is bad when children totally disregard every genuine wish of their parents and consider everything as their freedom and fundamental right to the extent of practicing sex before marriage and considering marriage as a mere contract that can be terminated by a divorce decree. They often have no respect for their religious values at all. According to a friend of mine, dating system is to help the youth to learn to divorce and not to marry. You date with some one, then reject the person and accept another one; so you learn to divorce. It is wonderful when there is sincere attempt to seek the partner for an intimate union. When this happens, there is respect for family and religion; and, they seek parent's advice.

Marrying a poor orphan girl is considered to be wonderful. Doesn't look like giving such a person an asylum? Compassion is a wonderful thing, but marrying somebody out of compassion is not good at all. Marriage is not a charitable work. It is mutual sharing of whole life. Each spouse has to feel equality and mutual respect. There is no place in marriage for superiority and inferiority. There is no meaning of one being submissive and the other being aggressive—although some people believe this to be an ideal marriage.

In India many people believe that by marriage a woman enters into a bondage, and in Indian situation this is pretty accurate—woman is not free. In arranged marriage, her consent is not sought; her desires have no importance; and, even if she loves somebody to be her husband, family not only doesn't give any consideration to that but also threatens her in many ways. After marriage, in many cases, she is like a slave. She must be submissive to the abuses of the husband and his family.

In America, on the contrary, too much freedom is given to person, even to the extent of disregarding the family or religion.

However, it should be noted that there is much stress on equality. Though this sense of equality is shown, sometimes to the extent of not having any humbleness to serve the other.

Whether it be arranged marriages or courtship marriage, people seek perfect husbands and perfect wives. A perfect husband or a perfect wife is a myth. No such person lives or ever lived in this world. We should not expect anyone to be 100 percent perfect. We are all called to be perfect, but we are only on the way to it. We have to accept each other with each one's weaknesses and failings. As there is no perfect wife or perfect husband, there is no perfect marriage either. Success of marriage is in mutual understanding and acceptance, and also in mutual love and respect.

Marriages in Indian Villages

India is a land of diverse culture and ethnicity, wherein the important occasions are celebrated in myriad ways. Throughout the length and breadth of the country, you will see that wedding is given a paramount importance in people's social life. Here, marriage is not only a legal bonding between and man and a woman, it is an auspicious occasion, which brings the families of the two, closer. The ceremony often takes the shape of a festive occasion that is observed with pomp and gaiety, in the Indian subcontinent. This is the reason why wedding is often celebrated lavishly and elaborately. Nonetheless, you will see a contrast in the ways in which the wedding rituals are observed in the rural and the urban areas of the country.

Weddings in Indian Villages

Just like urban areas of India, wedding is an elaborate affair in the rural parts of the country. The rituals conducted before, during and after wedding are conducted with special attention to the nuances of the same. Depending upon their belief, people in villages organize a number of pujas before the wedding, to ensure the smooth conduct of the ceremony. After the marriage, they conduct certain rituals to ensure that the newly wed couple leads a prospered life forever. If you go deep into the rural areas of the country, you would witness huge differences in the same rituals, because people in the villages are very particular in following the customs that are native to their community. Unlike cities, in Indian villages, the role of wedding planners is played by the family members of the bride and the groom. The expenses of wedding are generally borne by the bride's parents, while the groom's family arranges the reception party. Since the system of joint families is still prevalent in the villages, the arrangements for a wedding are conducted very smoothly. It is a joint effort of the family members, relatives and close friends, when it comes to organizing a wedding. All the people involved in the preparations for the wedding ensure that everything is conducted smoothly, before, during and after the ceremony.

Depending upon the financial status, the grandeur of the wedding ceremony varies. For instance, if the families of the prospective bride and the groom are not financially well settled, they would restrict the wedding to a short and crisp affair, inviting only the relatives and close friends. On the other hand, if it is the wedding of a renowned person of the village, who is financially well settled, then the wedding would be just like a festival for the village, wherein every villager is invited to mark his/her presence and grace the occasion. In general, weddings in Indian villages are as celebrated with pomp and gaiety, which is no less to those witnessed in urban parts of the country.

Till some times back, people in villages of India were strictly against love marriages. They strongly believed that two people should not tie the wedding knot without the consent of their elder members of the family and relatives. Due to this perception, arranged marriage is customary in Indian villages. However, with the passing times, people living even in the interiors of rural India are not so strictly against the concept of love marriage and hence, if persuaded, they would not hesitate to come forward and solemnize the wedding of the two loving souls. Therefore, the perception of wedding in the rural India has changed drastically.

6

Sociology of Caste System in India

The Indian caste system describes the system of social stratification and social restrictions in India in which social classes are defined by thousands of endogamous hereditary groups, often termed *jâtis* or castes. Within a jâti, there exist exogamous groups known as gotras, the lineage or clan of an individual. In a handful of sub-castes such as Shakadvipi, endogamy within a gotra is permitted and alternative mechanisms of restricting endogamy are used (e.g. banning endogamy within a surname).

The Indian caste system involves four castes and outcasted social groups. Although generally identified with Hinduism, the caste system was also observed among followers of other religions in the Indian subcontinent, including some groups of Muslims and Christians. Caste barriers have mostly broken down in large cities, though they persist in rural areas of the country, where 72% of India's population resides. None of the Hindu scriptuces endorses caste-based discrimination, and the Indian Constitution has outlawed caste-based discrimination, in keeping with the secular, democratic principles that founded the nation. Nevertheless, the caste system, in various forms, continues to survive in modern India because of a combination of political factors and social perceptions and behaviour.

History

There is no universally accepted theory about the origin of the Indian caste system. The Indian classes are similar to the ancient Iranian classes ("*pistras*"), wherein the priests are Brahmins, the warriors are Kshatriya, the merchants are Vastriya, and the artisans are Huiti.

Varna and Jati

According to the ancient Hindu scriptures, there are four "varnas". The Bhagavad Gita says varnas are decided based on Guna and Karma. Manusmriti and some other shastras name four varnas: the Brahmins (teachers, scholars and priests), the Kshatriyas (kings and warriors), the Vaishyas (agriculturists and traders), and Shudras (service providers, laborers).

This theoretical system postulated Varna categories as ideals and explained away the reality of thousands of endogamous Jâtis actually prevailing in the country as being the result of historical mixing among the "pure" Varnas – *Varna Sankara*. All those who did not subscribe to the norms of the Hindu society, including foreigners, tribals and nomads, were considered contagious and untouchables. Another group excluded from the main society was called Parjanya or Antyaja. This group of people formerly called "untouchables", the Dalits, was considered either the lowest among the Shudras or outside the Varna system altogether.

Several critics of Hinduism state that the caste system is rooted in the varna system mentioned in the ancient Hindu scriptures. However, many groups, such as ISKCON, consider the modern Indian caste system and the varna system two distinct concepts. Many European administrators from the colonial era incorrectly regarded the Manusmriti as the "law book" of the Hindus, and thus concluded that the caste system is a part of Hinduism, an assertion that is now rejected by most scholars, who state that it is a social practice, not a religious belief. Manusmriti was a work of reference for the Brahmins of north India, especially Bengal, and was largely unknown in southern India.

Although many Hindu scriptures contain passages that can be interpreted to sanction the caste system, they also contain indications that the caste system is not an essential part of Hinduism. The Vedas placed no importance on the caste system, mentioning caste only once (in the Purush Sukta) out of tens of thousands of verses. Most vedic scholars believe even this to be a subsequent and artificial insertion; B. R. Ambedkar concluded after a thorough study that this is a much later interpolation, giving strong evidence to support his conclusion. In the Vedic period, there was no prohibition against anyone, including the Shudras, listening to the Vedas or participating in any religious rite.

In *Early Evidence for Caste in South India*, George L. Hart stated that "the earliest Tamil texts show the existence of what seems definitely to be caste, but which antedates the Brahmins and the Hindu orthodoxy". He believes that the origins of the caste system can be seen in the "belief system that developed with the agricultural civilization", and was later profoundly influenced by "the Brahmins and the Brahmanical religion". These early Tamil texts also outline the concept of equality. Saint Valluvar has stated "pirapokkum ella uyirkkum", which means "all are equal at birth". Likewise, Saint Auvaiyaar has stated that there are only two castes in the world: those who contribute negatively and those who contribute positively. From these statements, it can be inferred that the caste system is a socio-economic class system.

Caste and Social Status

Traditionally, although the political power lay with the Kshatriyas, historians portrayed the Brahmins as custodians and interpreters of Dharma, who enjoyed much prestige and many advantages.

Fa Hien, a Buddhist pilgrim from China, visited India around 400 AD. "Only the lot of the Chandals he found unenviable; outcastes by reason of their degrading work as disposers of dead, they were universally shunned... But no other section of the population were notably disadvantaged, no other caste distinctions attracted comment from the Chinese pilgrim, and no oppressive caste 'system' drew forth his surprised censure.". In this period kings of Sudra and Brahmin origin were as common as those of Kshatriya *varna* and caste system was not wholly prohibitive and repressive.

The castes did not constitute a rigid description of the occupation or the social status of a group. Since British society was divided by class, the British attempted to equate the Indian caste system to their own social class system. They saw caste as an indicator of occupation, social standing, and intellectual ability. Intentionally or unintentionally, the caste system became more rigid during the British Raj, when the British started to enumerate castes during the ten year census and codified the system under their rule.

The Harijans, or the people outside the caste system, had the lowest social status. The Harijans, earlier referred to as *untouchables* by some, worked in what were seen as unhealthy, unpleasant or polluting jobs. In the past, the Harijans suffered from social segregation and restrictions, in addition to extreme poverty. They were not allowed temple worship with others, nor water from the same sources. Persons of higher castes would not interact with them. If somehow a member of a higher caste came into physical or social contact with an untouchable, the member of the higher caste was defiled, and had to bathe thoroughly to purge him or herself of the impurity. Social discrimination developed even among the Harijans; sub-castes among Harijans, such as the *dhobi* and *nai*, would not interact with lower-order Bhangis, who were described as "outcastes even among outcastes".

Sociologists have commented on the historical advantages offered by a rigid social structure as well as its drawbacks. While caste is now seen as anachronistic, in its original form the caste system served as an instrument of order in a society where mutual consent rather than compulsion ruled; where the ritual rights and the economic obligations of members of one caste or sub-caste were strictly circumscribed in relation to those of any other caste or sub-caste; where one was born into one's caste and retained one's station in society for life; where merit was inherited, where equality existed within the caste, but inter-caste relations were unequal and hierarchical. A well-defined system of mutual interdependence through a division of labour created security within a community. In addition, the division of labour on the basis of ethnicity allowed immigrants and foreigners to quickly integrate into their own caste niches. The caste system played an influential role in shaping economic activities, where it functioned much like medieval European guilds, ensuring the division of labour, providing for the training of apprentices and, in some cases, allowing manufacturers to achieve narrow specialisation. For instance, in certain regions, producing each variety of cloth was the speciality of a particular sub-caste. Additionally, some philosophers have argued that the majority of people would be comfortable in stratified endogamous groups, as they were in ancient times.

Caste Mobility

Some scholars believe that the relative ranking of other castes was fluid or differed from one place to another prior to the arrival of the British. Sociologists such as Bernard Buber and Marriott McKim describe how the perception of the caste system as a static and textual stratification has given way to the perception of the caste system as a more processual, empirical and contextual stratification. Other sociologists such as Y.B Damle have applied theoretical models to explain mobility and flexibility in the caste system in India. According to these scholars, groups of lower-caste individuals could seek to elevate the status of their caste by attempting to emulate the practices of higher castes. Flexibility in caste laws permitted very low-caste religious clerics such as Valmiki to compose the Ramayana, which became a central work of Hindu scripture. There is also precedent of certain Shudra families within the temples of the Sri Vaishnava sect in South India elevating their caste. The following is a list of changes in varna cited in Hindu texts:

- Manu eldest son [Priyavrata] became king, a Kshatriya. Out of his ten sons seven became kings while three became Brahman. Their names were Mahavira, Kavi and Savana.
- Kavash –ailush was born to a Sudra and attained varn of a Rishi. He became mantra-drashta to numerous Vedic mantras in Rig-Veda 10th Mandal.
- Jabala's son [Satyakama] born from unknown father became Rishi by his qualities.
- [Matanga] became a Rishi after his birth in low Varna.

According to some psychologists, mobility across broad caste lines may have been "minimal", though sub-castes (jatis) may have changed their social status over the generations by fission, re-location, and adoption of new rituals.

Sociologist M. N. Srinivas has also debated the question of rigidity in Caste. In an ethnographic study of the Coorgs of Karnataka, he observed considerable flexibility and mobility in their caste hierarchies. He asserts that the caste system is far from a rigid system in which the position of each component caste is fixed for all time; instead, movement has always been possible, especially in the middle regions of the hierarchy. It was always possible for groups born into a lower caste to "rise to a higher position by adopting vegetarianism and teetotalism" i.e. adopt the customs of the higher castes. While theoretically "forbidden", the process was not uncommon in practice. The concept of sanskritization, or the adoption of upper-caste norms by the lower castes, addressed the complexity and fluidity of caste relations.

The fact that many of the dynasties were of obscure origin suggests some social mobility: a person of any caste, having once acquired political power, could also acquire a genealogy connecting him with the traditional lineages and conferring Kshatriya status. A number of new castes, such as the Kayasthas (scribes) and Khatris (traders), are mentioned in the sources of this period. According to the Brahmanic sources, they originated from intercaste marriages, but this is clearly an attempt at rationalizing their rank in the hierarchy. Khatri appears to be unquestionably a Prakritised form of the Sanskrit Kshatriya. Many of these new castes played a major role in society. The hierarchy of castes did not have a uniform distribution throughout the country.

Reforms

There have been challenges to the caste system from the time of Buddha, Mahavira and Makkhali Gosala. Opposition to the system of varna is regularly asserted in the Yoga Upanisads and is a constant feature of Cîna-âcâra tantrism, a Chinese-derived movement in Asom; both date to the medieval era. The Nâtha system, which was founded by Matsya-indra Nâtha and Go-rakca Nâtha in the same era and spread throughout India, has likewise been consistently opposed to the system of varna.

Many Bhakti period saints rejected the caste discriminations and accepted all castes, including untouchables, into their fold.

During the British Raj, this sentiment gathered steam, and many Hindu reform movements such as Brahmo Samaj and Arya Samaj renounced caste-based discrimination. The inclusion of so-called untouchables into the mainstream was argued for by many social reformers. Mahatma Gandhi called them "Harijans" (children of God) although that term is now considered patronizing and the term Dalit (*downtrodden*) is the more commonly used. Gandhi's contribution toward the emancipation of the untouchables is still debated, especially in the commentary of his contemporary Dr. B.R. Ambedkar, an untouchable who frequently saw Gandhi's activities as detrimental to the cause of upliftment of his people.

The practice of untouchability was formally outlawed by the Constitution of India in 1950, and has declined significantly since then, to the point of a society allowing former untouchables to take high political office, like former President K. R. Narayanan, who took office in 1997, and former Chief Justice K. G. Balakrishnan.

British Rule

The fluidity of the caste system was affected by the arrival of the British. Prior to that, the relative ranking of castes differed from one place to another. The castes did not constitute a rigid description of the occupation or the social status of a group. The British attempted to equate the Indian caste system to their own class system, viewing caste as an indicator of occupation, social standing, and intellectual ability. During the initial days of the British East India Company's rule, caste privileges and customs were encouraged, but the British law courts disagreed with the discrimination against the lower castes. However, British policies of divide and rule as well as enumeration of the population into rigid categories during the 10 year census contributed towards the hardening of caste identities.

During the period of British rule, India saw the rebellions of several lower castes, mainly tribals that revolted against British rule. These were:

1. Halba rebellion (1774–79)
2. Bhopalpatnam Struggle (1795)

3. Bhil rebellion (1822–1857)
4. Paralkot rebellion (1825)
5. Tarapur rebellion (1842–54)
6. Maria rebellion (1842–63)
7. First Freedom Struggle (1856–57)
8. Bhil rebellion, begun by Tantya Tope in Banswara (1858)
9. Koi revolt (1859)
10. Gond rebellion, begun by Ramji Gond in Adilabad (1860)
11. Muria rebellion (1876)
12. Rani rebellion (1878–82)
13. Bhumkal (1910).

Modern Status of the Caste System

In some rural areas and small towns, the caste system is still very rigid. Caste is also a factor in the politics of India.

The Government of India has officially documented castes and sub-castes, primarily to determine those deserving reservation (positive discrimination in education and jobs) through the census. The Indian reservation system, though limited in scope, relies entirely on quotas. The Government lists consist of Scheduled Castes, Scheduled Tribes and Other Backward Classes:

Scheduled Castes (SC)

Scheduled castes generally consist of "Dalit". The present population is 16% of the total population of India (around 160 million). For example, the Delhi state has 49 castes listed as SC.

Scheduled Tribes (ST)

Scheduled tribes generally consist of tribal groups. The present population is 7% of the total population of India i.e. around 70 million.

Other Backward Classes (OBC)

The Mandal Commission covered more than 3000 castes

under OBC Category and stated that OBCs form around 52% of the Indian population. However, the National Sample Survey puts the figure at 32%. There is substantial debate over the exact number of OBCs in India; it is generally estimated to be sizable, but many believe that it is lower than the figures quoted by either the Mandal Commission or the National Sample Survey.

The caste-based reservations in India have led to widespread protests, such as the 2006 Indian anti-reservation protests, with many complaining of reverse discrimination against the forward castes (the castes that do not qualify for the reservation). Many view negative treatment of forward castes as socially divisive and equally wrong.

Caste System among Non-Hindus

In some parts of India, Christians are stratified by sect, location, and the castes of their predecessors, usually in reference to upper class Syrian Malabar Nasranis. Christians in Kerala are divided into several communities, including Syrian Christians and the so-called "Latin" or "New Rite" Christians.

Syrian Christians derive status within the caste system from the tradition that they are converted Namboodiris and Jews, who were evangelized by St. Thomas. Writers Arundhati Roy and Anand Kurian have written personal accounts of the caste system at work in their community. Syrian Christians, especially Knanaya Christians, tend to be endogamous and not to intermarry with other Christian castes.

The Latin Rite Christians were among the scheduled castes in the coastal belt of Kerala, where fishing was the primary occupation. They were actively converted by missionaries in the 16th and 19th centuries. These missionary activities were carried out by Western Latin Rite missionaries who did not understand the significance of the caste system in India; mone of the Syrian churches had participated in such activities among the scheduled castes of India because they were aware of the prejudices of the caste system. The government of India later granted this group OBC status. Very rarely are there intermarriages between Syrian Christians and Latin Rite Christians.

Anthropologists have noted that the caste hierarchy among Christians in Kerala is much more polarized than the Hindu practices in the surrounding areas, due to a lack of jatis. Also, the caste status is kept even if the sect allegiance is switched (i.e. from Syrian Catholic to Syrian Orthodox).

In the Indian state of Goa, mass conversions were carried out by Portuguese Latin missionaries from the 16th century onwards. The Hindu converts retained their caste practices. The continued maintenance of the caste system among the Christians in Goa is attributed to the nature of mass conversions of entire villages, as a result of which existing social stratification was not affected. The Portuguese colonists, even during the Goan Inquisition, did not do anything to change the caste system. Thus, the original Hindu Brahmins in Goa now became Christian *Bamons* and the Kshatriya became Christian noblemen called *Chardos*. The Christian clergy became almost exclusively Bamon. Vaishyas who converted to Christianity became *Gauddos*, and Shudras became *Sudirs*. Finally, the Dalits or "Untouchables" who converted to Christianity became *Maharas* and *Chamars*, the latter an appellation of the anti-Dalit ethnic slur *Chamaar*.

Units of social stratification, termed "castes" by many, have developed among Muslims in some parts of South Asia. Sources indicate that the castes among Muslims developed as the result of close contact with Hindu culture and Hindu converts to Islam. The Sachar Committee's report commissioned by the government of India and released in 2006 documents the continued stratification in Muslim society.

Among Muslims, those who are referred to as Ashrafs are presumed to have a superior status derived from their foreign Arab ancestry, while the Ajlafs are assumed to be converts from Hinduism, and have a lower status. In addition, the *Arzal* caste among Muslims was regarded by anti-caste activists like Ambedkar as the equivalent of untouchables. In the Bengal region of India, some Muslims stratify their society according to 'Quoms'. While many scholars have asserted that the Muslim castes are not as acute in their discrimination as those of the Hindus, some like Ambedkar argued that the social evils in Muslim society were "worse than those seen in Hindu society".

The Buddhists also had a caste system. In Sri Lanka, the Rodis might have been outcast by the Sri Lankan Buddhists due to the absence of *ahimsa* (*non-violence*), a central tenet of Buddhism, among their beliefs. The writer Raghavan notes, "That a form of worship in which human offerings formed the essential ritual would have been anathema to the Buddhist way of life goes without saying; and it needs no stretch of imagination that any class of people in whom the cult prevailed or survived even in an attenuated form would have been pronounced by the sangha (i.e. the Buddhist clergy) as exiles from the social order." Savarkar believed that the status of the backward castes (e.g. Chamar) that performed non-violence only worsened. When Ywan Chwang traveled to South India after the period of the Chalukyan Empire, he noticed that the caste system had existed among the Buddhists and Jains.

Jains also had castes in places such as Bihar. For example, in the village of Bundela, there were several *"jaats"* (*groups*) amongst the Jains. A person of one *"jaat"* cannot intermingle with a Jain or another *"jaat"*. They also could not eat with the members of other *"jaats"*.

The Sikh Gurus criticized the hierarchy of the caste system. While some castes were widely perceived as being better or higher than others (e.g. Brahmins being higher than others), they preached that all sections of society were valuable and that merit and hard-work were essential aspects of life. In the Shiromani Gurdwara Prabandhak Committee, out of 140 seats, 20 are reserved for low caste Sikhs. However, the quota system has attracted much criticism due to the lack of meritocracy, since merit is considered the single most important component of winning a seat.

Baha'i Faith has grown to prominence in India, since its philosophy of the unity of humanity attracted many of the lower castes.

Caste-related Violence

Independent India has witnessed a considerable amount of violence and hate crimes motivated by caste. Various incidents of violence against Dalits, such as Kherlanji Massacre have been reported from many parts of India. Many violent protests by Dalits, such as the 2006 Dalit protests in Maharashtra, have also been reported. Ranvir Sena, a caste-supremacist fringe paramilitary group based in Bihar, has committed violent acts against Dalits and other members of scheduled castes.

Phoolan Devi, who belonged to the *Mallah* lower caste, was mistreated and raped by upper-caste Thakurs at a young age. She became a bandit and carried out violent robberies against upper-caste people. In 1981, her gang massacred twenty-two Thakurs, most of whom were not involved in her kidnapping or rape. Later, she became a politician and Member of Parliament.

Caste Politics

B. R. Ambedkar and Jawaharlal Nehru had radically different approaches to caste, especially concerning constitutional politics and the status of untouchables. Since the 1980s, caste has become a major issue in the politics of India.

The Mandal Commission was established in 1979 to "identify the socially or educationally backward" and to consider the question of seat reservations and quotas for people to redress caste discrimination. In 1980, the commission's report affirmed the affirmative action practice under Indian law, whereby members of lower castes were given exclusive access to a portion of government jobs and slots in public universities. When V. P. Singh's administration tried to implement the recommendations of the Mandal Commission in 1989, massive protests were held in the country. Many alleged that the politicians were trying to cash in on caste-based reservations for purely pragmatic electoral purposes.

Many political parties in India have openly indulged in caste-based votebank politics. Parties such as Bahujan Samaj Party (BSP), the Samajwadi Party and the Janata Dal claim that they are representing the backward castes, and rely on OBC support, often in alliance with Dalit and Muslim support, to win elections. Remarkably, in what is called a landmark election in the history of India's biggest state of Uttar Pradesh, the Bahujan Samaj Party was able to garner a majority in the state assembly elections with the support of the brahmin community.

Criticism

There has been criticism of the caste system from both within and outside of India. Criticism of the Caste system in Hindu society came both from the Hindu fold and Dalit.

Historical Criticism

Many bhakti period saints, including Nanak, Kabir, Caitanya, Dnyaneshwar, Eknath, Ramanuja and Tukaram, rejected all caste-based discrimination and accepted disciples from all the castes. Many Hindu reformers such as Swami Vivekananda believe that there is no place for the caste system in Hinduism. The 15th century saint Ramananda accepted all castes, including untouchables, into his fold. Most of these saints subscribed to the Bhakti movements in Hinduism during the medieval period that rejected casteism. Nandanar, a low-caste Hindu cleric, also rejected casteism and accepted Dalits.

Some other movements in Hinduism have also welcomed lower-castes into their fold, the earliest being the Bhakti movements of the medieval period. Early Dalit politics involved many reform movements; these arose primarily as a reaction to the advent of Christian missionaries in India and their attempts to convert Dalits, who were attracted to the prospect of escaping the caste system.

In the 19th Century, the Brahmo Samaj under Raja Ram Mohan Roy actively campaigned against untouchability and casteism. The Arya Samaj founded by Swami Dayanand also renounced discrimination against Dalits. Sri Ramakrishna Paramahamsa and his disciple Swami Vivekananda founded the Ramakrishna Mission that participated in the emancipation of Dalits. Upper-caste Hindus such as Mannathu Padmanabhan participated in movements to abolish untouchability against Dalits; Padmanabhan opened his family temple to Dalits for worship. Narayana Guru, a pious Hindu and an authority on the Vedas, also criticized casteism and campaigned for the rights of lower-caste Hindus within the context of Hinduism.

The first upper-caste temple to openly welcome Dalits into their fold was the Laxminarayan Temple in Wardha in the year 1928; the move was spearheaded by reformer Jamnalal Bajaj. The caste system has also been criticized by many Indian social reformers. Some reformers, such as Jyotirao Phule and Iyothee Thass, argued that the lower caste people were the original inhabitants of India, who had been conquered in the ancient past by "Brahmin invaders." Mahatma Gandhi coined the term *Harijan*, a euphemistic word for untouchable, literally meaning *Sons of God*. B. R. Ambedkar, born in Hindu Dalit community, was a heavy critic of the caste system. He pioneered the Dalit Buddhist movement in India, and asked his followers to leave Hinduism, and convert to Buddhism. India's first Prime Minister, Jawaharlal Nehru, based on his own relationship with Dalit reformer Ambedkar, supported the eradication of untouchability for the benefit of the Dalit community. In 1936, the Maharaja proclaimed that "outcastes should not be denied the consolations and the solace of the Hindu faith". Even today, the Sri Padmanabhaswamy temple that first welcomed Dalits in the state of Kerala is revered by the Dalit Hindu community.

Contemporary Criticism

Kancha Ilaiah, a Christian professor at Osmania University, formerly of the Shephard caste in Andhra, is known for his public and often un-compromising statements on Hindus and the caste system and is considered an anti-Hindu by his critics. Similarly, Dalit rights activists, such as Buddhist convert Udit Raj, who have attacked Hindus for still maintaining their casteism, have achieved some popularity among evangelical Christian groups such as the Dalit Freedom Network in their criticism of Hinduism.

Many Hindus point out that the caste system is related to the Indian society, and not Hinduism, as is evident by presence of caste among Indian Christians and Muslims. Brahmin organizations such as the Rashtriya Swayamsevak Sangh have actively criticized the caste system.

Some activists consider the caste system a form of racial discrimination. At the United Nations Conference Against Racism in Durban, South Africa in March 2001, participants condemned discrimination based on the caste system and tried to pass a resolution declaring caste as a basis for segregation and oppression a form of apartheid. However, no formal resolution was passed. The alleged maltreatment of Dalits in India has been described by some authors as "India's hidden apartheid". Critics of the accusations point to substantial improvements in the position of Dalits in post-independence India, consequent to the strict implementation of the rights and privileges enshrined in the Constitution of India, as implemented by the Protection of Civil rights Act, 1955. They also note that India has had a Dalit president, K.R. Narayanan, and argue that the practise had disappeared in urban public life.

According to William A. Haviland, however: Although India's national constitution of 1950 sought to abolish cast discrimination and the practice of untouchability, the caste system remains deeply entrenched in Hindu culture and is still widespread throughout southern Asia, especially in rural India. In what has been called India's "hidden apartheid", entire villages in many Indian states remain completely segregated by caste. Representing about 15 percent of India's population—or some 160 million people—the widely scattered Dalits endure near complete social isolation, humiliation, and discrimination based exclusively on their birth status. Even a Dalit's shadow is believed to pollute the upper classes. They may not cross the line dividing their part of the village from that occupied by higher castes, drink water from public wells, or visit the same temples as the higher castes. Dalit children are still often made to sit in the back of classrooms.

Sociologists Kevin Reilly, Stephen Kaufman and Angela Bodino, while critical of casteism, conclude that modern India does not practice any apartheid since there is no state-sanctioned discrimination.

They write that casteism in India is presently "not apartheid. In fact, untouchables, as well as tribal people and members of the lowest castes in India benefit from broad affirmative action programmes and are enjoying greater political power." The Constitution of India places special emphasis on outlawing caste discrimination, especially the practice of untouchability. In addition, the Indian penal code inflicts severe punishments on those who discriminate on the basis of caste. Anti-Dalit prejudice and discrimination exists primarily in rural areas, where small societies can track the caste lineage of individuals and discriminate accordingly.

Caste and Race

Allegations that caste amounts to race were addressed and rejected by B.R. Ambedkar, an advocate for Dalit rights and critic of untouchability. He wrote that "The Brahmin of Punjab is racially of the same stock as the Chamar of Punjab. The Caste system does not demarcate racial division. The Caste system is a social division of people of the same race",

Such allegations have also been rejected by sociologists such as Andre Béteille, who writes that treating caste as a form of racism is "politically mischievous" and worse, "scientifically nonsensical" since there is no discernible difference in the racial characteristics between Brahmins and Scheduled Castes. He states, "Every social group cannot be regarded as a race simply because we want to protect it against prejudice and discrimination".

The Indian government also rejects the claims of equivalency between caste and racial discrimination, pointing out that the caste issues are essentially intra-racial and intra-cultural. Indian Attorney General Soli Sorabjee insisted that "[t]he only reason India wants caste discrimination kept off the agenda is that it will distract participants from the main topic: racism. Caste discrimination in India is undeniable but caste and race are entirely distinct".

Many scholars dispute the claim that casteism is akin to racism. Sociologist M. N. Srinivas has debated the question of rigidity in caste. Others have applied theoretical models to explain mobility and flexibility in the caste system in India. According to these scholars, groups of lower-caste individuals could seek to elevate the status of their caste by attempting to emulate the practices of higher castes.

In her book *Democracy and Authoritarianism in South Asia*, Pakistani-American sociologist Ayesha Jalal writes, "As for Hinduism, the hierarchical principles of the Brahmanical social order have always been contested from within Hindu society, suggesting that equality has been and continues to be both valued and practiced."

In India, some observers felt that the caste system must be viewed as a system of exploitation of poor low-ranking groups by more prosperous high-ranking groups. In many parts of India, land is largely held by high-ranking property owners of the dominant castes, who economically exploit low-ranking landless labourers and poor artisans.

Matt Cherry claims that karma underpins the caste system, which traditionally determines the position and role of every member of Hindu society. Caste determines an individual's place in society, the work he or she may carry out, and who he or she may marry and meet. According to him, Hindus believe that the karma of previous life will determine the caste an individual will be (re)born into.

On 29 March 2007, the Supreme Court of India, as an interim measure, stayed the law providing for 27% reservation for Other Backward Classes in educational institutions. This was done in response to a public interest litigation — Ashoka Kumar Thakur vs. Union of India. The Court held that the 1931 census could not be a determinative factor for identifying the OBCs for the purpose of providing reservation. The court also observed, "Reservation cannot be permanent and appear to perpetuate backwardness". However, the Supreme Court later upheld the reservation.

Genetic Analysis

There have been several studies examining caste members as discrete populations, examining the hypothesis that their ancestors have different origins. A 2002–03 study by T. Kivisild et al. concluded that the "Indian tribal and caste populations derive largely from the same genetic heritage of Pleistocene southern and western Asians and have received limited gene flow from external regions since the Holocene." Studies point to the various Indian caste groups having similar genetic origins and having negligible genetic input from outside south Asia. Because the Indian samples for this study were taken from a single geographical area, it remains to be investigated whether its findings can be safely generalized.

An earlier 1995 study by Joanna L. Mountain et al. of Stanford University had concluded that there was "no clear separation into three genetically distinct groups along caste lines", although "an inferred tree revealed some clustering according to caste affiliation". A 2006 study by Ismail Thanseem et al. of Centre for Cellular and Molecular Biology (India) concluded that the "lower caste groups might have originated with the hierarchical divisions that arose within the tribal groups with the spread of Neolithic agriculturalists, much earlier than the arrival of Aryan speakers", and "the Indo-Europeans established themselves as upper castes among this already developed caste-like class structure within the tribes." The study indicated that the Indian caste system may have its roots long before the arrival of the Indo-Aryans; a rudimentary version of the caste system may have emerged with the shift towards cultivation and settlements, and the divisions may have become more well-defined and intensified with the arrival of Indo-Aryans.

A 2006 genetic study by the National Institute of Biologicals in India, testing a sample of men from 32 tribal and 45 caste groups, concluded that the Indians have acquired very few genes from Indo-European speakers. More recent studies have also debunked the British claims that so-called Aryans and Dravidians have a racial divide. A study conducted by the Centre for Cellular and Molecular Biology in 2009 (in collaboration with Harvard Medical School, Harvard School of Public Health and the Broad Institute of Harvard and MIT) analysed half a million genetic markers across the genomes of 132 individuals from 25 ethnic groups from 13 states in India across multiple caste groups. The study establishes, based on the impossibility of identifying any genetic indicators across caste lines, that castes in South Asia grew out of traditional tribal organizations during the formation of Indian society, and was not the product of any Aryan invasion and subjugation of Dravidian people.

Untouchability

Untouchability is the social practice of ostracising a (usually) minority endogamous group by regarding them as "ritually polluted" and segregating them from the mainstream by social custom or legal mandate. The excluded group could be one that did not accept the norms of the excluding group and historically included foreigners, nomadic tribes, law-breakers and criminals. This exclusion was a method of punishing law-breakers and also protected against contagion from strangers. A member of the excluded group is known as an untouchable.

The term is commonly associated with treatment of the Dalit class among Hindus of India, Nepal and Bangladesh, but the term has been used for other groups as well, such as the Burakumin of Japan or the Al-Akhdam in Yemen. Untouchability has been made illegal in post-Independence India but prejudice continues.

Untouchability in Kerala

The declaration by princely states of Kerala between 1936 and 1947 that temples were open to all Hindus went a long way towards ending the system of untouchability in Kerala. However some historical forms of untouchability existed in Kerala, Nairs and Namboothiris, who constituted the forward castes forbid those belonging to lower castes within certain proximity to them, believing that the presence of lower castes would pollute them. Ezhava and other lower caste were untouchable people in Kerla. Savarna kept Ezhava from many feets than other lower caste.

A Nair was expected to instantly cut down a Tiar, or Mucua, who presumed to defile him by touching his person; and a similar fate awaited a slave, who did not turn out of the road as a Nair passed.

Historically, the people of the Nayadi, Kanisan and Mukkuvan caste were forbidden to come within 72, 32 and 24 feet respectively from Nairs. In modern India, observance of untouchability is a criminal offence.

Untouchability is a direct product of the caste system. It is not merely the inability to touch a human being of a certain caste or sub-caste. It is an attitude on the part of a whole group of people that relates to a deeper psychological process of thought and belief, invisible to the naked eye, translated into various physical acts and behaviours, norms and practices.

Untouchability is prompted by the spirit of social aggression and the belief in purity and pollution that characterises casteism. It is generally taken for granted that Dalits are considered polluted people at the lowest end of the caste order. The jobs considered polluting and impure are reserved for Dalits, and in many cases Dalits are prevented from engaging in any other work. These jobs include removing human waste (known as "manual scavenging"), dragging away and skinning animal carcasses, tanning leather, making and fixing shoes, and washing clothes. They are supposed to reside outside the village so that their physical presence does not pollute the "real" village. Not only are they restricted in terms of space, but their houses are also supposed to be inferior in quality and devoid of any facilities like water and electricity.

Untouchability is present in nearly every sphere of life and practiced in an infinite number of forms. At the village level Dalits are barred from using wells used by non-Dalits, forbidden from going to the barber shop and entering temples, while at the level of job recruitment and employment Dalits are systematically paid less, ordered to do the most menial work, and rarely promoted. Even at school, Dalit children may be asked to clean toilets and to eat separately.

As an instrument of casteism, Untouchability also serves to instill caste status to Dalit children from the moment they are born. Kachro (filth), Melo (dirty), Dhudiyo (dusty), Gandy (mad), Ghelo (stupid), Punjo (waste) are just some of the names given to Dalit boys in Gujarat. Of course, names with similar meanings are given to Dalit girls too. This shows the debilitating effect of Untouchability, as it becomes a conscious act of cooperation between two individuals of distinct caste or sub-caste identity. The person treated as untouchable submits himself or herself to untouchability practices because of a generational integrated belief that it is right, justified, religious and natural. Untouchability is in this sense a corollary of the caste system, and the only way to get rid of it seems to be to get rid of the caste system itself. Focusing on Untouchability ignores the root cause of the problem, all the more so as *Article 17* of the Indian Constitution, which bans Untouchability, confines its definition to individual discrimination against certain classes of persons not easily identifiable.

The 1950 national constitution of India legally abolishes the practice of "untouchability," and there are constitutional reservations in both educational institutions and public services for Dalits. Unfortunately, these measures have not changed the reality of daily life for most Dalits, as the Indian government frequently tolerates oppression and open discrimination aimed at this group. As the former Indian President K.R. Narayanan, himself a Dalit, noted in his public address to the nation on the eve of Republic Day, January 25, 2000, "these [Constitutional] provisions remain unfulfilled through bureaucratic and administrative deformation or by narrow interpretations of these special provisions." Dalits usually live in separate areas away from the caste Hindu communities, and they are often forbidden to access public wells. In many areas, when Dalits eat in public restaurants or patronize street vendors, they must use a special glass for drinking tea or coffee to prevent sharing between Dalits and caste Hindus. Dalits in different parts of India cannot enter Hindu temples or Christian churches, and many religious and caste leaders forbid inter-caste marriages.

Should a Dalit break one of these rules, frequently the entire Dalit community will be punished for the perceived individual transgression. Punishment often takes the form of denial of access to land or employment, physical attacks on Dalit women, and the burning down of Dalit homes. Despite a clear record of violence against the Dalits, there are numerous reports that police officials have refused to register complaints about violations of the law or to prosecute those responsible for the abuses. With little knowledge of their rights, limited access to attorneys, and no money for hearings or bail, Dalits are easy targets for human rights violations.

Who are these Untouchables?

— Defined by the Government of India as 'Scheduled Castes'

— Dalit ('down-trodden') is now the more generally accepted term for them

— About 150 million Dalits in India (1/6th of entire population)

— More than just prohibition of physical contact – what defines the Dalits is a much broader set of social sanctions

- Exclusion

- Humiliation–subordination
- Exploitation.

Dalit is a self-designation for a group of people traditionally regarded as of lower class and unsuitable for making personal relationships. Dalits are a mixed population of numerous caste groups all over South Asia, and speak various languages.

While the caste system has been abolished under the Indian constitution, there is still discrimination and prejudice against Dalits in South Asia. Since Indian independence, significant steps have been taken to provide opportunities in jobs and education. Many social organizations have encouraged proactive provisions to better the conditions of Dalits through improved education, health and employment.

Etymology

The word "Dalit" comes from the Marathi language, and means "ground", "suppressed", "crushed", or "broken to pieces". It was first used by Jyotirao Phule in the nineteenth century, in the context of the oppression faced by the erstwhile "untouchable" castes of the twice-born Hindus.

According to Victor Premasagar, the term expresses their "weakness, poverty and humiliation at the hands of the upper castes in the Indian society."

Mohandas Gandhi coined the word Harijan, translated roughly as "Children of God", to identify the former Untouchables. The terms "Scheduled castes and scheduled tribes" (SC/ST) are the official terms used in Indian government documents to identify former "untouchables" and tribes. However, in 2008 the National Commission for Scheduled Castes, noticing that "Dalit" was used interchangeably with the official term "scheduled castes", called the term "unconstitutional" and asked state governments to end its use. After the order, the Chhattisgarh government ended the official use of the word "Dalit".

"Adi Dravida", "Adi Karnataka" and "Adi Andhra" are words used in the states of Tamil Nadu, Karnataka and Andhra Pradesh, respectively, to identify people of former "untouchable" castes in official documents. These words, particularly the prefix of "Adi", denote the aboriginal inhabitants of the land.

The more general term, "Adivasi" derives from the Sanskrit words *adi* meaning primal, original, first + *bas* a verb root meaning to sit, settle, or stay, rendering Adivasi as "indigenous" people of India. People who identify themselves as Dalit may also identify themselves as Adivasi, but the distinction is analogous to that of Scheduled Tribes and Scheduled Castes in which there is some intersection but the two are distinct social identities.

Social Status of Dalits

In the context of traditional Hindu society, Dalit status has often been historically associated with occupations regarded as ritually impure, such as any involving leatherwork, butchering, or removal of rubbish, animal carcasses, and waste. Dalits work as manual labourers cleaning streets, latrines, and sewers. Engaging in these activities was considered to be polluting to the individual, and this pollution was considered contagious. As a result, Dalits were commonly segregated, and banned from full participation in Hindu social life. For example, they could not enter a temple nor a school, and were required to stay outside the village. Elaborate precautions were sometimes observed to prevent incidental contact between Dalits and other castes. Discrimination against Dalits still exists in rural areas in the private sphere, in everyday matters such as access to eating places, schools, temples and water sources. It has largely disappeared in urban areas and in the public sphere. Some Dalits have successfully integrated into urban Indian society, where caste origins are less obvious and less important in public life. In rural India, however, caste origins are more readily apparent and Dalits often remain excluded from local religious life, though some qualitative evidence suggests that its severity is fast diminishing.

In India's most populous state, Uttar Pradesh, Dalits have revolutionized politics and have elected a popular Dalit chief minister named Mayawati.

Dalits and similar groups are also found in Nepal and Bangladesh. In addition, the Burakumin of Japan, Al-Akhdam of Yemen, Baekjeong of Korea and Midgan of Somalia are similar in status to Dalits.

Genetics

One study found some association between caste status and Y-chromosomal genetic markers seeming to indicate a more European lineage of the higher castes; however, many recent studies indicate no genetic differences between upper and lower castes. Caste differentiation between Indians is regarded by many as a social construct between Indian people, and is claimed not to have a genetic basis. Genetic testing further indicates that, as a whole, Indian genetic groups do not show a great affinity to any non-South Asian groups.

Dalits and Religion

Sachar Committee report of 2006 revealed that scheduled castes and tribes of India are not limited to the religion of Hinduism. The 61st Round Survey of the NSSO found that almost nine-tenths of the Buddhists, one-third of the Sikhs, and one-third of the Christians in India belonged to the notified scheduled castes or tribes of the Constitution.

Religion	*Scheduled Caste*	*Scheduled Tribe*
Buddhism	89.50%	7.40%
Christianity	9.00%	32.80%
Sikhism	30.70%	0.90%
Hinduism	22.20%	9.10%
Zoroastrianism	-	15.90%
Jainism	-	2.60%
Islam	0.80%	0.50%

Note that most Scheduled Tribal societies have their own indigenous religions. Mundas have a Munda religion, for example. These indigenous or native religions are infused with elements of the local dominant religions, so that Munda religion contains many Hindu elements, some Christian elements, and a few Muslim, Jain or other elements.

Hinduism

The large majority of the Dalits in India are Hindus, although some in Maharashtra and other states have converted to Buddhism, often called Neo-Buddhism. Dalits in Sri Lanka can be Buddhist.

Historical Attitudes

The term, Chandala can be seen used in the Manu Smriti (codes of caste segregation) to the Mahabharata the religious epic. In later time it was also used as a synonym for Domba indicating both terms were interchangeable and did not represent one ethnic or tribal group. Instead, it was a general opprobrious term. In the early Vedic literature several of the names of castes that are spoken of in the Smritis as Antyajas occur. We have *Carmanna* (a tanner of hides) in the Rig Veda (VIII.8,38) the Chandala and Paulkasa occur in Vajasaneyi Samhita. *Vepa* or *Vapta* (barber) in the Rig Veda. Vidalakara or Bidalakar occurs in the Vajasaneyi Samhita. *Vasahpalpuli* (washer woman) corresponding to the Rajakas of the Smritis in Vajasaneyi Samhita. Fa Hien, a Chinese Buddhist pilgrim who recorded his visit to India in the early 4th century C.E., noted that Chandalas were segregated from the mainstream society as untouchables. Traditionally, Dalits were considered to be beyond the pale of Varna or caste system. They were originally considered as *Panchama* or the fifth group beyond the fourfold division of Indian people. They were not allowed to let their shadows fall upon a non-Dalit caste member and they were required to sweep the ground where they walked to remove the 'contamination' of their footfalls. Dalits were forbidden to worship in temples or draw water from the same wells as caste Hindus, and they usually lived in segregated neighborhoods outside the main village. In the Indian countryside, the dalit villages are usually a separate enclave a kilometre or so outside the main village where the other Hindu castes reside.

Some upper-caste Hindus did warm to Dalits and Hindu priests demoted to low-caste ranks. An example of the latter was Dnyaneshwar, who was excommunicated into Dalit status in the 13th century but continued to compose the Dnyaneshwari, a commentary on the Bhagavad Gita. Eknath, another excommunicated Brahmin, fought for the rights of untouchables during the Bhakti period. Historical examples of Dalit priests include Chokhamela in the 14th century, who was India's first recorded Dalit poet and Raidas, born into a family of cobblers. The 15th century saint Sri Ramananda Raya also accepted all castes, including untouchables, into his fold. Most of these saints subscribed to the Bhakti movements in Hinduism during the medieval period that rejected casteism. Nandanar, a low-caste Hindu cleric, also rejected casteism and accepted Dalits. Due to isolation from the rest of the Hindu society, many Dalits continue to debate whether they are 'Hindu' or 'non-Hindu'. Traditionally, Hindu Dalits have been barred from many activities that were seen as central to Vedic religion and Hindu practices of orthodox sects. Among Hindus each community has followed its own variation of Hinduism, and the wide variety of practices and beliefs observed in Hinduism makes any clear assessment difficult.

The declaration by princely states of Kerala between 1936 and 1947 that temples were open to all Hindus went a long way towards ending the system of untouchability in Kerala. According to Kerala tradition the Dalits were forced to maintain a distance of 96 feet from Namboothiris, 64 feet from Nairs and 48 feet from other upper castes (like Maarans and Arya Vysyas) as they were thought to pollute them. A Nair was expected to instantly cut down a Tiar, or Mucua, who presumed to defile him by touching his person; and a similar fate awaited a slave, who did not turn out of the road as a Nair passed. Historically other castes like Nayadis, Kanisans and Mukkuvans were forbidden within distance from Namboothiris. Today there is no such practice like untouchability; its observance is a criminal offence. However, educational opportunities to Dalits in Kerala remain limited.

Reform Movements

The earliest known historical people to have rejected the caste system were Gautama Buddha and Mahavira. Their teachings eventually became independent religions called Buddhism and Jainism. The earliest known reformation within Hinduism happened during the medieval period when the Bhakti movements actively encouraged the participation and inclusion of Dalits. In the 19th Century, the Brahmo Samaj, Arya Samaj and the Ramakrishna Mission actively participated in the emancipation of Dalits. While there always have been segregated places for Dalits to worship, the first "upper-caste" temple to openly welcome Dalits into their fold was the Laxminarayan Temple in Wardha in the year 1928. It was followed by the Temple Entry Proclamation issued by the last King of Travancore in the Indian state of Kerala in 1936.

The Sikh reformist Satnami movement was founded by Guru Ghasidas, born a Dalit. Other notable Sikh Gurus such as Guru Ravidas were also Dalits. Other reformers, such as Jyotirao Phule, Ayyankali of Kerala and Iyothee Thass of Tamil Nadu worked for emancipation of Dalits. The 1930s saw key struggle between Mahatma Gandhi and B. R. Ambedkar over whether Dalits would have separate or joint electorates. Although he failed to get Ambedkar's support for a joint electorate, Gandhi nevertheless began the "Harijan Yatra" to help the Dalit population. Palwankar Baloo, a Dalit politician and a cricketer, joined the Hindu Mahasabha in the fight for independence.

Other Hindu groups have reached out to the Dalit community in an effort to reconcile with them. On August 2006, Dalit activist Namdeo Dhasal engaged in dialogue with the Rashtriya Swayamsevak Sangh in an attempt to "bury the hatchet". Hindu temples are increasingly receptive to Dalit priests, a function formerly reserved for Brahmins. Suryavanshi Das, for example, is the Dalit priest of a notable temple in Bihar. Anecdotal evidence suggests that discrimination against Hindu Dalits is on a slow but steady decline. For instance, an informal study by Dalit writer Chandrabhan Prasad and reported in the New York Times states: "In rural Azamgarh District [in the state of Uttar Pradesh], for instance, nearly all Dalit households said their bridegrooms now rode in cars to their weddings, compared with 27 percent in 1990. In the past, Dalits would not have been allowed to ride even horses to meet their brides; that was considered an upper-caste privilege."

Many Hindu Dalits have achieved affluence in society, although vast millions still remain poor. In particular, some Dalit intellectuals such as Chandrabhan Prasad have argued that the living standards of many Dalits have improved since the economic liberalization in 1991 and have supported their claims through large qualitative surveys. Recent episodes of Caste-related violence in India have adversely affected the Dalit community. In urban India, discrimination against Dalits in the public sphere is greatly reduced, but rural Dalits are struggling to elevate themselves. Government organizations and NGO's work to emancipate them from discrimination, and many Hindu organizations have spoken in their favor. Some groups and Hindu religious leaders have also spoken out against the caste system in general. However, the fight for temple entry rights for Dalits is far from finished and continues to cause controversy. Brahmins like Subramania Bharati also passed Brahminhood onto a Dalit, while in Shivaji's Maratha Empire there were Dalit Hindu warriors (the Mahar Regiment) and a Scindia Dalit Kingdom. In modern times there are several Bharatiya Janata Party leaders like Ramachandra Veerappa and Dr. Suraj Bhan.

The Jajmani System

The notion of the jajmani system was popularized by colonial ethnography. It tended to conceptualize agrarian social structure in the framework of exchange relations. In its classical construct, different caste groups specialized in specific occupations and exchanged their services through an elaborate system of division of labor. Though asymmetry in position of various caste groups was recognized what it emphasized was not inequality in rights over land but the spirit of community. Wiser argued, each served the other. Each in turn was master. Each in turn was servant. This system of inter relatedness in service within Hindu community was called the Jajmani system. Central to such a construction of exchange is the idea of reciprocity (Gouldner) with the assumption that it was a non-exploitative system where mutual gratification was supposed to be the outcome of the reciprocal exchange.

The Concept of Jajmani System

Inter-caste relations at the village level constitute vertical ties. They may be classified into economic, ritual, political and civic ties. The castes living in a village are bound together by economic ties. Generally peasant castes are numerically preponderant in villages and they need the carpenter, blacksmith and leather worker castes to perform agricultural work. Servicing castes such as priest, barber, and washerman and water carrier cater to the needs of everyone except the Harijans.Artisan castes produce goods which are wanted by every one. Most Indian villages do not have more than a few of the essential castes and depend on neighboring villages for certain services, skills and goods.

In rural India with its largely subsistence and not fully monetized economy the relationship between the different caste groups in a village takes a particular form. The essential artisan and servicing castes are paid annually in grain at harvest time. In some parts of India the artisan and servicing castes are also provided with free food, clothing, fodder and residential site. On such occasions as birth, marriage and death, these castes perform extra duties for which they are paid customary money and some gifts in kind. This type of relationship is found all over India and is called by different names-jajmani in north,bara batute in Maharashtra,mirasi in Tamil Nadu and adade in Karnataka.

Oscar Lewis defined jajmani system as that under which each caste group within a village is expected to give certain standardized services to the families of other castes.Jajmani is more than a relationship between families than between castes.Jajmani is sort of mutual give and take form of relationship in which one family is hereditarily entitled to supply goods and render services to the other in exchange of the same. The person rendering the services or supplying the goods is known as kameen or prajan and the person to whom the services are rendered is called a jajman.Thus under jajmani system a permanent informal bond is made between jajman and kameen to meet each other's need for good and services.

Main Features of Jajmani System

The jajmani system is characterized by the following features:

- Unbroken relationship-Under the jajmani system the kameen remains obliged to render the services throughout his life to a particular jajman and the jajman in turn has the responsibility of hiring services of a kameen.
- Hereditary relationship-Jajmani rights are enjoyed hereditarily. After the death of a man his son is entitled to work as kameen for the same jajman family of

families. The son of a jajman also accepts the son of the kameen as his kameen.

- Multidimensional relationship-Due to the permanency of relationship both the jajman and kameen families become mutually dependent on each other. The relationship becomes very deep. They often take part in the personal and family affairs,family rituals and ceremonies.
- Barter exchange-Under jajmani system the payments are made mainly in terms of goods and commodities. The kameen gets his necessities from the jajman in return of his services.

The jajmani system has gradually decayed in modern society. There are many reasons responsible for it. Modern economic system that measures everything in terms of its monetary value. The decline of belief in caste system and hereditary occupation has given a strong blow to the system. Growth of better employment opportunities outside the village and introduction of new transport options.

7

Rural Chaupal

The chaupal is a common place, (constructed, semi-constructed, open space, the shadow of Banyan or peepal tree or a place in the orchard) owned by the all villagers. Even if the place belongs to some individual, he does not pose his authority to the panches. No individual or family can claim to have the individual ownership of the place identified as chaupal. It is place where villagers of all rank, age, castes, and faith sit together and discuss serious and non-serious issues. It is place where usually the village elders and traditional panches sit to solve the individual or communal disputes. Sometimes the chaupal has no fixed venue. The place where the village elders and panches sit to sort out some disputes or to take some collective decisions for the welfare of the villagers is called the chaupal. The chaupal is often identified with banyan tree.

As already discussed above, the concept of chaupal is not new to the Indian tradition; it has its root in the Vedic period. The Vedic administrators, perhaps, devised this universal system to maintain communal harmony and to ensure justice in every geographical and political area for every person with his satisfaction but within the limit of traditional as well as societal norms. Chaupal is place where all four doors or directions are open for everybody. Nobody, in its essentiality, can be denied the admittance of this place. It is a stage where everybody has the freedom irrespective of being associated with race, caste, religion, gender etc., to play the character without any fear and gets recognized by the jury members in a just and cordial atmosphere. I have substantiated my paper with the first hand examples of the villages of Mithila – a place located in the far away from the Indian big cities and modern world in eastern state of Bihar. The region is vast plane stretching north towards Nepal, south towards the Holly Ganga River and west towards Bengal.

Present-day Mithila is covered by the districts of Champaran, Saharsa, Muzaffarpur, Vaishali, Darbhanga. Madhubani, Samastipur; parts of Munger, Begusarai, Bhagalpur and Purnea. In Maithili language a chaupal is called chaupari. The word chaupari has multiple meanings.

It is used as seminary of scholars or students, as sacred place where some deities or other good spirits possesses a shaman or a diviner, a sacred place with the magical ability to cure the problems or diseases of the visitors.

But one thing is common in all forms of the chaupari: it is open for everybody. It is a public place and anybody, male or female, young or old, member of high caste or lower caste, well educated or most illiterate, can visit in order to get his/her problem listened and also to get the justice (or reward) in a fear free atmosphere. I have observed a shaman behaving as a Chief Justice, Dharmadhikari in the chaupal when in trance during the dispute resolution.

The disputants' come to him, touch the sacred soil of this place and as soon as the impersonator reaches into trance the disputants narrate their problem truthfully. Unlike modern courts they don't cook any story. The advocates, wearing black coats and white tie or any legal agent, has no role to play here. Cases or the causes of dispute are narrated in a very natural and realistic style. Both the involved parties keep doubtless faith on the judge – a person in trance, and the place. No unnecessary story or history of cause is cooked. Only truth is narrated before the deity.

The shaman in trance listens to the truth of both the disputants in the open space in front of many people who are assembled their for various reasons and gives his judgement which is usually acceptable to the both the disputants. If required he takes the help of other people sitting there. In Mithila, chaupal is also called bramhaasthan, devasthan, gahwarasthan, mahankarasthan, devithan etc. People are associated with it culturally, socially and emotionally. It is secular because of its sacred characteristics. During my fieldwork I collected one Udasikirtan about Ramvanvas, banishment, episode in which a small reference of chaupari comes:

- Hamra Rama lakhan dunu bhai
- Banma ke bhejalak ge dai
- Kinka bina sunna rasoia
- Kinka binu chupadi
- Sita bina sunna rasoia
- Laxaman bina chapadi
- Banma ke bhejlak ge dai.

(We do not know who is responsible for awarding banishment to our dearest Rama and Luxmana. In whose absence the kitchen is looking empty; who has caused the deserted look of the chuapari (chaupal)! The kitchen room is having a deserted look in absence of Sita and people have stopped visiting the chaupal because Luixamana has to gone to the jungle with his brother Rama. Dear, do you know who has sent our Rama and Luxmana to the jungle?)

The place or seminaries where traditional gurus used to teach their disciples are also called chaupari in Maithili language. In early thirteenth century there was a great scholar of Indian philosophy in the village of Sarisabpahi in Madhubani, Bihar – Mahamhopadhyaya Bhavanath Mishra. He had a rare distinction of being a non-suppliant. Not only that he never asked for anything but he flatly refused the presents made by others, including the King of Mithila. Though a prey to the proverbial poverty of pandits, he was contented with what meager resources he had. It was therefore that he was better known in the public by an alias of his, Ayachi. He was a great philosopher gifted with originality of thought.

People claim that there were over ten thousand students reading under his guidance in his native village, Sarisabpahi. He had a small piece of land; he was using it as his chaupari – seminary, locally known to the people as Ayachika chaupari. It was a real public space where the entry was open for all the bonafide, sincere and brilliant students of the region. The system of imparting education was a four-tier one. The great master gave lessons to ten selected extraordinary top ranking students, who, in their turn, trained ten students each and they taught ten students, who again taught ten students each. The King of Mithila never interfered in the academic activities, decision-making and selection of students in Ayachika chaupari and granted the autonomy of this seminary. The selection of students was democratic and it always took place without any bias. Is it not a wonderful example of public space in ancient Mithila?

In order to choose the qualified grooms, the people of Mithila initiated a tradition of Vivah-sabha (marriage mart), probably in 14th century AD. The Maharaja of Mithila once again sanctioned this idea and accordingly 14 villages were identified to hold such sabhas: Saurath, Khamgadi, Partapur, Sheohar, Govindpur, Fattepur, Sajhaul, Sukhasaina, Akhrarhi, Hemnagar, Balua, Baruali, Samsaul, and Sahsaula. While Saurath maintains the tradition, all other villages have discontinued holding thc marriage mart.

Almost every year, during suddha or auspicious days for the settling of marriages, thousands of Maithil Brahmans gather here. It is obligatory for every person desirous of marriage to get a certificate called asvajajanapatra (non-relationship) from a panjikara (genealogist), stating that there is no "blood relationship" (of course, fictitious blood relationship), as per the prescribed rules of prohibited degrees, between the two contracting parties. There is a fixed sitting place – dera – for every village in the sabha.

The timing and number of days etc. are decided in a general meeting of the scholars and pandits of Mithila in a complete democratic atmosphere as according to the traditional astrological diary – pachanga. Usually it is held for seven to 15 days every year or sometimes twice in a year during the auspicious period (months). After reaching at the dera the father or guardian of a bride starts searching for a suitable groom with the help of his relatives and a ghatak (middleman). The negation takes place in a complete democratic manner. The grooms also arrive at their respective deras. Here everybody is treated equally and given opportunity to negotiate with the guardians of appropriate groom of the bride in a democratic style in the sabha, public space. It appears to be influenced with the concept of chaupal.

As soon as we talk about chaupal it gives complete picture of traditional or conventional panchayat systems that have the capacity to keep real civil society in ordered or arranged style in Indian village.

Chaupal and Mahatma Gandhi

Mahatma Gandhi stands out in history as one of the greatest mobilizers of masses. It is one of the miracles to many of his biographers as to how he endeared himself to the millions of countrymen of various categories. His simple life, close association with the villagers, the sincerity with which he led them to social action, the idiom that he spoke, the loin cloth that he wore were genuine expressions of Gandhi's profound conviction to identify himself with the poorest of the poor. Mahatma Gandhi's own life became an exemplar of not only higher values of life but also the fountainhead of a new source of inspiration and passion for collective action.

He decided to begin his journey of freedom struggle from the villages of India. His Gramaswaraj and Hindswarj are in fact rooted in Chaupal. He always wanted that power should be given to he local bodies of villages. In 1931 when he visited England in connection with the Second Round Table Conference, he was asked at Oxford, "what is the greatest obstacle in the way of Swaraj?" he replied, "It is the British officers' unwillingness to part with power and our incapacity to wrest power from unwilling hands." The whole concept of Panchayati Raj was evolved on the Gandhian principle of Gram Swaraj in which the village was made the centre for planning and implementation of development activities.

In his ashrams and camps as well as in Khadi spinning and weaving centres his prayers and meetings and dining all held in a chaupal like atmosphere. The untouchables and the Brahmans all were eating together in a common place. All use to clean their toilets themselves. He opted to choose the conventional Indian measures for creating an atmosphere of civil society. He visioned Rama rajya instead of liberal society.

Non-Hindus and a section among his admirers failed to understand what Gandhi meant by Ram Rajya. He said, "By Ram Rajya, I do not mean Hindu Raj, I mean by Ram Rajya, a Divine Raj, the Kingdom of God." His faith in God was unshakable. His God was not a personal god. Ram, for him, the almighty God which guides to noble action and whose presence can be felt everywhere. The Ram Rajya he was promoting was an ideal social order where an ideal king rules over his subjects without any distinction whatsoever. Truth, dharma and justice will be the dominant characteristics of such a society. Both the Pandit and the poorest of the poor will have equal say in the governance. Nobody will be discriminated against anybody. Gandhi's Ram Rajya was not a utopia where idealism alone will prevail. There was much in common, if one can stretch it, between Plato's Ideal Republic and Gandhiji's Ram Rajya though Tolstoy's influence on Gandhiji could also be discrenible in formulating his vision of a new society. The major difference between the appraoches of Gandhi and Plato is that while Plato is philosophical Gandhji is pragmatic and down to earth a realist.

For Mahatma Gandhi rights and duties are complementary and a citizen who is not conscious of his duties has no right to think of his rights. He believed, "There can be no Ram Raj in the present state of iniquitous inequalities in which only a few roll in riches, while the masses do not get even enough to eat." Does this Gandhian passion for social justice remain a far cry? No one knows. In the modern context a king like Ram, Gandhiji's ideal king, is the Custodian of not only the physical domain of the people but also the inspirer of his people of higher reals of spiritual attainments. To him, a real devotee of Ram is he who feels the pains and sufferings of the poor and the helpless. He rightly preferred to use Narsimha Mehta's devotional song, Vainav jana to tene kahiye jo pira parai jane re. He initiated changes that could really groomed the way for civil society in a conventional but innovative manner. Coming to his ashramas all people, mainly those with rural background felt to come in the native atmosphere and made themselves ready for freedom struggle in a peaceful manner. It was his connection with the rural setups that made truly the Father of the Nation, Rastrapita. He took three major initiatives: first, motivated people to fight for freedom struggle in a peaceful and non-violent way; second, created an atmosphere through his experiments for women's freedom and participation in all walks of life; third, fought for the evil practices of the traditional Indian society such as untouchability, child marriage etc. People liked his experiments. Men and women all became the committed members of his movements and swadeshi initiatives to get freedom from the colonial rule of India in peaceful and non-violent measures. Even non-literate Indians had no problem to understand his objectives of non-violence, satyagraha, civil-disobedience movement, self rule and spinning and weaving Khadi clothes. During my recent fieldwork in Mithila I collected a wonderful folksong from an octogenarian non-literate woman:

- Ham nai pahirab meelak saari
- Ham ta charkha katbai na
- Baat karab gramswarajak
- Gandhi ke sunbai na
- Ham nahi pahirab meelak saari
- Hama ta charkha katbai naa
- Hamhu katbai piyo ji katthinha
- Dunu mile katabai na
- Ham.

(We will now never wear the mill-weaved saree, we would rather spin thread on spinning wheal. We will talk about the possibility of Gramsvaraj and listen to Gandhi. I will spin and request my dear husband also to spin; we will spin together.)

Naturally Gandhi was treated as the pradhan, mukhia or chief of the chaupal of India – a truly semi-global village. As early as 1936 he remarked, "I would say that if villages perish India would perish too. I believe and repeat times without number that India is to be found not in few cities but in its 7,00,000 villages." His role was crucial in awakening the most dormant and stagnant sector of Indian society, i.e., villages of India.

Gandhi's Gramsvaraj was not the resurrection of the old village but the formation of fresh independent units of villages having a self-sufficient economy. Self-suffiency in basic needs was one of the fundamental conditions of Gandhian village reconstruction. Food, clothing and other basic necessities should be produced at the village itself, which would lead to full employment of almost each able-bodied person and would prevent the rural – urban migration in search of employment and better opportunities.

Illustrating the idea of Gramswaraj Gandhi speaks: "My idea of village swaraj is that it is a complete republic, independent of its neighbours for its vital wants, and yet interdependent for many others in which dependence is a necessity. Thus the village's first concern will be to grow its own food crops and cotton for its cloth. It should have a reserve for its cattle, recreation and playground for adults and children. Then if there is more land available, it will grow useful money crops, thus excluding ganja, tobacco, opium and the like. The village will maintain a village theatre, school and public hall. It will have its own water works ensuring a clean water supply. This can be done through controlled wells or tanks. Education will be compulsory upto the final basic course. As far as possible, every activity will be conducted on cooperative basis. There will be no caste, such as we have today with their graded untouchability. Nonviolence with its technique of satygraha and non-cooperation will be the sanction of the village community. There will a compulsory service of village guards who will be selected by rotation from the register maintained by the village. The government of the village will be conducted by the Panchayat of five persons annually elected by the adult villagers, male and female, possessing minimum prescribed qualifications. They will have all the authority and jurisdiction required. Since there will be no system of punishment in the accepted sense, this Panchayat will be the legislature, judiciary and executive combined to operate for its year of office. Any village can become such republic without much interference, even from the present Government whose sole effective connection with the villages is the exaction of village revenue. I have not examined here the question of relations with the neighbouring villages of the centre, if any. My purpose is to present an outline of village government. Here there is perfect democracy based upon individual freedom. The individual is the architect of his own government. The law of non-violence rules him and the government. He and his village are able to defy the might of a world. For the law governing every villager is that he will suffer death in the defence of his and his village's honour." His imagination of "Self Government" came to reality in 1992 when the Indian Parliaments gave rights, power and duties to the Gram Panchayats through 73rd amendment in the Constitution. Here the Panchayats are defined as "institutions of self-government." The Act provides for a three-tier Panchayati Raj system at the village, block and district level with a fixed tenure of five years. Seats have been reserved in favour of SC/ST and women so as to enhance their participation. The Act also provides for setting up a Finance Commission and an Election Commission.

Chaupal and Bhoodan/Gramdaan Movement

As a true or the best disciple of Gandhi, Vinaoba Bhave also tried to create an alternative agrarian civil society using the traditional system of India. He used the basic concept of Chaupal to begin his bhoodan (gift of land) movement in India in 1951. It was a very unique approach for alternative development. The major aim of this movement was to bring about a peaceful agrarian revolution in the country. The bhoodan movement consisted of collection of land from bog zamindars or landlords as gift and distribution of the same to the landless persons. According to him in a just and equitable order of society, the land must belong to all and that was why he did not beg for gifts but demanded a share to which the landless or poor are rightly entitled. For him the real owner of the entire land of this universe is nobody but almighty Gopala alone: Sabai bhumi Gopal ke. A therefore has no right according to Vinoba to get the ownership of the land. What they can do is to use or cultivate the pieces of land as per their requirement. It was an initiative to propagate the right thought, by which social and economic maladjustment could be corrected without serious conflict. Later, he went one step ahead and started motivating people to donate the entire village land as gramdan. This was a wonderful approach to create a real and just civil society in an alternative style. He gave his slogan of jai jagat: hail to the world. Like Mahatma Gandhi, Vinoba also decided to begin his journey from the village. And to get his entry into any village he took the help of chaupal and its panches.

In 1958 his followers came to know about a village in Munger district in North Bihar. This village, known as Berain, was a village of backward and underprivileged communities. The villagers did not have proper food and shelter. No job opportunity, no land to plough. Their economic condition was so wretched that many of them had to live on theft and robbery. Such behaviour of people defamed it as a village of thieves and notorious people.

Discussion and discord frequent quarrels, mutual jealousies marred the village, occasional conflicts permeated the social life of Berain. The villagers usually stole standing crops etc There were 83 families before 1958. 36 families owned about 11 acres of land. Of these only one family had little over 4 acres and three had about 2 acres.

People of Berain provided the necessary labor force for the big absentee zamindars. The favorites were given land on batai, share cropping. They were working as agents for the zamindars to manage cheap labor for cultivation and to help generate disharmony among people so that they might not unite. So long as there was discard among them, the zamindars were free to rule and control them.

The rebel laborers were ill-treated. All of a sudden there was a famine-like situation in the village. It was difficult to manage even subhuman standard food one time a day. Some young men realized the grim situation of utter helplessness in Berain. Realizing the game plan of the zamindars they were collected in the village Chaupal and decided unanimously to approach the sarvodaya workers. In those days the bhoodan and gramdan movement was at its peak.

The sarvodaya volunteers were moving from one village to other asking for land of one kattha in a bigha from the landowners for the landless people and organizing people for a change in the society to alleviate their pangs and to teach them how to stand against exploitation by peaceful means. On the request of the youths of the village they visited with Vonoba Bhave under the leadership of Laxmi Sahu, a sarvodaya leader and the Chairman of Khadi and Village Industries Commission of India on February 4th, 1958. The villagers warmly welcomed their visit with drums and other musical instruments. The next day i.e., on 5th February almost entire village: men and women, young and old, big castes and small castes, all gathered on a

Chaupal and meeting took place under the banyan tree to listen to Vinoba and his associates. The lectures of Vinoba created a deep impression on them. It was finally decided to declare Beraian as gramdan village. In a way Berain was declared first gramdan village in Bihar in 1958. A new beginning initiated to create a just, democratic and fearless civil society by the peaceful measures.

The sarvodaya workers, with the help of villagers created job opportunities in the for of charkha spinning, weaving, oil-pressing, collective farming; awareness on hygiene and sanitation, Basic school and other facilities and now within few months all starving villagers were able to eat their two meals and live in harmony without any fear. That tool place because of the inspiration of Sarvodaya workers made it a model village. Many leaders and dignitaries of India and other countries visited this village to see the alternative model of development. Jayprakash Narayan, Sri Krishna Singh, the then Chief Minister of Bihar, Dr. Jakir Hussain, Vice President of India and many representatives of England, America Switzerland, Yugoslavia, Ghana and other countries visited and praised the efforts of villagers. Once I visited this village with my father who is a Gandhian in 1981.

Vinoba's experiment however did not work completely. It has many reasons. Emergency posed by Late Smt. Indira Gandhi compelled Jayprakash to join the active politics but Vinoba continued doing his experiments without any political intention. Many of his committed workers saw their disinterest in the Gramadan and Bhoodan movement. Government also did not take any serious step to patronize this great approach of alternative development. Vinoba was getting old. So it actually could not bloom the way Vinoba wanted it to grow but the concept was acknowledged and praised everywhere in the world.

Chaupal and Hindi Literature

In Hindi literature many writers have made attempts to make people aware about civil society using Chapal as platform for conveying the message of change. Here I have taken three examples: two short stories – Pancha Parameshwar by Munshi Premchand, Panchalight by Phanishwarnath "Renu" and one novel Baba Bateshwarnath by Nagarjuna. The conventional panches are treated as god because in their decision both the disputants come with the hope to get their problem (dispute) solved. In most of the cases their hopes are fulfilled. Interestingly both the parties go back as friends after the decision given by the panches. Such situation is hardly seen or observed in constitutional courts in India or elsewhere in the world. All decisions are given in the Chaupal. The Indian villagers are emotionally as well as socially attached it. Premchand has used this relationship in his story, Pancha Parameshwar very effectively. His intention is to propagate the message of egalitarian society through it in India. And the story was well received. Even today it is an integral part of school curriculum. That shows the significance of it.

Phanishwarnatha "Renu", known as anchalik kathakar, country writer, has tired to show how change, if required, is accepted in the conventional society in India through his well-known short story, Panchalite. Briefly speaking, it is a story about a low caste youth in a typical north Indian village who only knows how to operate and repair patro-max.

This man falls in love with a village girl who does not belong to his caste and elopes with her to some unknown place. He comes back to his village after a few month but the panches sit in the Chaupal and do not sanction their marriage as social. They order him to live outskirt of the village. He abides by the decision and constructs his hut in the last boundary of the village. All of sudden, the head of Gram Panchayat dies. The villagers and his family members decide to give a big feast in his memory.

A huge number of people from the village and neighbouring villages are invited. Interestingly nobody knows how to operate panchalite. The village elders are now helpless because a feast of such time cannot be organized at night without proper arrangement of light. Now this man is summoned in the Chaupal before the panches. He is said to operate the panchalite but this man put a condition before them, "I will do this job if the panches are ready to accept my marriage as socially sanctioned and also permit me to once again construct my house in the village. " "I should also be permitted to dine with the village elders", he concluded. The panches finally takes unanimous decision to admit him with his wife in the village. He is also allowed to dine with the villagers.

This story shows, as has been stated earlier, how the conventional society accepts the change in its fore fold. The author tries to convey the message of unity, individual freedom to choose life partner without any caste prejudices etc., in a very convincing style. As the Indian people are rooted with the tradition of panches and Chaupal, he uses it as a platform to reach to the audience.

Nagarjun in his novel, originally written in Maithili and later translated into Hindi, Baba Bateshamatha, tries to explain the cause of the lower castes and landless community of a particular village of Mithila.

This village, however, is representative of almost all the villages of India. A small banyan tree is planted in a gairmajarua aam, common land in the village by a lower caste youth. This tree becomes a public space where everybody come and shares his pain and pleasure. It is also used a Chaupal. In the novel, this tree has been used as a grand old tree with a divine merit. It talks like an old man and tells the story of zamindars's exploitation of poor and lower caste people. It talks also about Gandhian approach and freedom struggle, it talks about creating a democratic society. This experiment of Nagarjuna liked by the readers in India.

Chaupal and Radio and Television

Popularity of chaupal influenced the creative people to develop and transmit some programmes addressing development issues such as health, hygiene, community awareness drive on literacy, numeracy, untouchability, gender equality etc., through chaupal. Right from the very beginning, the All India Radio (AIR) has been airing such programmes. Most famous among them is called chaupal. Here, in this programme, men, women – of course from villages – participate and share the news and information with their fellow village brothers and sisters. This is even today one of the most interesting programmes of the AIR. Television has also been transmitting such programmes.

Chaupal in Indian Cinemas

Many creative and intelligent directors and produces of Indian cinemas have very minutely read the psychology of the villagers of India and tried to used chaupal as a platform to convey their message of any form: gender equality, child labour, relationship, bad impact of caste system and untouchability jut to name a few. An innovative example of using chaupal as a platform to initiate change in order to create an atmosphere of women's freedom in a conventional society is seen in a well-known Hindi Cinema, Ashta.

Mansi, a role played by Rekha, is a beautiful lady and a homely housewife of her Professor husband, Amar – a role played by Om Puri. She has a charming school going girl child. This family is a typical lower middle class urban family in India. The lady wants to buy many things for her husband, baby girl and for herself but the family income does not allow her to buy all that she desires to buy. Once she comes closure to a well-off neighbouring lady. She lives a very happy life and owns all possible luxuries – car, ornaments, costly clothes etc. Mansi admires her and dreams to have all that this lady owns. She repents on her poor economic status. The neighbouring lady is smart enough to read her psychology. Playing with the daughter of Mnasi, one day she comes to her house, enquires about them. Mansi likes her generosity and they are become very friendly.

One day she takes Mansi and her daughter in a market. Mansi's daughter selects a costly sandal. Mansi too likes it but she does not buy as it is beyond their imagination. The lady immediately buys that pair of sandal for her the baby girl. Initially Mansi opposes it to accept that gift from her but after a little persuasion the lady manages to convince her to accept this. Now, a new chapter begins.

With her behaviour and costly gifts, she creates a sense of guilty consciousness in Mansi's mind. She wants to have money so that she can live her life in a happy way. The neighbouring lady also buys some costly items for her. One day she takes her to a rich man who wants to have always-new women for his sexual urge, a role played by Naveen Nischal. This man reads her palms and creates a compulsive atmosphere and she ultimately surrenders herself before him, knowing that she is doing wrong. He develops physical relationship with her.

Mansi comes back to her house and repents for the entire episode. She does not want to repeat this incidence again but once trapped, it is hard to get rid off such trap. The neighbouring lady now takes her to the rich man regularly. She also threatens her if she does not go to the rich man she would let her husband know the entire episode. Helpless Mansi succumbs herself to her out of fear and societal prestige. Many times she thinks to confess all that she has done before her husband but social fear does not permit her to do so.

Poor Mansi gets an opportunity after her husband's journalist friend comes to their house from a remote village and shares his wonderful experience of how traditional justice given to a lady in a village chaupal by the elders and traditional panches. He narrates that in a remote tribal village a poor man with no means to cultivate and no opportunity to earn his livelihood decides to go to some urban city to earn but he has no money to travel. He goes to a village moneylender requesting him to lend a few hundred rupees loan on interest. The moneylender wants something, which can be mortgaged. The poor man has nothing to be mortgaged. The moneylender suggests if he can mortgage his wife he may take the loan and his wife would be returned as soon as he comes back and return the money, of course with interest. With little hesitation he agrees to his proposal and mortgages his wife. He goes to the urban city finds a job, earns and comes back to his village. On his return, he is informed that his wife is pregnant and the baby in her womb is moneylender's baby. He returns the money to the moneylender and says he is willing to accept his wife not the baby because the baby (in the womb) is not his baby it belongs to moneylender. The moneylender however is willing to wave off his entire loan and keeps the lady as his wife but for this also he is not agreed.

Finally they go to the chaupal and request the panches for justice. It is a very hard issue to be settled. The meeting goes for many hours. The panches ultimately ask with whom she wants to live. Now she breaks her silence: "My husband has used me, say my body and mind, as a commodity. He has mortgaged me to get money. I am a human being; naturally I had gone to the house of moneylender with my emotion, flesh and womanhood. He has loved me, cared for me, which brought me much closer to him – mentally, physically and emotionally. We have shared our moments together and as a result I am now expecting a baby. The baby, I am expecting, belongs to the moneylender who is ready to accept me as his wife with my baby. My husband mortgaged me as ornament or a piece of land. Now once again he wants me to go to his house so that in future also he can use me as commodity. I, if allowed, would love to live with the moneylender as his wife because he has given me emotional healing, social recognition and worldly things."

Hearing her argument and getting it confirm from her first husband, the panches of chaupal give a historic decision and allowing her to live with the moneylender.

This story shows how the film media has used chaupal to initiate change in the society and honor the individual freedom of a woman, an essential element of civil society. This story encourages Mansi to confess the entire situation before her husband. She tells him the truth and as expected he forgives her as he knows Mansi has done this but her intention was not bad.

Similarly, in a recent Hindi Cinema, the GodMother, the young director has made a good attempt to use chaupal for propagating the role of women equal to men in all fields. He has tried to give the message that if need be an innocent and soft spoken housewife of a lower middle class family from a village can play all the tricks and weave good and bad plots to sustain her position and also very skilfully she can take revenge.

In the film, an honest village Sarpanch is killed brutally by his rival group with the help of professional killers and guns. The innocent wife of the slain Sarpanch now decides to jump in the politics. She does it. Knowingly, she develops her nexus with the professional killers, rowdy elements, and political guns and also begins smoking, drinking etc. She takes the help of anti-social elements in order to take revenge from the killers of her husband and to create a position of woman in the politics.

The young director has perhaps taken the responsibility to paint the role of a female politician as a strong character who may take any tough, legal or anti-social, decision or direction to show her work in the society or the nation.

Use of Chaupal in Indian Judiciary: Lok Adalat

Delay in judgment, created, and it is still creating a sense of havoc, helplessness in the mind of common people, mainly poor and those living in the remote villages. In countless number of litigations both the parties were willing to sort out their problems, but because of lawyers vested interest and the unnecessary technicality of the official process of the courts they were not allowed to do so. In the states like Bihar, Madhya Pradesh and Uttar Pradesh many accused spent more than 20 years in jail without any judgment. And when final judgment came they were found innocent. Such situations compelled the social thinkers, judges, legal experts and specialists of our constitution to think for an attentive method by which the pending cases should be finalized immediately and chief Justice Bhagwati has rightly observed that courts in India should not be guided by any verbal or formalistic canons of construction but by the permanent object and purpose for which the Constitution has been enacted. He too has made law as a tool of social transformation for creating a new social order imbued with social justice. He made a prophetic observation, which has inspired the poor, the weak and the destitute to seek protection of the court against exploitation, injustice and tyranny. Chief Justice Bhagwati highlighted the new swing and significance of judicial process in these wards:

"Today a vast revolution is taking place in the judicial process, the theatre of law is fast changing and the problems of the poor are coming to the forefront. The Court has to innovate new methods; and device new strategies for the purpose of providing access to the justice to large masses of the people who are denied their basic human rights and to whom, freedom and liberty has no meaning. (Quoted in Road of Justice, Public Interest Litigation and Media, 2001.)

And some other legal experts are of the opinion that too Indians need to resurrect the judicial conscience on the line of social philosophy envisaged in the Indian National Charter, rather than to the live of erstwhile British Colonial rulers. It has now become imperative for the Courts that their decisions are animated with the philosophy of human rights enshrined in the constitution. What is expected from the Courts is that Courts weave a home-spun jurisprudence shaking its link from Anglo-Saxon jurisprudence by making law and legal institutions the delivery system of human liberty, social equality and social justice. The harsh reality is that only privileged classes have been to approach the courts for protecting their vested interests. It is only for the moneyed who have so far had the golden key to unlock the doors of justice. To once again quote Justice Bhagwati: "The time has come when the courts must become the courts of poor and struggling masses of this country. They must shed their character as upholders of the established order and status-quos. They must be sensitized to the need of doing justice to the large masses of the people to whom justice has been denied by cruel and heartless society for generations. The realization must come to them that social justice is the signature tune of the constitution and it is their solemn duty under the Constitution to enforce the basic human rights of the poor and the vulnerable sections of the community and actively help in the realization of the Constitutional goals. This new change has to come if the judicial system is to become an effective instrument of social justice, for without it can not survive for long."(ibid).

And finally chief Justice Bhagwati worked seriously on the idea of Lok Adalat, and the result may magnetic. In a single day, I witnessed how he finalized more than 396 cases in a small mela like function in a small district town Giridih – of Jharkhand during his tenure as Chief Justice of India. The idea, philosophy and mode of functioning of Lok Adalat is cent percent similar to traditional judiciary'. And the atmosphere in which decisions are taken before giving the judgment is very much similar to mahachaupal (the great chaupal).

Chaupal as a Forum for the Politicians to get Public Support

Many politicians have used chaupal in last 55 years as a platform or catchword to get the public support. Famous among them are Choudhury Charan Singh and Choudhury Devilal. Choudhury Charan Singh always did his politics in a chaupal like atmosphere and behaved himself as the elder of chaupal. This practice worked well with him and he could always managed to maintain his political supremacy in his constituency and neighbouring regions. Choudhury Devilal also played the same politics. He was truly regarded as the Tau, big uncle, in Haryana, Punjab and western Uttar Pradesh. He used to run his chaupal during his tenure as Deputy Prime minister in a five star Hotel in Delhi.

Maheder Singh, the founder of Bhartiya Kisaan Union (BKU), developed his personality as a savior of the farmers of northern in India, and now when the famous south Indian leaders such as ex-Prime minister H.D. Devegoda has joined him, he has developed his image as a unique leader who represents the countless number of farmers of India. Very brilliantly he uses all the metaphors of the chaupal – the hookah, the safa, the dhoti, and the words spoken by him are the words of a village folk or a village elder that he speaks in the chaupal. Tikait is very successful in his mission and he has achieved many successes for himself and also for the group of people he has been working. In him farmer see their honest representative everywhere.

Very recently, Sheila Dixit, the Chief Minister of Delhi, has announced the achievements of her Government during the last four years. She listed the construction works that her Government did under her leadership in a heading, entitled, "Facts at a glance", and claimed to have constructed following infrastructure for the common citizens of Delhi. In the details of development she claims to have constructed chaupals in various localities of Delhi. These chaupals are created mainly for rural poor and among the rural poor also attempts are made to construct the chaupals for the Harijans in order to create the atmosphere of social justice for them through their participation.

E-Choupal

e-Choupal is an initiative of ITC Limited, a large multi business conglomerate in India, to link directly with rural farmers via the Internet for procurement of agricultural and aquaculture products like soybeans, wheat, coffee, and prawns. e-Choupal was conceived to tackle the challenges posed by the unique features of Indian agriculture, characterized by fragmented farms, weak infrastructure and the involvement of numerous intermediaries. The programme involves the installation of computers with Internet access in rural areas of India to offer farmers up-to-date marketing and agricultural information.

Problems Addressed

Traditionally, commodities were procured in *mandis* (major agricultural marketing centres in rural areas of India), where the middleman used to make most of the profit. These middlemen used unscientific and sometimes outright unfair means to judge the quality of the product to set the price. The difference in price between good quality and inferior quality was little, and therefore there was no incentive for the farmers to invest and produce good quality output. With e-Choupal, the farmers have a choice and the exploitative power of the middleman is neutralised.

Effects of e-Choupal

ITC Limited has now provided computers and Internet access in rural areas across several agricultural regions of the country, where the farmers can directly negotiate the sale of their produce with ITC Limited. This online access enables farmers to obtain information on mandi prices, and good farming practices, and to place orders for agricultural inputs like seeds and fertilizers. This helps farmers improve the quality of their products, and helps in obtaining a better price. Each ITC Limited kiosk having Internet access is run by a sanchalak — a trained farmer. The computer is housed in the sanchalak's house and is linked to the Internet via phone lines or by a VSAT connection. Each installation serves an average of 600 farmers in the surrounding ten villages within about a 5 km radius. The sanchalak bears some operating cost but in return earns a service fee for the e-transactions done through his e-Choupal. The warehouse hub is managed by the same traditional middlemen, now called samyojaks, but with no exploitative power due to the reorganisation. Indeed these middlemen make up for the lack of infrastructure and fulfil critical jobs like cash disbursement, quantity aggregation and transportantion.

Since the introduction of e-Choupal services, farmers have seen a rise in their income levels because of a rise in yields, improvement in quality of output, and a fall in transaction costs. Even small farmers have gained from the initiative. Customized and relevant knowledge is offered to the farmers despite heterogeneous cultures, climates and scales of production. Farmers can get real-time information despite their physical distance from the *mandis*. The system saves procurement costs for ITC Limited. The farmers do not pay for the information and knowledge they get from e-Choupals; the principle is to inform, empower and compete. At the same time ITC Limited has obtained benefits from the programme:

1. elimination of non value added activities
2. differentiated product through identity preserved supply chains
3. value added products traceable to farm practices
4. e-market place for spot transactions and support services to futures exchange.

There are presently 6,500 e-Choupals in operation. ITC Limited plans to scale up to 20,000 e-Choupals by 2012 covering 100,000 villages in 15 states, servicing 15 million farmers.

Rural Factions

It seems nothing can stop the rise of India. India supplies the world with a robust knowledge-based economy, challenges US economic dominance, and acts as an important counterweight to China. Its controversial US-backed nuclear program has given it a primary place on the global energy front as well as granted its military new pull abroad. India's telecommunication, information technology, and service sector have played a strong role in redefining global trade and communication routes. Graduates from India's universities and those now returning from abroad generate substantial wealth for the country. A newly minted middle class fuels India's blistering economy, furnishing it with the fifth-largest purchasing power in the world. This, in hand with its diplomatic legitimacy abroad, seems the perfect storm for unfettered national growth.

Yet India is a country in contradiction. Sagging infrastructure, a shortage of Internet connections in rural areas, and large disparities in education threaten its stability. While India's educated urbanites see their salaries quadruple, much of India's poor live in poverty worse than that found in sub-Saharan Africa. Undereducation fuels fundamental factions rooted deep within rural and urban states alike. Environmental problems such as water shortages, sanitation-related illnesses, and pollution threaten to topple India's forward momentum—no matter how mighty it may seem.

Many predict a catastrophe for the country unless these issues are effectively dealt with—soon. The World Trade Organization (WTO) predicts a major national health crisis for India as soon as 2020 if it does not curb its inefficient redistribution and regulation of water resources immediately. Despite this serious cautionary tale, India continues to rise. The world—whether in concordance or not—has no choice but to accommodate India in the new global order—and this is a role India is more than eager to occupy.

8

Rural Leadership

Leadership has played an important role in the human history since earliest times. The historians have glorified heroes in battle and valued the importance of their deeds for the future generations.

Importance of Rural Leadership

The utilization of rural leaders is essential because of the following reasons:

- Extension has a long tradition of using leader in extension work. Extension worker as an outsider may not have complete knowledge about different aspects of village community nor they are supposed to have similar perceptions and feelings about village problems as local people may have. Thus, there are good reasons to use such people who belong to the community.
- Leaders by virtue of their influences can convey messages of development more convincingly in the people's language. They can use arguments and styles of presentation most appropriate for the target population. They can also help to get social sanction for development. Besides, they can also serve as mouthpiece of people before extension workers, they can explain elaborately the needs and aspirations of people.
- Number of extension workers is proportionately far less than required. Thus use of leader can help to multiply effects of extension work conveniently and convincingly.

- Leaders can help in enlisting participation of people in programmes of their own development. It is possible to organize people around concrete problems. Leaders can use their influence and skills to bring people together and empower them to take action for their development.
- Villages in India are still haunted by deep rooted beliefs, customs, superstitions and ignorance which influence development negatively. It calls for different types of efforts to overcome social barriers. Leaders, if positively inclined, can play prominent roles in master minding development in right earnest.

Every social group has certain people who command respect. They have influence and undisputed following.

Their opinions count. They have people flock around them for information, advice or inspiration or otherwise influence members to action. Such people are called as leaders and such activity is called as leadership. They are also known as power holders, men of power, power centres and power elite. If they are somehow linked with development programmes, the task of development would become very easy.

Leadership is an act that causes others to act or respond in a shared direction. A rural leader is the one who can inspire, persuade, influence and motivate useful changes. Bringing about change is a critical goal because most improvements demand a departure from routine ways. A rural leader creates a vision for others and then directs them towards achieving that. A rural leader has followers who have confidence in him and give him support and commitment to a goal. This is what leadership really means.

Leadership in rural areas is a key dynamic force that motivates and capture the cooperation of people. A rural leader must have a magnetic personality. Persuasion is another key aspect of leaders role. A leader must often get people to change their minds or take actions they had not considered. Influence is almost synonymous with leadership. Leadership is often defined as the process of influencing others to achieve objectives. He influences others to accomplish such things as taking on more responsibility, achieving high quality standards and raising ethical standards. Many leaders, unfortunately in rural areas influence group members to engage in negative, unethical acts that hurt the community in the long run.

Leaders have to motivate their followers to work harder. Top rural leaders are generally tough as their jobs are immensely demanding of time, concentration, sheer grinding brain power and physically tiring. He is supposed to make decisions on his own, strong willed, ambitious, energetic and motivated by power. He is full of courage, emotionally and physically strong and has ability to empathies with others. He is sensitive to other people's needs, values, cultures, beliefs and tradition. He takes on responsibility and is credible. He is dependable and loyal to his followers.

A good rural leader has all the relevant knowledge, keen mind, analytical ability. He has good interpersonal skills with sound relationships with rural people. He is full of energy.

Charismatic Rural Leaders

Charisma comes from a combination of emotional expressiveness, self confidence, determination and freedom from inner conflict. They have strong conviction in the essential rightness of their own convictions. They are radical, unconventional, risk taking, visionary, entrepreneurial and exemplary. There is intense emotional attachment to them on the part of their followers which goes beyond such things as trust, respect or admiration to embrace awe, devotion and loyalty. It is most important ingredient of leadership. Rural charismatic leaders make their followers more productive.

The effective leader is the one who sees leadership as responsibility rather than privilege. They have integrity and consistency. They are usually modest, loosing no opportunity to stress that real achievement has come from team work and not from inspiration of just one individual.

Why People Like to become Leader?

The main advantage of being a leader is that it gives you a feeling of power and prestige. The prestige comes from the fact that so many people admire leaders. Leaders are in a position to help others, thereby finding their jobs satisfying. Rural leaders are very well respected and control resources of the village and those coming from outside. Rural leadership does make a difference to the performance of individuals, groups and organisations. It helps to build teams and generates pride in collective achievements. It brings about changes in people's attitudes and behaviour as a consequence of interaction between leaders and followers. Leadership is widely distributed. Rural leaders are important because they are involved in maintaining traditional values in the face of challenges from those who wish to bring change in enabling groups of people to endues hardships

It shall not be wrong to say that it is almost impossible to have effective rural programme without involving rural leaders. They have to be involved in the programme from day one at planning stage. They are the one who will tell you how successful you will be in the programme implementation. They will give suggestions about how, where and what to change in the programme. They will be the ones who will explain in their own way to villagers about the benefits of the programme and also about what role they will play in the project. It is essential that development agencies develop an instant rapport with rural leaders and show the true picture to them. The good leader tends to share decision making and share responsibility. The good rural leader is visionary and is able to develop a shared vision with his followers.

Rural leaders help you to overcome obstacles and setbacks. With his unique communication skills, he talks to villagers and solves problems. This is because he is connected to the group in every possible way and empathise to them in his unique style.

Rural leaders are important since they help their followers to decide an important issue. They give direction for group action. They resort to group decision making, participative decision making and consensus decision making. A consensus decision making means that the leader encourages group discussion about an issue and then makes a decision that reflects general agreement and is supported by group members.

There is also complete agreement about how significant the leadership factor is in determining success and failure in village programmes. A leader helps others to improve their performance by providing suggestions and encouragement.

Types of Leaders

There are two broad categories of leaders in villages viz., 'traditional' and emergent leaders.

Traditional leaders command influence on the basis of land, wealth or certain inherited status belonging to tradition like caste leaders, land lord, priest. Emergent leaders are those persons who command influence on the basis of their personal qualities, specialization or office of power, political influence or such other acquired traits such as progressive farmers, head of village council (panchayat), cooperatives or member of a voluntary or political organization.

Traditional Leaders

They are respected because they possess wealth or power to conduct social rituals/ceremonies. Thus, they fulfil social and religions needs of the people. They up hold those values. There are many other terms to indicate various types of traditional leaders as given below:

Caste Leaders

If the influence of some leaders extend to particular caste group, such individuals have interest and active role in social and economic development of their own caste. They are more acceptable by members of their own caste.

Sacred Leaders

The term specifically refers to those who officiate in various religions and social ceremonies. They are prominent in sacred or spiritual field such as priests or ojhas (exorcists). Such traditional leaders, however, have influence over a section of society. They are characterized by inherited status due to birth in a family. However, their role in development programme can be limited due to their value orientations and pernicious interests.

Emergent Leaders

Emergent leaders have come on the rural scene due to new opportunities available in the villages such as village council (panchayat), cooperatives, voluntary organizations, rural branches of political parties etc.

Personal Leaders

Those leaders who are valued due to their specialized skills such as progressive farmers.

Professional Leaders

They are people who command respect or influence by virtue of their professional status, training etc. such as village extension workers or village school teachers.

Political Leaders

They are affiliated with an ideology or political party and command respect by virtue of their initiatives in the party.

Social Leaders

Leaders of various social organizations located in the villages command influence because of their involvement in development of people. There are sharp differences in leadership pattern among progressive and non-progressive villages. Leadership in one progressive villages are polymorphic in nature i.e. one person is sought for advice on a variety. In non-progressive villages, leadership is monomorphic or specialized in nature.

Leadership structure in rural India has undergone a sea change during post-independence era. The planned national development efforts, democratically elected governments and policy of involving people in institutions of development have created consciousness at the village level. The strong hold of traditional caste-oriented leadership is on the wane. Many youths from backward caste have emerged prominently, of late, in villages due to opportunities available in panchayat, cooperative, village schools and voluntary organizations.

Qualities of Leadership

Potential leaders can be selected on the basis of their attribute. Leaders for extension work must possess a blend of following qualities. Volunteer: The incumbent must come out on his/her own to work for the cause of the community. In every society there are people with altruistic tendency. Secular: People with partisan interest cannot serve for the cause of the whole village.

Democratic: Basic belief in individual supremacy and need for equal involvement of one and all in development programme is a must. Honesty: Sense of honesty and reliability builds trust for the leader in a group. Positive Enthusiasm: An abounding sense of joy and natural interest in development work sustains involvement of leader in hours of stress. Friendliness: Good leader feels deeply for those with whom he works. Friendly attitude inspires others to seek his contact. Scientific Outlook: Development work demands appreciation for breaking away from shackles of traditional beliefs and systems of living. A number of other attributes have been mentioned by various experts such as intelligence, tact, patience, poise, sense of humour, health, fairness, dependability, originality, sincerity, loyalty, integrity, vision, ethics, perseverance, impartiality, decisiveness, etc. However, it is for a potential leader to be a experienced farmer himself to be able to command natural influence.

How to identify and select potential leaders?

There are many ways to locate people with desirable qualities and potential to play leadership role, as given below:

Discussion Method

An opportunity for discussion on real issue gets people in action giving expression to their knowledge, group skill and power of conviction. This is said to be a live laboratory to see display of power and influence in natural condition.

The Workshop Method

Through this method, where the large group breaks up into smaller unit, leadership emerges, in each group over a period of time, the extension worker can spot certain leaders who come to the fore in taking responsibilities. The extension worker or professional leader in workshop has the position of consultant observer, discussion group leader etc.

Participative Observation

Even though observation is part of both discussion and workshop methods, leaders can be selected through close observation in the community by observer being a part of the scene for a period of time. This provide him enough data regarding conditions of the community opportunities of leadership and skills.

Sociometric Technique

The term 'sociometry' refers to the pattern of attraction among members of a group. Sociometric technique is meant for determining the extent to which individuals are accepted in a group. This helps in revealing the relationship structure within a group.

The technique can be applied if all the members of the group know each other well. In order to seek preference for leader the specific content is explained to each member and he is asked to give a number of preference (say 1st, 2nd and 3rd,) alongwith rating. Thus people are given a situation narrating whom do you consult from your village if you have problems regarding cultivation, name three persons from community in order of preference.

Sociometric score is calculated by multiplying number of incoming choices for each person and total of scores obtained in terms of preferences. Thus individuals are ranked on the basis of sociometric score.

Key Informants Method

A community or its members may be asked to indicate opinion leaders in that area. This is cost saving and time saving when compared to sociometric method.

Self-designating Techniques

It consists of asking a respondent a series of questions to determine the degree to which he perceives himself to be an opinion leader.

Training of Village Leaders

The task of developing villages cannot be achieved without trained democratic leaders with secular and social outlook. While potential leaders should be selected from the village communities concerned, they would require training to play enabling role. Training of potential leaders is essential for strengthening local initiative for development.

This will accelerate implementation of on-going efforts. Training, however should not be thought as one-stroke affair. It would rather be a continuous process although various levels of training may be designed. However, to start with the goal of training would be as below:

- To motivate local leaders to commit themselves for the cause of development
- To create general awareness in them about the problems of villages, current approaches of development, national policy, organization etc.
- To indicate in them basic skills of communication and group work.
- To provide them knowledge and skills in technical subject matter area relevant to the programme.

Content Area of Leader's Training

- Theoretical information should always be related at every step to practical situations.
- The subject matter should be in the nature of problems encountered by the local leaders in their respective area. Hence content of the programme should be problem centred.

The following general outline of content has been indicated in one of the United Nations Reports on training of rural leaders:

- Basic principles and aims of rural development and the practical set-up needed for effective rural development work.
- Leadership in rural society.
- Community organization principles, methods & techniques including method of stimulating group thinking, group planning and group action.
- Co-operatives, principles of co-operation and methods of organizing various types of co-operative enterprises and services.
- Local government principles and methods with particular reference to co-ordination of local bodies.

- Central government and other enternal machinery services. What facilities are available and how local efforts can be coordinated with national programme.

Essential Features of Leaders Training

The training to full fill the above mentioned objectives must adopt approach essential for bringing desired impact.

- The leaders must be trained through process of dialogue or group interaction rather than traditional lectures and notes, in order to inculcate right skills for facilitating participative leadership.
- The training should create an open and participative atmosphere. There should be enough opportunity to reach decisions through critical discussion among trainers and trainees with open mind and not take anything for granted.
- The training should help in acquiring and reinforcing values like justice, equality, honesty, solidarity through day-to-day working.
- The discussion and analysis should be based on the realities expressed by the participants in their life and work. They should begin with the known and lead to unknown.
- The training venue and set-up should be realistic, closer to the village life so that they can relate with their own situation.
- Practical involvement in workshop site visit, role playing and cultural programmes should be used more frequently.
- The period of training may vary from a day to a few weeks depending upon the intent.

In the beginning intensive training of long duration may be desirable for preparing adequately in the techniques of organizations, group working and practical vocational skills.

However, the training for development of leadership would be continuous affair to be imparted from time to time, though in varying forms.

Meaning of Administration, Coordination and Team Work

Administration: It is mainly concerned with organizational processes, procedures and rules. It focuses on attaining the existing goals and standard of performance and is tied to organizational goals and culture. It emphasizes rationality and control. It is normally reactive to current situation. It believes in manipulation and control. It believes in solving problems generally relying as time tested traditional methods. It has less emotional involvement with organizational members. It avoids conflicts and struggles and is satisfied with status quo. It includes planning, organizing, controlling, budgeting and counseling.

Coordination: It is the process of ensuring that all parts of project undertaken are well linked and balanced. This is ensured by planning in such a way that no part of the project is ignored or left out. There is some way of coordination between different units, so that they progress simultaneously. Coordination can be defined as the process of integrating the activities of separate parts or units of an organization to pursue organizational goals effectively. Without coordination people would loose sight of their goals within the total organization and tempted to pursue their own departmental interests at the expense of organizational goals. Hence coordination means harmonious adjustment or functioning. Coordination is between equals or near equals working together. In this each agency retains its dignity, objectives, functions and responsibility. It, however, willingly surrenders a small part of individuality in return for the advantage of working together with other agencies, thereby ultimately securing better service for all concerned. The coordinator, therefore, is a general purpose man charged with the responsibility of ensuring a total balance effort but is not expected to control or guide the technical details of the programme and the policies of the technical agencies or departments.

Herbert Simon has referred to two kinds of coordination:

1. Procedural coordination is exemplified by the design of the organization itself that establishes the lines of authority, delimits the sphere of activity and specifies.

The relationships among the members of the organization.

2. Substantive coordination is related to the content of the organisation's activities. The organizational form for Small Farmers Development Agency (SFDA) symbolizes procedural coordination. An Animal husbandry project (e.g. Sheep Development Programme) that designs different activities in the interrelations involved in the project represents substantive coordination.

A Team is a group of people with a high degree of interdependence focused on the achievement of some common goal. Effective team has unified common and meaningful purpose that provides direction, momentum and commitment for members. It usually results in better products, faster and at lower costs. Teams are flexible and responsive to the changing events. Pfeiffer and Jones (1974) suggest the following hypothesis in relation to successful cooperation in problem solving groupsa).

Each individual should understand the total problem.

a) Each individual should understand how he can contribute towards solving the problem

b) Each individual should be aware of the potential contribution of other individuals.

c) There is need to recognize the problems of other individuals in order to aid them in making their maximum contribution.

Groups that pay attention to their own problem solving processes are likely to be more effective than the groups which do not.

Team Building

It is data based intervention which assess the strengths and improvement opportunities of a work team and then prepares and implements plans to increase the effectiveness of the Team. It also increases the ability of the team to diagnose and solve its problems. Team effectiveness training is a programme that increases the ability of people to function as a member or leader of the team. It provides the participants with skills and knowledge to increase their personal effectiveness and ultimately the effectiveness of the team. The training will include topics such as problem solving, decision making, communication, goal setting, meeting management, conflict resolution, research tools, presentation skill and team success factor.

Team is basically a small group of people who meet more or less regularly in face to face interaction, who possess a common identity or exclusiveness of purpose and who share a set of standards governing their activities. One must realize that the team members can make 2+2=5. Of course they have also capability of making 2+2=3. Oral interaction involving speech communication via both verbal and non-verbal is the soul of team building. Their interaction is continuous during a discussion so that the members are constantly reaching, adapting and modifying their actions in response to each other. Impromptu speaking rather than prepared speeches is the essence of small group discussion.

It entails give and take. A sense of cooperation exist among the members. Despite the differences, members are engaged in search of group outcome. Agreement is taken as means to select best idea. Group Dynamics or process deals with morale, feeling, tone, atmosphere, influence, participation, style of influence, leadership struggles, conflict and competition. Sensitivity to group processes enables one to diagnose group problems early and deal with them more effectively. Leaders become more aware of differences of opinions and explore all sides of issues and alternatives. They are more sensitive to group norms, pressures and feelings. A good leader should have the ability to form a team as it typically outperform individuals when the task being done require multiple skills, judgement and experience. Teams are more flexible and responsive to changing events. They have capability to quickly assemble, deploy, refocus and disband.

Teams are an effective means for management to demoralize their organizations and increase employee's motivation. Extensive use of teams creates potential in a village to generate greater outputs with no increase in inputs.

Public Administration and Extension Administration

Administration is ordinarily defined as the one of "getting things done". Emphasis is placed upon processes and methods for ensuring decisive action. Principles are set forth for securing concrete action from groups of men. The task of deciding pervades the entire administrative organization quite as much as the task of 'doing'. Indeed it is integrally tied up with the later. A general theory of administration must include principle of organization that will ensure correct decision making, just as it must include principles.

Meaning of Administration

The term administration is derived from the latin words 'administrative' meaning 'to serve', 'to care for' or 'to look after people'. To administer is to manage or to direct affairs. The term administration, therefore, refers to the direction and management of affairs and to the activities of group cooperating to accomplish common goals.

It is a process of management which is practiced by all kinds of organizations from the household to the most complex system of government. Even in primitive societies, simple activities like hunting, food gathering etc., could not be carried out without some form of organisation. Somebody had to determine as to who will do what. Certain norms of behaviour had to be laid down to decide the distribution of work among the members of the primitive groups. Of course, the administration at that time was rather simple because the tasks to be carried out were also simple. With the growing complexity of modern life and administration of private as well as public affairs has become more and more complex. However administration is a collective activity directed towards the attainment of a specific goals. This means that it is a rational action, an endeavour to maximize one's goal or achievement by rationally relating means to ends. The term 'administration' has been variously defined by different writers. Some definitions of the word 'administration' are as follows:

"Administration can be defined as the activities of groups cooperating to accomplish common goals" – Herbert Simon.

"Administration has to do with getting things done, with the accomplishment of defined objectives" – Luther Gulick.

"Administration is determined action taken in pursuit of a conscious purpose. It is the systematic ordering of affairs and the calculated use of resources aimed at making things happen which one wants to happen and foretelling everything to the contrary."-F.M. Marx. (1998)

Thus, it is clear from above definitions that "administration" is only that type of collective activity which involves a rational organisation and management of men and material. In simplest terms, administration is determined action taken in pursuit of a conscious purpose. It is the specialized vocation of managers who have skills of organizing and directing men and materials just as definitely as an engineer has the skill of building structures. E.N. Gladden (1992) has rightly observed that administration "is a long and slightly pompous word, but it has an humble meaning, for it means to care for or to look after people, to manage affairs.

Public Administration

Public administration as an aspect of governmental activity is very old. It is as old as human history in European languages the term Public Administration began to creep in during the 17th century to separate the absolute monarch's administration of public affairs from his management of his private household. It was a period when the church was separated from the State and the government was super imposed on all other societal institutions within a definite territory.

In every society there are some activities like maintenance of Law and order, revenue collection, social welfare, agriculture and rural development etc. which have to be undertaken in public interest. Public Administration as an instrument of government is mainly concerned with the performance of these activities.

The origin and evolution of Public administration as distinctive subject can be traced from 1887 onwards. In India, there are evidences to suggest that there existed a good literature on the aspects of administration even before 1887. Written in the fourth century, Kautilya's Arthashastra is the oldest text on Public Administration. Akbar's time is another note worthy treatise on Public Administration. At present stage of man's evolution, Public Administration has expanded with the rise of the modern administrative stage. Its growing importance in the conduct of human affairs is evident in the birth of numerous public laws, growth of public profession, increasing coverage of taxes and public expenditure.

Public Administration is a part of the wider field of 'administration'. The term 'administration' is a collective activity directed towards the attainment of a specific goal. When the term refers to the activities of a club, an association etc. it is called 'Private Administration', and when it refers to those of the activities of local, State and Central government, it is called Public Administration. Public Administration is a specialized academic field. It essentially deals with the machinery and procedure of governmental activities. Administration has been defined as a cooperative human effort towards achieving some common goals. Thus defined, administration can be found in various institutional settings such as business firm, a hospital, a university, a government department such as Department of Agriculture, Department of Horticulture and so on. As an aspect of this more generic concept, public administration is that branch of administration which operates within a specific political setting. It is a means by which the policy decisions made by the political policy makers are carried out. It is the action part of the government, means by which the purposes and goals of government are realized.

Government activities are undertaken for public good, so administration of the governmental affairs is known as Public Administration. The collection of tax, maintenance of Law & order, construction of public roads, highways, river bridges, canals and even provision of Extension services to the farmers are some of the activities of Public administration. Public administration is distinguished that its ultimate purpose is general interest and public good.

Extension Administration

The principles of Public administration when applied to Extension are called Extension Administration. This is linked with development issues and can be done by Govt. or non-Govt.

agencies. The set up is generally participatory and democratic. Everything from planning to implementation is done through active participation of farmers.

POSDCORB

This concept of Management was profounded by Luther Gullick. He was of the view that administration is to be identified with managerial techniques, be sums up those techniques in the word or acronym 'POSDCORB', each letter of which describes one techniques namely – planning, organizing, staffing, directing, co-ordinating, reporting and budgeting.

Planning

Planning is decision making and involves selecting and integrating the courses of action that an organisation will follow to attain its objectives. Planning is deciding in advance what to do, how to do, when to do, who is to do and with what result. Although the future can seldom be predicted with accuracy and unforeseen events may interfere with the best prepared plans, unless there is planning, actions of people tend to be aimless and left to chance.

Elements in Planning

Planning in an extension organisation is not done for its own sake, but for the purpose of improving conditions of rural life. There are some basic elements through the interaction contribution by which a good plan may be developed. Planning results from the interaction of the two systems – the change agent system' and 'the client agent system' in the context of their objectives, resources, facilities and constraints is time.

Organisation

After planning the activities of administration (i.e. extension organisation) one should think of the structure of administration, namely, organisation through which the activities are operationalised and objectives achieved. In all the writing of management thinkers there is an excessive importance attached to the structural aspects of organisation. The problems of formal organisation are related to matters like levels of organisation, delegation of authority, hierarchy, span of control and work division.

Staffing

Staffing is concerned with all aspects of 'personnel administration'. Thus recruitment, appointment, promotion, discipline, retirement etc. are functions which must receive due attention of the managers. As the efficiency of organisation largely depends upon personnel, most of the time of the executive usually is devoted to this function. However, the motivational factors behind employees behaviour have not received the attention of the classical theorists.

Directing

Directing relates to the orders issued by the managers or superiors to the subordinates, directing the activities of administration or an organisation.

Coordination

Coordination means establishing harmonious relationship between the efforts of individuals and groups for the accomplishment of enterprise objectives. For smooth running of an organisation coordination is necessary within the organisation as well as with outside organizations. For instance, Extension organisation need coordination of organizations such as Department of Animal Husbandry, Department of Agriculture, Horticulture, Forest Department etc., in order to be effective in transfer of technologies to the farmers. Some sort of basic coordination is essential within an organisation throughout its lifetime for its survival and for unified action.

The need for coordination generally increases with increase in the size of organisation and the complexity of its functioning. Voluntary coordination may be encouraged amongst employees by clarifying the objectives of the organisation and by motivating them. Coordination may also be achieved externally by the use of committees and supervision etc. Coordination aims at combining individuals, groups and organisations as 'Team' to attain the organizational objectives.

Reporting

It is the responsibility of the executive to keep himself posted with the progress of activities in the organisation. It is through reporting that the executive becomes aware of the problems in the organisation for which he may initiate corrective measures by issuing necessary directions.

A 'report' is a formal record of activities or performance. It generally reflects the achievement or otherwise of a performance. Preparation of too many reports may hinder the day-to-day work, particularly field extension work. Reporting should be standardized as far as possible, so that comparable data are obtained from all the units and summarized for the organisation. However, there should be provision for reporting both i.e. something significant and the usual.

An annual report provides for some amount of functional control in an organisation and also as a documentation for its work. The annual report furnishes the needed feedback information to the funding agency, other organizations and the general public. The annual reports also serves as an integrating factor by providing information about the total organisation to its different units, which may be located at various places.

Budgeting

Budgeting means stating the objectives in numerical and financial terms. It indicates the allocation of funds for different sectors of the programme and is essentially a part of the planning process. Budgeting aims at arriving at least cost and most effective model for implementation of a project. Budgeting provides for pre-expenditure control of funds. For the Extension Programme Director, budgeting means that the persons in position shall spend the resources and money properly as per directive of the functioning agency, shall not divert or misuse funds and shall be responsible for the audit for their proper utilization. Thus, the concept of POSDCORB profounded by Luther (1999) is an comprehensive one which gives insight into the various activities of the management in any organisation.

These POSDCORB activities are common to all large scale organisations. They are the common problems of management which are found in the different agencies regardless of the peculiar nature of the work they do. These common activities are performed by Public Administration irrespective of the fact whether it is involved in military or in civil or state government or in the administration of local bodies.

Reorganised Extension System

By the middle of 1970s it was felt that Extension Services in the developing countries were suffering from a number of weaknesses (Benor, 1984) including the dissipation of extension workers' energies on low priority tasks, lack of a single clear line of command and a low level of agricultural knowledge in expertise among field level functionaries.

Apart from these, many factors were responsible for impeding efforts for measuring agricultural production through the spread of new technology. One such factor was inadequecy of extension machinery in the states. Steps required for strengthening agricultural extension administration in the states have been examined by various high powered committees by National Commission on Agriculture. They have stressed the need for gearing up agricultural administration all along the line.

In this context, a centrally sponsored scheme for "strengthening and re-organisation of Agricultural Extension administration in the States", had been approved by the Government of India for implementation in all the States during the sixth Plan period (i.e. 1978-79). This scheme is based on the new agricultural extension methodology known as the "Training and visit system".

The Training and Visit System

The training & Visit (T & V) System has been one of the most significant Extension organizational developments in the last decades. Billions of dollars have been invested in this system by the World bank since 1975. The system has been diffused very rapidly, first in South & South East Asia including India where it has been shown to increase the effectiveness of Agricultural Extension in irrigated areas in a number of countries. Thus contributing to rapid increases in Food production, and later in Africa where it was not always so successful.

The system tries to achieve changes in production technologies used by the majority of farmers through assistance from well trained Extension agents who have closelinks with agricultural research system.

Organisation

The T & V system has on hierarchial organisation with one Extension agent (VEW) for about 800 farmers. In turn, eight Extension agents are supervised by an Agricultural Extension Officer (AEO) and eight AEOs are supervised by a provincial Extension Officer who is assisted by three to five Subject Matter Specialists (SMS). In a large country there may also be several higher level supervisors, each in charge of about eight subordinates and assisted by SMSs.

It is physically impossible for Extension agents to meet all their farmers regularly. Hence, about 80 contact farmers are selected and visited every 2 weeks on a fixed day, preferably in their fields where other farmers can attend and join the discussion or demonstration of improved practices. Each supervisor, even those responsible for an area with several million farmers, is supposed to spend atleast half his or her time in the field to check on work progress and to identify problems to be solved by management. Paper work does not increase agricultural production, hence should be kept to a minimum.

Key Features

Staff are professionals with a sound knowledge of Agricultural research, farmer's experience & factors limiting the productivity in agriculture.

There is no Extension service for all aspects of agriculture. The service is responsible only for Extension. All other tasks required for agricultural & rural development (inputs, marketing) are performed by other organisation or by private business. The Extension service should cooperate closely with these organizations.

National Extension Service

The Grow More Food Inquiry Committee, after examining the results of the Campaign for increased food production, had identified issues in relation to extension work and extension workers. It had indicated that "no plan can have any chance of success unless the millions of small farmers in the country accept its objective, share in its making, regard it as their own, and are prepared to make the sacrifices necessary for implementing it". The integrated production programme of the Campaign failed to arouse such enthusiasm.

This analysis and the ideal led the Grow More Food Enquiry Committee to propose the establishment of a National Extension Organisation for intensive rural work which would reach every farmer and assist him in coordinated development of rural life as a whole. The First Plan made necessary provisions to support the ideal and the proposals associated with that ideal. The idea was that the Central Government would assist the State Governments in establishing the extension organizations so as to bring the entire area under extensive development within a period of about ten years. The Central and the State Governments were expected to frame detailed programmes for reorganizing the existing extension services, recruiting further needed extension staff, and arranging for their training.

Training of Extension Staff

The task of establishing a network of Gram Sevak Training Centres, and that for the training of farmers and their leaders, was actively supported. The main defect of the extension work in the pre-Plan period had been its reliance on propaganda rather than actual demonstrations to the cultivators under their field conditions. For training of senior officials involved in the functions of community development and agricultural improvement, the National Institute of Community Development (NICD), was proposed to be set up at Hyderabad. This institute later adopted various modes of imparting training including sophisticated and research based seminars, workshops, and conferences as tools of extension education.

Logic of Extension

The First Plan articulated that the training of extension workers required the closest attention, and must be related to the services that they were required to perform.

The Second Plan: Expansion of Community Development

The Second Plan acknowledged that community development and the national extension programme had made good progress in terms of extended coverage ;of development blocks and number of villages, and had achieved promising results on the movement.

Taking Benefits of Freedom to People

The Second Plan continued with the earlier spirit of taking benefits of freedom to rural people without delay, and decided to serve the entire country during the plan period by national extension service. Not less than 40 per cent of the blocks were to be converted into community development blocks, which are more intensive in development inputs needed to improve the quality of rural life.

Harnessing People's Initiatives

Unfortunately, the Second Plan gave differential treatment to the agricultural investment in favour of the industrial development.

Third Plan: Resurgence Continued

Combating poverty and building a technologically mature society by the application of science and scientific temper set tone for the Third Plan (1961-66). Diversified and efficient system of agriculture including animal husbandry, dairy, and production of meat, fish, and poultry was highlighted. It was hoped that besides achieving self-sufficiency in foodgrains, the Third Plan should increase the production of commercial crops like cotton, oilseeds, and jute. People's participation in soil conservation works, supply of fertilizers, benefits of irrigation infrastructure, and field level extension efforts were still problematic.

Agricultural Research Support

ICAR was further reorganized to strengthen All India Coordinated Research Projects to deal with problems visualized for the country as a whole taking into account the distinct agroclimatic zones. The ICAR's expenditure on agricultural research jumped from a mere Rs. 6 crore in 1947 to Rs. 237 crores in 1966, and thereafter to Rs. 2589 crore in 1972.

National Demonstration

Introduced in 1965, the National Demonstration Programme

further aimed at achieving a specific minimum yield target at the block level by increased productivity per unit area and per unit of time, and giving a reasonable opportunity to research workers to demonstrate in farmer's field what science can do to transform the Indian agriculture.

Multiple Methods of Extension Communication

Besides, the non-formal education and Krishi Vigyan Kendras (KVKs), introduction of agricultural education in schools, and education through non-degree institutional programmes to impart vocational skills were also experimented as a part of the larger extension strategy.

Fourth Plan Priorities

In view of the shortfalls, the Fourth Five Year Plan continued to give priority to agricultural sector and expected to achieve a target of 120 million tons of foodgrains production at the end of the Plan period. Yield per acre were expected to go up significantly for selected foodgrains, oilseeds, sugarcane, cotton, and jute crops. To achieve this, the Plan proposed fourfold increase in the use of fertilizers, twofold increase in the use of improved seeds, threefold increase in green manuring, and doubling of soil conservation works. The programme of community development and *Panchayati Raj* was to be more closely linked with the economic development.

The Intensive Agricultural District Programme (IADP) which was initiated in the Third Plan to induce cultivators to adopt a package of improved agricultural practices and to bring aout significant increase in yields had not matched the expectations. Similarly Intensive Agricultural Area Programme (IAAP) was introduced in the middle of the Third Plan for selected crops like paddy, millets, and wheat. This programme in the Fourth Plan was to deal with total crop economy of the entire area of IADP and IAAP districts rather than only the dominant crops.

Dwindling Impact

Inspite of continuous and unintegrated flow of resourceful schemes and programmes like Grow More Food Campaign, Community Development and National Extension Service,

Intensive Agricultural District Programme, High Yielding Varieties Programme, Multiple Cropping Programme, Small Farmers' Development Agency, Marginal Farmers' and Agricultural Labourers' Development Agency, and Dryland Farming, Integrated Rural Development Programme, the impact of strategies developed for diffusion of agricultural information in the pre-Training and Visit (T & V) period was slowly dwindling because of organizational and administrative arrangements.

Entry of Pilot Training and Visit Approach

A new approach was introduced in Rajasthan Canal and Chambal Irrigation projects in 1974-75, in Rajasthan on a pilot basis in the form of Training and Visit (T & V) system.

Institutional Restructuring

It is clear that no one uniform extension system will serve as a panacea for all States. A menu of various models will be available to the States to select and adapt to their own requirements. States have before them several models namely, (i) the ATMA model (7 States), (ii) Single Window – Broad Based extension model (Maharashtra), (iii) Panchayati Raj Institutions (Kerala, West Bengal and Madhya Pradesh) and (iv) the SAU-Farmer Direct Contact (Punjab). With Technology, the public extension service would be made leaner and professional.

District Level Agriculture Technology Management Agency (ATMA) model: A key concept is to decentralize decision-making to the district level through the creation of the ATMA as a registered society. A second goal is to increase farmer input into programme planning and resource allocation, especially at the block level and to increase accountability to stakeholders. A third major goal is to increase programme coordination and integration between departments so that the following programme thrusts can be implemented more effectively and efficiently.

Group Approach to Extension : The contact farmer approach to extension popularized by the T & V is to be replaced by the group approach. Formation and mobiliation of Farmer Interest Groups (FIG), Farmers Co-operatives and Self-Help Groups will be encouraged with the support of NGOs. Group extension will help to replace the top down approach with bottomup approach in technology transfer, as FIGs. This would lead to a farmer-extension worker participatory process with emphasis on problem solving rather than disseminating routine messages. The group approach in extension would also be in line with the Self-Help Groups of rural credit delivery, water user associations and co-operatives. Links with KVKs will be strengthened at the district level through institutions such as ATMAs.

Management Reforms in Agricultural Extension

Central Government Support to State Governments for Extension Services on their *Undertaking Policy and Institutional Reforms:* After the close of the World Bank supported NAEP, Central support to the State extension services dried-up, leaving them with the operation and maintenance of personnel and infrastructure created under T & V. It is proposed to support the State extension services provided, policy reforms and institutional restructuring is undertaken with demonstrated ability to develop a demand-driven, farmeraccountable, sustainable & farming systems with broad-based integrated delivery.

Funds from the Central Government together with State share for all technology transfer and extension activities would be pooled at these district level agencies and released for various activities according to the Strategic Research and Extension Plan prepared for the district. At present, about Rs.200 crore worth of funds are released annually to the States under 100 Centrally sponsored schemes (crops, horticulture, inputs, soil & water management) for the purpose of transfer of technology. Wherever ATMAs have been established, they should be conduit of these funds.

9

Rural Economy

The success story of Indian economy is spreading its wings towards India's districts and rural areas which accounts for over 65% of the nation's total populace. Currently, the rural sector of India is not only observing a massive increase in its per capita income but also in its expenditure and production. To enhance the rural economy of India, the Indian government has increased the monetary incentives allotted for the National Rural Employment Guarantee Act (NREGA) to USD 8.04 bn in its 2009 Union Budget. Moreover, the government has also allotted USD 34.74 bn in its Bharat Nirman Programme for enhancing rural road and rail network.

Surprisingly, the rural economy was unaffected by the recent global financial meltdown as per the research conducted by Rural Marketing Association of India (RMAI). The research also revealed that the rural economy in India is soon to witness an increase in its earnings which will be largely triggered by the incessant expansion in agriculture for the last four successive years.

Rural Consumer Market of India

The rural consumer market of India is expected to attain its target of USD 425 bn by 2010-2011, which can be translated as double of 2004-05 economy size, as per the report by CII-Technopark.

Indian Rural Retail Industry

As per the report by Associated Chambers of Commerce and Industry of India (ASSOCHAM), the Indian rural retail economy is worth USD 113 bn which can be translated as 40% of the total Indian retail market worth USD 280 bn. Some of the firms which have already established their base in rural areas are Reliance, AV Birla and Godrej, while firms like DCM, Pantaloon-Godrej JV, Tata, Hindustan Unilever, etc. are all set to expand their retail business in rural market.

Demand for FMCG in Indian Rural Areas

During the fourth quarter of the FY 2009, the demand for fast moving consumer goods (FMCG) increased steadily as compared to its urban counterparts, as per the research conducted by AC Nielsen.

Companies like Dabur, HUL, Godrej, etc have started recruiting more and more deserving candidates from rural districts in an attempt to elevate their network and market. Firms like Nestle and GlaxoSmithkline Consumer Healthcare (GSK) are all set to introduce new products for the rural areas in order to promote their brand.

This indicates that the FMCG firms no longer treat rural markets as an appendage to their metropolitan strongholds and are targeting the market for positioning their brands and for industrial set-ups.

Indian rural Healthcare Industry

The Indian rural Healthcare market is expected to expand at a pace of 44% by 2015, totaling its worth to USD 8.8 bn, according to a survey carried out by McKinsey. Conglomerates like Sanofi-Aventis, has currently introduced a promotional activity to advertise generics in rural provinces called 'Prayas'. This initiative is considered as an attempt to share medicinal information with practicing medicos in rural districts through seminars.

Indian Rural Automobiles Industry

The recent development that the Indian rural Automobiles Industry saw was the declaration of the establishment of new sales and service channels in rural India by the President of Mahindra and Mahindra Group (M&M) Rajeev Dubey. These service outlets have a premeditated target of manufacturing 1,00,000 automobiles by FY 2015.

Indian Rural Services Industry

Surprisingly, more than 60% of the services industry of the nation is based in the rural areas, as per the research conducted by National Sample Survey Organisation (NSSO). In the fiscal year 2007, there were around 85% of the own account enterprises (OAEs) in India which deployed 76% of the manpower in rural districts of India.

Indian Rural Telecommunication Industry

According to the research carried out by Confederation of Indian Industries (CII), the Indian rural Telecommunication Industry is expected to account for more than 65% of the entire telecom subscribers in India.

In an attempt to envelop rural subscribers, many telecom giants in India have willingly invested in rural telecom industry to benefit from its massive potential. Mobile equipments manufacturing firms like Intex Technologies, Karbonn, etc have allocated USD 21.03 mn for its promotional activities for 2010.

Indian Rural Agricultural System

Although agriculture contributes only 21% of India's GDP, its importance in the country's economic, social, and political fabric goes well beyond this indicator. The rural areas are still home to some 72 percent of the India's 1.1 billion people, a large number of whom are poor. Most of the rural poor depend on rain-fed agriculture and fragile forests for their livelihoods.

The sharp rise in foodgrain production during India's Green Revolution of the 1970s enabled the country to achieve self-sufficiency in foodgrains and stave off the threat of famine. Agricultural intensification in the 1970s to 1980s saw an increased demand for rural labor that raised rural wages and, together with declining food prices, reduced rural poverty.

Sustained, although much slower, agricultural growth in the 1990s reduced rural poverty to 26.3 percent by 1999/00. Since then, however, the slowdown in agricultural growth has become a major cause for concern. India's rice yields are one-third of China's and about half of those in Vietnam and Indonesia. With the exception of sugarcane, potato and tea, the same is true for most other agricultural commodities.

The Government of India places high priority on reducing poverty by raising agricultural productivity.

However, bold action from policymakers will be required to shift away from the existing subsidy-based regime that is no longer sustainable, to build a solid foundation for a highly productive, internationally competitive, and diversified agricultural sector.

Issues and Challenges

Slow Down in Agricultural and Rural Non-Farm Growth: Both the poorest as well as the more prosperous 'Green Revolution' states of Punjab, Haryana and Uttar Pradesh have recently witnessed a slow-down in agricultural growth. Some of the factors hampering the revival of growth are:

- Poor composition of public expenditures: Public spending on agricultural subsidies is crowding out productivity-enhancing investments such as agricultural research and extension, as well as investments in rural infrastructure, and the health and education of the rural people. In 1999/2000, agricultural subsidies amounted to 3 percent of GDP and were over 7 times the public investments in the sector.
- Over-regulation of domestic agricultural trade: While economic and trade reforms in the 1990s helped to improve the incentive framework, over-regulation of domestic trade has increased costs, price risks and uncertainty, undermining the sector's competitiveness.
- Government interventions in labor, land, and credit markets: More rapid growth of the rural non-farm sector is constrained by government interventions in factor markets — labor, land, and credit — and in output markets, such as the small-scale reservation of enterprises.
- Inadequate infrastructure and services in rural areas.

Weak Framework for Sustainable Water Management and Irrigation:

- Inequitable allocation of water: Many states lack the incentives, policy, regulatory, and institutional framework for the efficient, sustainable, and equitable allocation of water.

- Deteriorating irrigation infrastructure: Public spending in irrigation is spread over many uncompleted projects. In addition, existing infrastructure has rapidly deteriorated as operations and maintenance is given lower priority.

Inadequate Access to Land and Finance:

- Stringent land regulations discourage rural investments: While land distribution has become less skewed, land policy and regulations to increase security of tenure (including restrictions or bans on renting land or converting it to other uses) have had the unintended effect of reducing access by the landless and discouraging rural investments.
- Computerization of land records has brought to light institutional weaknesses: State government initiatives to computerize land records have reduced transaction costs and increased transparency, but also brought to light institutional weaknesses.
- Rural poor have little access to credit: While India has a wide network of rural finance institutions, many of the rural poor remain excluded, due to inefficiencies in the formal finance institutions, the weak regulatory framework, high transaction costs, and risks associated with lending to agriculture.

Weak Natural Resources Management: One quarter of India's population depends on forests for at least part of their livelihoods.

- A purely conservation approach to forests is ineffective: Experience in India shows that a purely conservation approach to natural resources management does not work effectively and does little to reduce poverty.
- Weak resource rights for forest communities: The forest sector is also faced with weak resource rights and economic incentives for communities, an inefficient legal framework and participatory management, and poor access to markets.

Weak delivery of basic services in rural areas:

- Low bureaucratic accountability and inefficient use of public funds: Despite large expenditures in rural development, a highly centralized bureaucracy with low accountability and inefficient use of public funds limit their impact on poverty. In 1992, India amended its Constitution to create three tiers of democratically elected rural local governments bringing governance down to the villages. However, the transfer of authority, funds, and functionaries to these local bodies is progressing slowly, in part due to political vested interests. The poor are not empowered to contribute to shaping public programs or to hold local governments accountable.

Priority Areas for the World Bank Support

Enhancing Agricultural Productivity, Competitiveness, and Rural Growth

Enhancing productivity: Creating a more productive, internationally competitive and diversified agricultural sector would require a shift in public expenditures away from subsidies towards productivity enhancing investments.

Second it will require removing the restrictions on domestic private trade to improve the investment climate and meet expanding market opportunities.

Third, the agricultural research and extension systems need to be strengthened to improve access to productivity enhancing technologies. The diverse conditions across India suggests the importance of regionally differentiated strategies, with a strong focus on the lagging states.

Improving Water Resource and Irrigation/Drainage Management: Increase in multi-sectoral competition for water highlights the need to formulate water policies and unbundle water resources management from irrigation service delivery. Other key priorities include: (i) modernizing Irrigation and Drainage Departments to integrate the participation of farmers and other agencies in irrigation management; (ii) improving cost recovery; (iii) rationalizing public expenditures, with priority to completing schemes with the highest returns; and (iv) allocating sufficient resources for operations and maintenance for the sustainability of investments.

Strengthening rural non-farm sector growth: Rising incomes are fueling demand for higher-value fresh and processed agricultural products in domestic markets and globally, which open new opportunities for agricultural diversification to higher value products (e.g. horticulture, livestock), agro-processing and related services. The government needs to shift its role from direct intervention and overregulation to creating the enabling environment for private sector participation and competition for agribusiness and more broadly, the rural non-farm sector growth. Improving the rural investment climate includes removing trade controls, rationalizing labor regulations and the tax regime (i.e. adoption of the value added tax system), and improving access to credit and key infrastructure (e.g. roads, electricity, ports, markets).

Improving Access to Assets and Sustainable Natural Resource use

Balancing poverty reduction and conservation priorities: Finding win-win combinations for conservation and poverty reduction will be critical to sustainable natural resource management. This will involve addressing legal, policy and institutional constraints to devolving resource rights, and transferring responsibilities to local communities.

Improving access to land: States can build on the growing consensus to reform land policy, particularly land tenancy policy and land administration system. States that do not have tenancy restrictions can provide useful lessons in this regard. Over the longer term, a more holistic approach to land administration policies, regulations and institutions is necessary to ensure tenure security, reduce costs, and ensure fairness and sustainability of the system.

Improving access to rural finance: It would require improving the performance of regional rural banks and rural credit cooperatives by enhancing regulatory oversight, removing government control and ownership, and strengthening the legal framework for loan recovery and the use of land as collateral.

It would also involve creating an enabling environment for the development of micro-finance institutions in rural areas.

Strengthening Institutions for the Poor and Promoting Rural Livelihood

Promoting Community-Based Rural Development: State Government efforts in scaling up livelihood and community-driven development approaches will be critical to build social capital in the poorest areas as well as to expand savings mobilization, promote productive investments, income generating opportunities and sustainable natural resource management. Direct support to self-help groups, village committees, user's associations, savings and loans groups and others can provide the initial 'push' to move organizations to higher level and access to new economic opportunities. Moreover, social mobilization and particularly the empowerment of women's groups, through increased capacity for collective action will provide communities with greater "voice" and bargaining power in dealing with the private sector, markets and financial services.

Strengthening Accountability for Service Delivery: As decentralization efforts are pursued and local governments are given more prominence in the basic service delivery, the establishment of accountability mechanisms becomes critical. Local governments' capacity to identify local priorities through participatory budgeting and planning needs to be strengthened. This, in turn, would improve the rural investment climate, facilitating the involvement of the private sector, creating employment opportunities and linkages between farm and non-farm sectors.

Agriculture Sector

Agriculture in India has a long history dating back to ten thousand years.

Today, India ranks second worldwide in farm output. Agriculture and allied sectors like forestry and logging accounted for 16.6% of the GDP in 2007, employed 52% of the total workforce and despite a steady decline of its share in the GDP, is still the largest economic sector and plays a significant role in the overall socio-economic development of India. India is the largest producer in the world of milk, cashew nuts, coconuts, tea, ginger, turmeric and black pepper. It also has the world's largest cattle population (281 million). It is the second largest producer of wheat, rice, sugar, groundnut and inland fish. It is the third largest producer of tobacco. India accounts for 10% of the world fruit production with first rank in the production of banana and sapota.

India's population is growing faster than its ability to produce rice and wheat.

Initiatives

The required level of investment for the development of marketing, storage and cold storage infrastructure is estimated to be huge. The government has not been able to implement various schemes to raise investment in marketing infrastructure. Among these schemes are *Construction of Rural Go downs*, *Market Research and Information Network*, and *Development/Strengthening of Agricultural Marketing Infrastructure, Grading and Standardization*.

The Indian Agricultural Research Institute (IARI), established in 1905, was responsible for the research leading to the "Indian Green Revolution" of the 1970s. The Indian Council of Agricultural Research (ICAR) is the apex body in agriculture and related allied fields, including research and education. The Union Minister of Agriculture is the President of the ICAR. The Indian Agricultural Statistics Research Institute develops new techniques for the design of agricultural experiments, analyses data in agriculture, and specializes in statistical techniques for animal and plant breeding. Recently Government of India has set up Farmers Commission to completely evaluate the agriculture program.. However the recommendations have had a mixed reception.

Mixed Farming

In August 2001 India's Parliament passed the Plant Variety Protection and Farmers' Rights Act, a sui generis legislation. Being a WTO member, India had to comply with TRIPS and include PVP. However, farmers' rights are of particular importance in India and thus the Act also allows for farmers to save, sow and sell seeds as they always have, even if it is of a protected variety. This not only saves the livelihoods of many farmers, it also provides an environment for the continuing development and use of landraces, says Suman Sahai. The way it always was

Problems

Slow agricultural growth is a concern for policymakers as some two-thirds of India's people depend on rural employment for a living. Current agricultural practices are neither economically nor environmentally sustainable and India's yields for many agricultural commodities are low. Poorly maintained irrigation systems and almost universal lack of good extension services are among the factors responsible. Farmers' access to markets is hampered by poor roads, rudimentary market infrastructure, and excessive regulation. —World Bank: "India Country Overview 2008".

The low productivity in India is a result of the following factors:

- According to World Bank, Indian Branch: Priorities for Agriculture and Rural Development", India's large agricultural subsidies are hampering productivity-enhancing investment. Overregulation of agriculture has increased costs, price risks and uncertainty. Government intervenes in labour, land, and credit markets. India has inadequate infrastructure and services. World Bank also says that the allocation of water is inefficient, unsustainable and inequitable. The irrigation infrastructure is deteriorating. The overuse of water is currently being covered by over pumping aquifers, but as these are falling by foot of groundwater each year, this is a limited resource.
- Illiteracy, general socio-economic backwardness, slow progress in implementing land reforms and inadequate or inefficient finance and marketing services for farm produce.
- Inconsistent government policy. Agricultural subsidies and taxes often changed without notice for short term political ends.

- The average size of land holdings is very small (less than 20,000 m^2) and is subject to fragmentation, due to land ceiling acts and in some cases, family disputes. Such small holdings are often over-manned, resulting in disguised unemployment and low productivity of labour.
- Adoption of modern agricultural practices and use of technology is inadequate, hampered by ignorance of such practices, high costs and impracticality in the case of small land holdings.
- Irrigation facilities are inadequate, as revealed by the fact that only 52.6% of the land was irrigated in 2003–04, which result in farmers still being dependent on rainfall, specifically the Monsoon season. A good monsoon results in a robust growth for the economy as a whole, while a poor monsoon leads to a sluggish growth. Farm credit is regulated by NABARD, which is the statutory apex agent for rural development in the subcontinent. At the same time overpumping made possible by subsidized electric power is leading to an alarming drop in aquifer levels.

History

Indian agriculture began by 9000 BC as a result of early cultivation of plants, and domestication of crops and animals. Settled life soon followed with implements and techniques being developed for agriculture. Double monsoons led to two harvests being reaped in one year. Indian products soon reached the world via existing trading networks and foreign crops were introduced to India. Plants and animals—considered essential to their survival by the Indians—came to be worshiped and venerated.

The middle ages saw irrigation channels reach a new level of sophistication in India and Indian crops affecting the economies of other regions of the world under Islamic patronage. Land and water management systems were developed with an aim of providing uniform growth. Despite some stagnation during the later modern era the independent Republic of India was able to develop a comprehensive agricultural program.

Agricultural Produces

Agriculture is the production, processing, marketing, and use of foods, fibers and byproducts from plant crops and animals. Agriculture was the key development that led to the rise of human civilization, with the husbandry of domesticated animals and plants (i.e. crops) creating food surpluses that enabled the development of more densely populated and stratified societies. The study of agriculture is known as agricultural science. Agriculture is also observed in certain species of ant and termite.

Agriculture encompasses a wide variety of specialties and techniques, including ways to expand the lands suitable for plant raising, by digging water-channels and other forms of irrigation. Cultivation of crops on arable land and the pastoral herding of livestock on rangeland remain at the foundation of agriculture. In the past century there has been increasing concern to identify and quantify various forms of agriculture. In the developed world the range usually extends between sustainable agriculture (e.g. permaculture or organic agriculture) and intensive farming (e.g. industrial agriculture).

Modern agronomy, plant breeding, pesticides and fertilizers, and technological improvements have sharply increased yields from cultivation, but at the same time have caused widespread ecological damage and negative human health effects. Selective breeding and modern practices in animal husbandry such as intensive pig farming (and similar practices applied to the chicken) have similarly increased the output of meat, but have raised concerns about animal cruelty and the health effects of the antibiotics, growth hormones, and other chemicals commonly used in industrial meat production.

The major agricultural products can be broadly grouped into foods, fibers, fuels, and raw materials. In the 21st century, plants have been used to grow biofuels, biopharmaceuticals, bioplastics, and pharmaceuticals. Specific foods include cereals, vegetables, fruits, and meat. Fibers include cotton, wool, hemp, silk and flax. Raw materials include lumber and bamboo. Other useful materials are produced by plants, such as resins. Biofuels include methane from biomass, ethanol, and biodiesel. Cut flowers, nursery plants, tropical fish and birds for the pet trade are some of the ornamental products.

In 2007, one third of the world's workers were employed in agriculture. The services sector has overtaken agriculture as the economic sector employing the most people worldwide. Despite the size of its workforce, agricultural production accounts for less than five percent of the gross world product (an aggregate of all gross domestic products).

Overview

Agriculture has played a key role in the development of human civilization. Until the Industrial Revolution, the vast majority of the human population labored in agriculture. Development of agricultural techniques has steadily increased agricultural productivity, and the widespread diffusion of these techniques during a time period is often called an agricultural revolution. A remarkable shift in agricultural practices has occurred over the past century in response to new technologies. In particular, the Haber-Bosch method for synthesizing ammonium nitrate made the traditional practice of recycling nutrients with crop rotation and animal manure less necessary.

Synthetic nitrogen, along with mined rock phosphate, pesticides and mechanization, have greatly increased crop yields in the early 20th century. Increased supply of grains has led to cheaper livestock as well. Further, global yield increases were experienced later in the 20th century when high-yield varieties of common staple grains such as rice, wheat, and corn (maize) were introduced as a part of the Green Revolution. The Green Revolution exported the technologies (including pesticides and synthetic nitrogen) of the developed world to the developing world. Thomas Malthus famously predicted that the Earth would not be able to support its growing population, but technologies such as the Green Revolution have allowed the world to produce a surplus of food.

Many governments have subsidized agriculture to ensure an adequate food supply. These agricultural subsidies are often linked to the production of certain commodities such as wheat, corn (maize), rice, soybeans, and milk. These subsidies, especially when instituted by developed countries have been noted as protectionist, inefficient, and environmentally damaging.

In the past century agriculture has been characterized by enhanced productivity, the use of synthetic fertilizers and pesticides, selective breeding, mechanization, water contamination, and farm subsidies. Proponents of organic farming such as Sir Albert Howard argued in the early 20th century that the overuse of pesticides and synthetic fertilizers damages the long-term fertility of the soil. While this feeling lay dormant for decades, as environmental awareness has increased in the 21st century there has been a movement towards sustainable agriculture by some farmers, consumers, and policymakers.

In recent years there has been a backlash against perceived external environmental effects of mainstream agriculture, particularly regarding water pollution, resulting in the organic movement. One of the major forces behind this movement has been the European Union, which first certified organic food in 1991 and began reform of its Common Agricultural Policy (CAP) in 2005 to phase out commodity-linked farm subsidies, also known as decoupling. The growth of organic farming has renewed research in alternative technologies such as integrated pest management and selective breeding. Recent mainstream technological developments include genetically modified food.

In late 2007, several factors pushed up the price of grains consumed by humans as well as used to feed poultry and dairy cows and other cattle, causing higher prices of wheat (up 58%), soybean (up 32%), and maize (up 11%) over the year. Food riots took place in several countries across the world. Contributing factors included drought in Australia and elsewhere, increasing demand for grain-fed animal products from the growing middle classes of countries such as China and India, diversion of foodgrain to biofuel production and trade restrictions imposed by several countries.

An epidemic of stem rust on wheat caused by race Ug99 is currently spreading across Africa and into Asia and is causing major concern. Approximately 40% of the world's agricultural land is seriously degraded. In Africa, if current trends of soil degradation continue, the continent might be able to feed just 25% of its population by 2025, according to UNU's Ghana-based Institute for Natural Resources in Africa.

History

Agricultural practices such as irrigation, crop rotation, fertilizers, and pesticides were developed long ago, but have made great strides in the past century. The history of agriculture has played a major role in human history, as agricultural progress has been a crucial factor in worldwide socio-economic change. Division of labor in agricultural societies made commonplace specializations rarely seen in hunter-gatherer cultures. So, too, are arts such as epic literature and monumental architecture, as well as codified legal systems. When farmers became capable of producing food beyond the needs of their own families, others in their society were freed to devote themselves to projects other than food acquisition. Historians and anthropologists have long argued that the development of agriculture made civilization possible.

Ancient Origins

The Fertile Crescent of Western Asia, Egypt, and India were sites of the earliest planned sowing and harvesting of plants that had previously been gathered in the wild. Independent development of agriculture occurred in northern and southern China, Africa's Sahel, New Guinea and several regions of the Americas. The eight so-called Neolithic founder crops of agriculture appear: first emmer wheat and einkorn wheat, then hulled barley, peas, lentils, bitter vetch, chick peas and flax.

By 7000 BC, small-scale agriculture reached Egypt. From at least 7000 BC the Indian subcontinent saw farming of wheat and barley, as attested by archaeological excavation at Mehrgarh in Balochistan. By 6000 BC, mid-scale farming was entrenched on the banks of the Nile. About this time, agriculture was developed independently in the Far East, with rice, rather than wheat, as the primary crop. Chinese and Indonesian farmers went on to domesticate taro and beans including mung, soy and azuki. To complement these new sources of carbohydrates, highly organized net fishing of rivers, lakes and ocean shores in these areas brought in great volumes of essential protein. Collectively, these new methods of farming and fishing inaugurated a human population boom that dwarfed all previous expansions and continues today.

By 5000 BC, the Sumerians had developed core agricultural techniques including large-scale intensive cultivation of land, monocropping, organized irrigation, and the use of a specialized labor force, particularly along the waterway now known as the Shatt al-Arab, from its Persian Gulf delta to the confluence of the Tigris and Euphrates. Domestication of wild aurochs and mouflon into cattle and sheep, respectively, ushered in the large-scale use of animals for food/fiber and as beasts of burden. The shepherd joined the farmer as an essential provider for sedentary and seminomadic societies. Maize, manioc, and arrowroot were first domesticated in the Americas as far back as 5200 BC.

The potato, tomato, pepper, squash, several varieties of bean, tobacco, and several other plants were also developed in the New World, as was extensive terracing of steep hillsides in much of Andean South America. The Greeks and Romans built on techniques pioneered by the Sumerians, but made few fundamentally new advances. Southern Greeks struggled with very poor soils, yet managed to become a dominant society for years. The Romans were noted for an emphasis on the cultivation of crops for trade.

In the Americas, a parallel agricultural revolution occurred, resulting in some of the most important crops grown today. In Mesoamerica wild teosinte was transformed through human selection into the ancestor of modern maize, more than 6000 years ago. It gradually spread across North America and was the major crop of Native Americans at the time of European exploration. Other Mesoamerican crops include hundreds of varieties of squash and beans. Cocoa was also a major crop in domesticated Mexico and Central America. The turkey, one of the most important meat birds, was probably domesticated in Mexico or the U.S. Southwest. In the Andes region of South America the major domesticated crop was potatoes, domesticated perhaps 5000 years ago. Large varieties of beans were domesticated, in South America, as well as animals, including llamas, alpacas, and guinea pigs. Coca, still a major crop, was also domesticated in the Andes.

A minor center of domestication, the indigenous people of the Eastern U.S. appear to have domesticated numerous crops.

Sunflowers, tobacco, varieties of squash and Chenopodium, as well as crops no longer grown, including marshelder and little barley were domesticated. Other wild foods may have undergone some selective cultivation, including wild rice and maple sugar. The most common varieties of strawberry were domesticated from Eastern North America.

Middle Ages

During the Middle Ages, farmers in North Africa, the Near East, and Europe began making use of agricultural technologies including irrigation systems based on hydraulic and hydrostatic principles, machines such as norias, water-raising machines, dams, and reservoirs. This combined with the invention of a three-field system of crop rotation and the moldboard plow greatly improved agricultural efficiency.

In the European medieval period, agriculture was considered part of the set of *seven mechanical arts*.

Modern Era

After 1492, a global exchange of previously local crops and livestock breeds occurred. Key crops involved in this exchange included the tomato, maize, potato, manioc, cocoa bean and tobacco going from the New World to the Old, and several varieties of wheat, spices, coffee, and sugar cane going from the Old World to the New. The most important animal exportation from the Old World to the New were those of the horse and dog (dogs were already present in the pre-Columbian Americas but not in the numbers and breeds suited to farm work). Although not usually food animals, the horse (including donkeys and ponies) and dog quickly filled essential production roles on western-hemisphere farms.

The potato became an important staple crop in northern Europe. Since being introduced by Portuguese in the 16th century, maize and manioc have replaced traditional African crops as the continent's most important staple food crops.

By the early 19th century, agricultural techniques, implements, seed stocks and cultivated plants selected and given a unique name because of its decorative or useful characteristics had so improved that yield per land unit was many times that seen in the Middle Ages. Although there is a vast and interesting history of crop cultivation before the dawn of the 20th century, there is little question that the work of Charles Darwin and Gregor Mendel created the scientific foundation for plant breeding that led to its explosive impact over the past 150 years.

With the rapid rise of mechanization in the late 19th century and the 20th century, particularly in the form of the tractor, farming tasks could be done with a speed and on a scale previously impossible. These advances have led to efficiencies enabling certain modern farms in the United States, Argentina, Israel, Germany, and a few other nations to output volumes of high-quality produce per land unit at what may be the practical limit.

The Haber-Bosch method for synthesizing ammonium nitrate represented a major breakthrough and allowed crop yields to overcome previous constraints. In the past century agriculture has been characterized by enhanced productivity, the substitution of labor for synthetic fertilizers and pesticides, water pollution, and farm subsidies. In recent years there has been a backlash against the external environmental effects of conventional agriculture, resulting in the organic movement.

The cereals rice, corn, and wheat provide 60% of human food supply. Between 1700 and 1980, "the total area of cultivated land worldwide increased 466%" and yields increased dramatically, particularly because of selectively bred high-yielding varieties, fertilizers, pesticides, irrigation, and machinery. For example, irrigation increased corn yields in eastern Colorado by 400 to 500% from 1940 to 1997.

However, concerns have been raised over the sustainability of intensive agriculture. Intensive agriculture has become associated with decreased soil quality in India and Asia, and there has been increased concern over the effects of fertilizers and pesticides on the environment, particularly as population increases and food demand expands. The monocultures typically used in intensive agriculture increase the number of pests, which are controlled through pesticides. Integrated pest management (IPM), which "has been promoted for decades and has had some notable successes" has not significantly affected the use of pesticides because policies encourage the use of pesticides and IPM is knowledge-intensive.

Although the "Green Revolution" significantly increased rice yields in Asia, yield increases have not occurred in the past 15–20 years. The genetic "yield potential" has increased for wheat, but the yield potential for rice has not increased since 1966, and the yield potential for maize has "barely increased in 35 years". It takes a decade or two for herbicide-resistant weeds to emerge, and insects become resistant to insecticides within about a decade. Crop rotation helps to prevent resistances.

Agricultural exploration expeditions, since the late 19th century, have been mounted to find new species and new agricultural practices in different areas of the world. Two early examples of expeditions include Frank N. Meyer's fruit-and nut-collecting trip to China and Japan from 1916-1918 and the Dorsett-Morse Oriental Agricultural Exploration Expedition to China, Japan, and Korea from 1929-1931 to collect soybean germplasm to support the rise in soybean agriculture in the United States.

In 2009, the agricultural output of China was the largest in the world, followed by the European Union, India and the United States, according to the International Monetary Fund. Economists measure the total factor productivity of agriculture and by this measure agriculture in the United States is roughly 2.6 times more productive than it was in 1948.

Six countries-the US, Canada, France, Australia, Argentina and Thailand-supply 90% of grain exports. The United States controls almost half of world grain exports. Water deficits, which are already spurring heavy grain imports in numerous middle-sized countries, including Algeria, Iran, Egypt, and Mexico, may soon do the same in larger countries, such as China or India.

Crop Production Systems

Cropping systems vary among farms depending on the available resources and constraints; geography and climate of the farm; government policy; economic, social and political pressures; and the philosophy and culture of the farmer. Shifting cultivation (or slash and burn) is a system in which forests are burnt, releasing nutrients to support cultivation of annual and then perennial crops for a period of several years.

Then the plot is left fallow to regrow forest, and the farmer moves to a new plot, returning after many more years (10-20). This fallow period is shortened if population density grows, requiring the input of nutrients (fertilizer or manure) and some manual pest control. Annual cultivation is the next phase of intensity in which there is no fallow period. This requires even greater nutrient and pest control inputs. Further industrialization lead to the use of monocultures, when one cultivar is planted on a large acreage. Because of the low biodiversity, nutrient use is uniform and pests tend to build up, necessitating the greater use of pesticides and fertilizers. Multiple cropping, in which several crops are grown sequentially in one year, and intercropping, when several crops are grown at the same time are other kinds of annual cropping systems known as polycultures. In tropical environments, all of these cropping systems are practiced. In subtropical and arid environments, the timing and extent of agriculture may be limited by rainfall, either not allowing multiple annual crops in a year, or requiring irrigation. In all of these environments perennial crops are grown (coffee, chocolate) and systems are practiced such as agroforestry. In temperate environments, where ecosystems were predominantly grassland or prairie, highly productive annual cropping is the dominant farming system.

The last century has seen the intensification, concentration and specialization of agriculture, relying upon new technologies of agricultural chemicals (fertilizers and pesticides), mechanization, and plant breeding (hybrids and GMO's). In the past few decades, a move towards sustainability in agriculture has also developed, integrating ideas of socio-economic justice and conservation of resources and the environment within a farming system. This has led to the development of many responses to the conventional agriculture approach, including organic agriculture, urban agriculture, community supported agriculture, ecological or biological agriculture, integrated farming and holistic management, as well as an increased trend towards agricultural diversification.

Crop Statistics

Important categories of crops include grains and pseudograins, pulses (legumes), forage, and fruits and vegetables. Specific crops are cultivated in distinct growing regions throughout the world. In millions of metric tons, based on FAO estimate.

Top Agricultural Products, by crop types (million tonnes) 2004 data

Cereals	2,263
Vegetables and melons	866
Roots and Tubers	715
Milk	619
Fruit	503
Meat	259
Oilcrops	133
Fish (2001 estimate)	130
Eggs	63
Pulses	60
Vegetable Fiber	30

Source: *Food and Agriculture Organization (FAO)*

Top agricultural products, by individual crops (million tonnes) 2004 data

Sugar Cane	1,324
Maize	721
Wheat	627
Rice	605
Potatoes	328
Sugar Beet	249
Soybean	204
Oil Palm Fruit	162
Barley	154
Tomato	120

Source: *Food and Agriculture Organization (FAO)*

Livestock Production Systems

Animals, including horses, mules, oxen, camels, llamas, alpacas, and dogs, are often used to help cultivate fields, harvest crops, wrangle other animals, and transport farm products to buyers. Animal husbandry not only refers to the breeding and raising of animals for meat or to harvest animal products (like milk, eggs, or wool) on a continual basis, but also to the breeding and care of species for work and companionship. Livestock production systems can be defined based on feed source, as grassland-based, mixed, and landless.

Grassland based livestock production relies upon plant material such as shrubland, rangeland, and pastures for feeding ruminant animals. Outside nutrient inputs may be used, however manure is returned directly to the grassland as a major nutrient source. This system is particularly important in areas where crop production is not feasible because of climate or soil, representing 30-40 million pastoralists. Mixed production systems use grassland, fodder crops and grain feed crops as feed for ruminant and monogastic (one stomach; mainly chickens and pigs) livestock. Manure is typically recycled in mixed systems as a fertilizer for crops. Approximately 68% of all agricultural land is permanent pastures used in the production of livestock.

Landless systems rely upon feed from outside the farm, representing the de-linking of crop and livestock production found more prevalently in OECD member countries. In the U.S., 70% of the grain grown is fed to animals on feedlots. Synthetic fertilizers are more heavily relied upon for crop production and manure utilization becomes a challenge as well as a source for pollution.

Production Practices

Tillage is the practice of plowing soil to prepare for planting or for nutrient incorporation or for pest control. Tillage varies in intensity from conventional to no-till. It may improve productivity by warming the soil, incorporating fertilizer and controlling weeds, but also renders soil more prone to erosion, triggers the decomposition of organic matter releasing CO_2, and reduces the abundance and diversity of soil organisms.

Pest control includes the management of weeds, insects/ mites, and diseases. Chemical (pesticides), biological (biocontrol), mechanical (tillage), and cultural practices are used. Cultural practices include crop rotation, culling, cover crops, intercropping, composting, avoidance, and resistance. Integrated pest management attempts to use all of these methods to keep pest populations below the number which would cause economic loss, and recommends pesticides as a last resort.

Nutrient management includes both the source of nutrient inputs for crop and livestock production, and the method of utilization of manure produced by livestock. Nutrient inputs can be chemical inorganic fertilizers, manure, green manure, compost and mined minerals. Crop nutrient use may also be managed using cultural techniques such as crop rotation or a fallow period. Manure is used either by holding livestock where the feed crop is growing, such as in managed intensive rotational grazing, or by spreading either dry or liquid formulations of manure on cropland or pastures.

Water management is where rainfall is insufficient or variable, which occurs to some degree in most regions of the world. Some farmers use irrigation to supplement rainfall. In other areas such as the Great Plains in the U.S. and Canada, farmers use a fallow year to conserve soil moisture to use for growing a crop in the following year. Agriculture represents 70% of freshwater use worldwide.

Processing, Distribution, and Marketing

In the United States, food costs attributed to processing, distribution, and marketing have risen while the costs attributed to farming have declined. This is related to the greater efficiency of farming, combined with the increased level of value addition (e.g. more highly processed products) provided by the supply chain. From 1960 to 1980 the farm share was around 40%, but by 1990 it had declined to 30% and by 1998, 22.2%. Market concentration has increased in the sector as well, with the top 20 food manufacturers accounting for half the food-processing value in 1995, over double that produced in 1954. As of 2000 the top six US supermarket groups had 50% of sales compared to 32% in 1992. Although the total effect of the increased market concentration is likely increased efficiency, the changes redistribute economic surplus from producers (farmers) and consumers, and may have negative implications for rural communities.

Crop Alteration and Biotechnology

Crop alteration has been practiced by humankind for thousands of years, since the beginning of civilization. Altering crops through breeding practices changes the genetic make-up of a plant to develop crops with more beneficial characteristics for humans, for example, larger fruits or seeds, drought-tolerance, or resistance to pests. Significant advances in plant breeding ensued after the work of geneticist Gregor Mendel. His work on dominant and recessive alleles gave plant breeders a better understanding of genetics and brought great insights to the techniques utilized by plant breeders. Crop breeding includes techniques such as plant selection with desirable traits, self-pollination and cross-pollination, and molecular techniques that genetically modify the organism.

Domestication of plants has, over the centuries increased yield, improved disease resistance and drought tolerance, eased harvest and improved the taste and nutritional value of crop plants. Careful selection and breeding have had enormous effects on the characteristics of crop plants. Plant selection and breeding in the 1920s and 1930s improved pasture (grasses and clover) in New Zealand. Extensive X-ray an ultraviolet induced mutagenesis efforts (i.e. primitive genetic engineering) during the 1950s produced the modern commercial varieties of grains such as wheat, corn (maize) and barley.

The green revolution popularized the use of conventional hybridization to increase yield many folds by creating "high-yielding varieties". For example, average yields of corn (maize) in the USA have increased from around 2.5 tons per hectare (t/ha) (40 bushels per acre) in 1900 to about 9.4 t/ha (150 bushels per acre) in 2001. Similarly, worldwide average wheat yields have increased from less than 1 t/ha in 1900 to more than 2.5 t/ha in 1990. South American average wheat yields are around 2 t/ha, African under 1 t/ha, Egypt and Arabia up to 3.5 to 4 t/ha with irrigation. In contrast, the average wheat yield in countries such as France is over 8 t/ha. Variations in yields are due mainly to variation in climate, genetics, and the level of intensive farming techniques (use of fertilizers, chemical pest control, growth control to avoid lodging).

Genetic Engineering

Genetically Modified Organisms (GMO) are organisms whose genetic material has been altered by genetic engineering techniques generally known as recombinant DNA technology. Genetic engineering has expanded the genes available to breeders to utilize in creating desired germlines for new crops. After mechanical tomato-harvesters were developed in the early 1960s, agricultural scientists genetically modified tomatoes to be more resistant to mechanical handling. More recently, genetic engineering is being employed in various parts of the world, to create crops with other beneficial traits.

Herbicide-tolerant GMO Crops

Roundup Ready seed has a herbicide resistant gene implanted into its genome that allows the plants to tolerate exposure to glyphosate. *Roundup* is a trade name for a glyphosate-based product, which is a systemic, nonselective herbicide used to kill weeds. *Roundup Ready* seeds allow the farmer to grow a crop that can be sprayed with glyphosate to control weeds without harming the resistant crop. Herbicide-tolerant crops are used by farmers worldwide. Today, 92% of soybean acreage in the US is planted with genetically modified herbicide-tolerant plants.

With the increasing use of herbicide-tolerant crops, comes an increase in the use of glyphosate-based herbicide sprays. In some areas glyphosate resistant weeds have developed, causing farmers to switch to other herbicides. Some studies also link widespread glyphosate usage to iron deficiencies in some crops, which is both a crop production and a nutritional quality concern, with potential economic and health implications.

Insect-resistant GMO Crops

Other GMO crops used by growers include insect-resistant crops, which have a gene from the soil bacterium *Bacillus thuringiensis* (Bt), which produces a toxin specific to insects. These crops protect plants from damage by insects; one such crop is Starlink. Another is cotton, which accounts for 63% of US cotton acreage.

Some believe that similar or better pest-resistance traits can be acquired through traditional breeding practices, and resistance to various pests can be gained through hybridization or cross-pollination with wild species. In some cases, wild species are the primary source of resistance traits; some tomato cultivars that have gained resistance to at least nineteen diseases did so through crossing with wild populations of tomatoes.

Costs and benefits of GMOs

Genetic engineers may someday develop transgenic plants which would allow for irrigation, drainage, conservation, sanitary engineering, and maintaining or increasing yields while requiring fewer fossil fuel derived inputs than conventional crops. Such developments would be particularly important in areas which are normally arid and rely upon constant irrigation, and on large scale farms. However, genetic engineering of plants has proven to be controversial. Many issues surrounding food security and environmental impacts have risen regarding GMO practices. For example, GMOs are questioned by some ecologists and economists concerned with GMO practices such as terminator seeds, which is a genetic modification that creates sterile seeds. Terminator seeds are currently under strong international opposition and face continual efforts of global bans.

Another controversial issue is the patent protection given to companies that develop new types of seed using genetic engineering. Since companies have intellectual ownership of their seeds, they have the power to dictate terms and conditions of their patented product. Currently, ten seed companies control over two-thirds of the global seed sales. Vandana Shiva argues that these companies are guilty of biopiracy by patenting life and exploiting organisms for profit Farmers using patented seed are restricted from saving seed for subsequent plantings, which forces farmers to buy new seed every year. Since seed saving is a traditional practice for many farmers in both developing and developed countries, GMO seeds legally bind farmers to change their seed saving practices to buying new seed every year.

Locally adapted seeds are an essential hertitage that has the potential to be lost with current hybridized crops and GMOs. Locally adapted seeds, also called land races or crop eco-types, are important because they have adapted over time to the specific microclimates, soils, other environmental conditions, field designs, and ethnic preference indigenous to the exact area of cultivation. Introducing GMOs and hybridized commercial seed to an area brings the risk of cross-pollination with local land races Therefore, GMOs pose a threat to the sustainability of land races and the ethnic heritage of cultures. Once seed contains transgenic material, it becomes subject to the conditions of the seed company that owns the patent of the transgenic material. There is also concern that GMOs will cross-pollinate with wild species and permanently alter native populations' genetic integrity; there are already identified populations of wild plants with transgenic genes. GMO gene flow to related weed species is a concern, as well as cross-pollination with non-transgenic crops. Since many GMO crops are harvested for their seed, such as rapeseed, seed spillage in is problematic for volunteer plants in rotated fields, as well as seed-spillage during transportation.

Modern Agriculture

Modern agriculture is a term used to describe the wide majority of production practices employed by America's farmers. The term depicts the push for innovation, stewardship and advancements continually made by growers to sustainably produce higher-quality products with a reduced environmental impact. Intensive scientific research and robust investment in modern agriculture during the past 50 years has helped farmers double food production while essentially freezing the footprint of total cultivated farmland.

Safety

The agriculture industry works with government agencies and other organizations to ensure that farmers have access to the technologies required to support modern agriculture practices. Farmers are supported by education and certification programs that ensure they apply agricultural with care and only when required.

Sustainability

Technological advancements help provide farmers with tools and resources to help reduce their environmental footprint and to make farming more sustainable.

New technologies have given rise to innovations like conservation tillage, a farming process which helps prevent land loss to erosion, water pollution and enhances carbon sequestration.

The World Bank, the Bill & Melinda Gates Foundation and others have noted that integrated crop management is based on agro-ecological principles and can increase yields while reducing environmental damage.

Affordability

Modern agriculture practices help farmers to provide an affordable supply of nutritious food to meet the demands of a growing population. With modern agriculture, more crops can be grown on less land allowing farmers to provide an increased supply of food at an affordable price.

Food Safety, Labeling and Regulation

Food security issues also coincide with food safety and food labeling concerns. Currently a global treaty, the BioSafety Protocol, regulates the trade of GMOs. The EU currently requires all GMO foods to be labeled, whereas the US does not require transparent labeling of GMO foods. Since there are still questions regarding the safety and risks associated with GMO foods, some believe the public should have the freedom to choose and know what they are eating and require all GMO products to be labeled.

The Food and Agriculture Organization of the United Nations (FAO) leads international efforts to defeat hunger and provides a neutral forum where nations meet as equals to negotiate agreements and debate food policy and the regulation of agriculture. According to Dr. Samuel Jutzi, director of FAO's animal production and health division, lobbying by "powerful" big food corporations has stopped reforms that would improve human health and the environment. The "real, true issues are not being addressed by the political process because of the influence of lobbyists, of the true powerful entities," he said, speaking at the Compassion in World Farming annual forum. For example, recent proposals for a voluntary code of conduct for the livestock industry that would have provided incentives for improving standards for health, and environmental regulations, such as the number of animals an area of land can support without long-term damage, were successfully defeated due to large food company pressure.

Environmental Impact

Agriculture imposes external costs upon society through pesticides, nutrient runoff, excessive water usage, and assorted other problems. A 2000 assessment of agriculture in the UK determined total external costs for 1996 of £2,343 million, or £208 per hectare. A 2005 analysis of these costs in the USA concluded that cropland imposes approximately $5 to 16 billion ($30 to $96 per hectare), while livestock production imposes $714 million. Both studies concluded that more should be done to internalize external costs, and neither included subsidies in their analysis, but noted that subsidies also influence the cost of agriculture to society. Both focused on purely fiscal impacts. The 2000 review included reported pesticide poisonings but did not include speculative chronic effects of pesticides, and the 2004 review relied on a 1992 estimate of the total impact of pesticides.

A key player who is credited to saving billions of lives because of his revolutionary work in developing new agricultural techniques is Norman Borlaug. His transformative work brought high-yield crop varieties to developing countries and earned him an unofficial title as the father of the Green Revolution.

Livestock Issues

A senior UN official and co-author of a UN report detailing this problem, Henning Steinfeld, said "Livestock are one of the most significant contributors to today's most serious environmental problems". Livestock production occupies 70% of all land used for agriculture, or 30% of the land surface of the planet. It is one of the largest sources of greenhouse gases, responsible for 18% of the world's greenhouse gas emissions as measured in CO_2 equivalents. By comparison, all transportation emits 13.5% of the CO_2. It produces 65% of human-related nitrous oxide (which has 296 times the global warming potential of CO_2) and 37% of all human-induced methane (which is 23 times as warming as CO_2. It also generates 64% of the ammonia, which contributes to acid rain and acidification of ecosystems. Livestock expansion is cited as a key factor driving deforestation, in the Amazon basin 70% of previously forested area is now occupied by pastures and the remainder used for feedcrops. Through deforestation and land degradation, livestock is also driving reductions in biodiversity.

Land Transformation and Degradation

Land transformation, the use of land to yield goods and services, is the most substantial way humans alter the Earth's ecosystems, and is considered the driving force in the loss of biodiversity. Estimates of the amount of land transformed by humans vary from 39–50%. Land degradation, the long-term decline in ecosystem function and productivity, is estimated to be occurring on 24% of land worldwide, with cropland overrepresented. The UN-FAO report cites land management as the driving factor behind degradation and reports that 1.5 billion people rely upon the degrading land. Degradation can be deforestation, desertification, soil erosion, mineral depletion, or chemical degradation (acidification and salinization).

Eutrophication

Eutrophication, excessive nutrients in aquatic ecosystems resulting in algal blooms and anoxia, leads to fish kills, loss of biodiversity, and renders water unfit for drinking and other industrial uses. Excessive fertilization and manure application to cropland, as well as high livestock stocking densities cause nutrient (mainly nitrogen and phosphorus) runoff and leaching from agricultural land. These nutrients are major nonpoint pollutants contributing to eutrophication of aquatic ecosystems.

Pesticides

Pesticide use has increased since 1950 to 2.5 million tons annually worldwide, yet crop loss from pests has remained relatively constant. The World Health Organization estimated in 1992 that 3 million pesticide poisonings occur annually, causing 220,000 deaths. Pesticides select for pesticide resistance in the pest population, leading to a condition termed the 'pesticide treadmill' in which pest resistance warrants the development of a new pesticide.

An alternative argument is that the way to 'save the environment' and prevent famine is by using pesticides and intensive high yield farming, a view exemplified by a quote heading the Center for Global Food Issues website: 'Growing more per acre leaves more land for nature'. However, critics argue that a trade-off between the environment and a need for food is not inevitable, and that pesticides simply replace good agronomic practices such as crop rotation.

Climate Change

Climate change has the potential to affect agriculture through changes in temperature, rainfall (timing and quantity), CO_2, solar radiation and the interaction of these elements. Agriculture can both mitigate or worsen global warming. Some of the increase in CO_2 in the atmosphere comes from the decomposition of organic matter in the soil, and much of the methane emitted into the atmosphere is caused by the decomposition of organic matter in wet soils such as rice paddies. Further, wet or anaerobic soils also lose nitrogen through denitrification, releasing the greenhouse gas nitric oxide. Changes in management can reduce the release of these greenhouse gases, and soil can further be used to sequester some of the CO_2 in the atmosphere.

International Economics and Agriculture

Differences in economic development, population density and culture mean that the farmers of the world operate under very different conditions.

A US cotton farmer may receive US$230 in government subsidies per acre planted (in 2003), while farmers in Mali and other third-world countries do without. When prices decline, the heavily subsidized US farmer is not forced to reduce his output, making it difficult for cotton prices to rebound, but his Mali counterpart may go broke in the meantime.

A livestock farmer in South Korea can calculate with a (highly subsidized) sales price of US$1300 for a calf produced.

A South American Mercosur country rancher calculates with a calf's sales price of US$120–200 (both 2008 figures). With the former, scarcity and high cost of land is compensated with public subsidies, the latter compensates absence of subsidies with economics of scale and low cost of land.

In the Peoples Republic of China, a rural household's productive asset may be one hectare of farmland. In Brazil, Paraguay and other countries where local legislature allows such purchases, international investors buy thousands of hectares of farmland or raw land at prices of a few hundred US$ per hectare.

Energy and Agriculture

Since the 1940s, agricultural productivity has increased dramatically, due largely to the increased use of energy-intensive mechanization, fertilizers and pesticides. The vast majority of this energy input comes from fossil fuel sources. Between 1950 and 1984, the Green Revolution transformed agriculture around the globe, with world grain production increasing by 250% as world population doubled. Modern agriculture's heavy reliance on petrochemicals and mechanization has raised concerns that oil shortages could increase costs and reduce agricultural output, causing food shortages.

Modern or industrialized agriculture is dependent on fossil fuels in two fundamental ways: 1) direct consumption on the farm and 2) indirect consumption to manufacture inputs used on the farm. Direct consumption includes the use of lubricants and fuels to operate farm vehicles and machinery; and use of gas, liquid propane, and electricity to power dryers, pumps, lights, heaters, and coolers. American farms directly consumed about 1.2 exajoules (1.1 quadrillion BTU) in 2002, or just over 1 percent of the nation's total energy.

Indirect consumption is mainly oil and natural gas used to manufacture fertilizers and pesticides, which accounted for 0.6 exajoules (0.6 quadrillion BTU) in 2002. The energy used to manufacture farm machinery is also a form of indirect agricultural energy consumption, but it is not included in USDA estimates of U.S. agricultural energy use. Together, direct and indirect consumption by U.S. farms accounts for about 2 percent of the nation's energy use. Direct and indirect energy consumption by U.S. farms peaked in 1979, and has gradually declined over the past 30 years.

Food systems encompass not just agricultural production, but also off-farm processing, packaging, transporting, marketing, consumption, and disposal of food and food-related items. Agriculture accounts for less than one-fifth of food system energy use in the United States.

Oil shortages could impact this food supply. Some farmers using modern organic-farming methods have reported yields as high as those available from conventional farming without the use of synthetic fertilizers and pesticides. However, the reconditioning of soil to restore nutrients lost during the use of monoculture agriculture techniques made possible by petroleum-based technology takes time.

In 2007, higher incentives for farmers to grow non-food biofuel crops combined with other factors (such as over-development of former farm lands, rising transportation costs, climate change, growing consumer demand in China and India, and population growth) to cause food shortages in Asia, the Middle East, Africa, and Mexico, as well as rising food prices around the globe. As of December 2007, 37 countries faced food crises, and 20 had imposed some sort of food-price controls. Some of these shortages resulted in food riots and even deadly stampedes.

The biggest fossil fuel input to agriculture is the use of natural gas as a hydrogen source for the Haber-Bosch fertilizer-creation process. Natural gas is used because it is the cheapest currently available source of hydrogen. When oil production becomes so scarce that natural gas is used as a partial stopgap replacement, and hydrogen use in transportation increases, natural gas will become much more expensive. If the Haber Process is unable to be commercialized using renewable energy (such as by electrolysis) or if other sources of hydrogen are not available to replace the Haber Process, in amounts sufficient to supply transportation and agricultural needs, this major source of fertilizer would either become extremely expensive or unavailable. This would either cause food shortages or dramatic rises in food prices.

Mitigation of Effects of Petroleum Shortages

One effect oil shortages could have on agriculture is a full return to organic agriculture. In light of peak-oil concerns, organic methods are more sustainable than contemporary practices because they use no petroleum-based pesticides, herbicides, or fertilizers. Some farmers using modern organic-farming methods have reported yields as high as those available from conventional farming. Organic farming may however be more labor-intensive and would require a shift of the workforce from urban to rural areas. It has been suggested that rural communities might obtain fuel from the biochar and synfuel process, which uses agricultural *waste* to provide charcoal fertilizer, some fuel *and* food, instead of the normal food vs fuel debate. As the synfuel would be used on-site, the process would be more efficient and might just provide enough fuel for a new organic-agriculture fusion.

It has been suggested that some transgenic plants may some day be developed which would allow for maintaining or increasing yields while requiring fewer fossil-fuel-derived inputs than conventional crops. The possibility of success of these programs is questioned by ecologists and economists concerned with unsustainable GMO practices such as terminator seeds, and a January 2008 report shows that GMO practices "fail to deliver environmental, social and economic benefits." While there has been some research on sustainability using GMO crops, at least one hyped and prominent multi-year attempt by Monsanto Company has been unsuccessful, though during the same period traditional breeding techniques yielded a more sustainable variety of the same crop. Additionally, a survey by the bio-tech industry of subsistence farmers in Africa to discover what GMO research would most benefit sustainable agriculture only identified non-transgenic issues as areas needing to be addressed. Nevertheless, some governments in Africa continue to view investments in new transgenic technologies as an essential component of efforts to improve sustainability.

Position of Farmers

A farmer is a person, engaged in agriculture, who raises living organisms for food or raw materials, generally including livestock husbandry and growing crops such as produce and grain. A farmer might own the farmed land or might work as a labourer on land owned by others; but in advanced economies, a farmer is usually a farm owner, while employees of the farm are farm workers, farmhands, etc.

India is an agricultural country. India lives in villages. The villagers depend on agriculture. They are either farmers or workers on the agricultural fields. Ours industries and urban business also depend on agriculture. Thus, an Indian farmer truly represents India. He can be called the son of the soil. It is on his sweet and labour that our progress and prosperity depend.

It is he who feeds and clothes the people. An Indian farmer is very hard working. He is very busy throughout the year. For him there is no rest. He is engaged in tilling the soil, sowing the seeds, watering the fields, reaping and harvesting the crop and then taking it to the market to sell it. And yet he is very poor. He is being exploited by the money-lenders, the middlemen and the government servants.

His needs are few and simple and yet they are not met. Most of the Indian farmers or tenants. Their exploitation should be stopped. They should be distributed agricultural land. They should be given cheap loans and other facilities. They should be given better seeds, fertilizers and return for their produce. The irrigation facilities should be improved.

India cannot prosper until Indian farmer is poor and miserable. He is the very soul of the country. He is as important as a soldier, a doctor or an engineer. That is why the then Prime Minister Lal Bahadur Shastri gave us the slogan: "Jai Jawan, Jai Kisan." But it should not remain only a slogan. The Indian farmer should be given his due regard and status. Every effort should be made to make him happy, rich and comfortable. His labours and sweat should not go unrewarded.

He should be taught how to read and write. Education should be taken to his door-steps so that his children do not remain illiterate. He should be provided with better medical and health facilities. He is the bread-earner of the country and should be treated accordingly. If he himself remains hungry, illcad or ignorant how India can make progress? Some schemes have been started to improve his economic and social condition. But many more such schemes need to be started.

Indian Farmers Position on WTO

The farmers of India are very much concerned with the recent developments in the WTO negotiations on agriculture. In the current negotiations to conclude the modalities on agriculture before the General Council in end July, it is becoming clearer that once again the interest of India and other developing countries and their farmers are in danger. And we fear that the Indian government, driven by its offensive interest in services, would try to push through a deal for conclusion of the Doha round even at the cost of its million of farmers and industry workers. We had witnessed this in Hong Kong where India betrayed other developing countries in joining hands with US and EU to protect services text in exchange of minor gains in agriculture.

Today it is clear that the Indian position in WTO is driven by its offensive interest in services negotiations. India has no stake in agricultural negotiations and we are quite apprehensive that any tradeoff in services negotiations can change Indian position in agriculture.

When UPA government came in power largely with the support of farmers and rural India, Indian farmers were quite hopeful that their interest would be paramount in its agenda. But last two years of UPA rule has brought misery and destitution for the rural community and never before there were such severe agrarian crisis as it is today. Every day dozens of farmers are committing suicide yet Mr. Sharad Pawar, Union Minister for Agriculture, in a live television interview (CNN-IBN-June 4) said that "100,000 farmers suicide per year is a normal thing that we have been seeing for a number of years". This is the height of government's apathy towards farmers. And ironically even the relief packages announced by this government to deal with agrarian crisis are corporate driven and only promote the interest of the US biotech industries like Monsanto and their agribusiness like Cargill and ADM. And quite obviously three giant US corporations (Monsanto, Wal-Mart and Archer Daniels Midland) along with an Indian agribusiness ITC have got formal entry in the Indian government system as board members of the "Indo-US Knowledge Initiative on Agricultural Research and Education", launched during the US President's recent visit to India.

In last two years the UPA government has done a lot to protect interest of the corporate India at the cost of the poor and marginal class. Most of the agricultural related policy introduced by the UPA government has been to further the agenda of corporate globalization. The introduction of seed bills 2004; changes in the agriculture produce marketing act (APMC Act); the food safety and standards bill; withdrawal of food subsides for the poor under BPL programme; the contract farming; liberalization of imports for seeds and planting material; increased commercialization of GM cotton and field trials for GM food crops; providing data exclusivity to MNCs in agro-chemicals; and completely liberalizing imports of food grains are some of those decisions which favours only the corporations. Recently we witnessed a classic example of anti farmer and pro corporate policy of the UPA government when it signed a deal with AWB Ltd of Australia for import of 5 lakh tonne of wheat, at the time of harvest in India and at a price much above the MSP price for procurement of wheat from farmers. Though the government refused to pay an MSP of above Rs. 7000/-per tonne to Indian farmers but it is paying Rs. 10500 per tonne to AWB, which is procuring wheat from Indian mandies at a little extra price than the MSP and supplying the same Indian wheat to the government.

In view of the above, we fear that in the ongoing negotiations on agriculture as well, the UPA government will jeopardize the interest of Indian farmers by accepting whatever scrap being offered by US and EU. And this will be done on the name of protecting the export interest of an small section of big "farmers" and corporations like ITC.

In the current negotiations on agriculture, the main issue is about deciding the formulae for tariff cuts and subsidy cuts. In view of the impact of removal of quantitative restrictions, Indian farmer stand to lose from the proposed large tariff cuts under negotiations. Any further lowing of tariff on agricultural goods would be disastrous for small and marginal farmers of the country and would lead to an epidemic of farmers' suicide. It would jeopardize our self-sufficiency in food, increase our dependency on agricultural imports and reduce the margin between applied and bound rates, thereby restricting future governments from freely changing tariffs.

In return for the increased market access, the US and EU are offering artificial reduction in their domestic support and the proposed cut will not make any change in their applied level of support. Instead it allows them to raise their overall subsidies level. This was made clear in the recent Domestic Support Simulations conducted by Canada which proved that neither the U.S. nor the E.C. will have to make reductions in their domestic support payments (as per their current proposals) and the U.S. in particular, will be able to increase overall spending in the amber and blue boxes and the de minimis. It found that under the U.S. proposal, U.S. agriculture spending could legally increase to $22.5 billion a year, from last year's estimated $19.6 billion, simply by re-categorizing existing payments.

The US trade official also claim that they are under extreme pressure from number of leading U.S. agriculture organizations who demand lowering of U.S. ambitions on domestic support. That means there can't be any further increase in the current US offer for reduction in domestic support. Moreover, the US is not ready to concede an effective protection for the developing countries through SPs and allows only five tariff lines (against a demand of 20% by the G20) to be self designated as SPs (US framework paper on SP of 6th April 2006) which is less than 1% of India's total tariff line (680) in agriculture. Even on Special Safeguard Mechanism (SSM), US intentions are not very clear and it is trying to limit the scope of this safeguard to an extent that recourse to such mechanism becomes useless (US proposal of 24th April 2006).

In fact all the so-called gains from the Hong Kong Declaration are proving to be illusionary. Even though SP and SSM are not effective safeguard mechanisms to deal with cheap subsidized imports, but these are the only safeguard available to the developing nations given the proposed deepest cut in import tariff. But US and EU does not want to offer even these minimal safeguard to the developing countries to protect their farmers from cheap subsidized imports. Therefore there going to be a complete disaster for the farmers and agriculture of the developing countries if this present offers on the table goes through.

It is now clear how tough it is to get so little from the developed countries on any issues which is of the interest of the developing countries and LDCs in the agricultural negotiations. We therefore reassert our demand that agriculture must be kept out of the perview of the WTO.

Several recent studies have also indicated the same and predicted loses for developing countries including India from the Doha Development Round, in the agriculture as well as industrial sectors. Contrary to commonly held view, research from the World Bank, the Carnegie Endowment and the European Commission reveal that the majority in Asia and Africa will be faced with losses in both agriculture and industrial goods liberalisation. Even EU's own impact assessment of the Doha Round foresee that many of the world's developing economies will lose out from the Round, including parts of South Asia and much of Sub-Saharan Africa.

10

Rural Recreation

Recreation is any activity performed during one's leisure or free time. Recreational activities are often done for amusement, enjoyment or pleasure and are considered to be 'fun'. Almost any activity can be considered recreational when engaged in during one's free time.

Rural tourism focuses on participating in a rural lifestyle. It can be a variant of ecotourism. Any village can be a tourist attraction, and many villagers are very hospitable. Agriculture is becoming highly mechanized and therefore requires less manual labor. This is causing economic pressure on some villages, leading to an exodus of young people to urban areas.

Benefits

Rural tourism allows the creation of an alternative source of income in the non-agricultural sector for rural dwellers. The added income from rural tourism can contribute to the revival of lost folk art and handicrafts. It is an ideal and natural method of rural and urban economic exchange.

Relevance in Developing Nations

Rural tourism is particularly relevant in developing nations wherein farmland has become fragmented due to population growth.

Relevance in Developed Nations

Rural tourism exists in developed nations in the form of providing accommodation in a scenic location ideal for rest and relaxation.

United States: Niche Tourism in Rural Areas

Many niche tourism programs are located in rural areas. From wine tours and eco-tourism, to agritourism and seasonal events, tourism can be a viable economic component in rural community development. According the USDA, Cooperative State, Education and Extension Service, "Tourism is becoming increasingly important to the U.S. economy. A conservative estimate from the Federal Reserve Board in Kansas, based on 2000 data, shows that basic travel and tourism industries accounted for 3.6 percent of all U.S. employment. Even more telling, data from the Travel Industry Association of America indicate that 1 out of every 18 people in the U.S. has a job directly resulting from travel expenditures."

The publication *Promoting Tourism in Rural America* explains the need for planning and marketing rural community and to weigh the pros and cons of the impacts of tourism. Local citizen participation is helpful and should be included in starting any kind of a tourism program. Being prepared by planning tourism can assist in a successful program that enhances the community.

Folk Art

Folk art encompasses art produced from an indigenous culture or by peasants or other laboring tradespeople. In contrast to fine art, folk art is primarily utilitarian and decorative rather than purely aesthetic.

As a phenomenon that can chronicle a move towards civilization yet rapidly diminish with modernity, industrialization, or outside influence, the nature of folk art is specific to its particular culture. The varied geographical and temporal prevalence and diversity of folk art make it difficult to describe as a whole, though some patterns have been demonstrated.

Antique Folk Art

Antique folk art is distinguished from traditional art in that while it is collected today based mostly on its artistic merit; it was never intended as a category to be art for art's sake. Examples include: weathervanes, old store signs and carved figures, itinerant portraits, carousel horses, fire buckets, painted game boards, cast iron doorstops and many other similar lines of highly collectible "whimsical" antiques.

Characteristics

Characteristically folk art is not influenced by movements in academic or fine art circles, and, in many cases, folk art excludes works executed by professional artists and sold as "high art" or "fine art" to the society's art patrons. On the other hand, many 18th and 19th century American folk art painters made their living by their work, including itinerant portrait painters, some of whom produced large bodies of work.

Other terms that overlap with folk art are naïve art, Arts Primitive, Pop art, outsider art, traditional art, Tribal art, "self-taught" art and even "working class" art. As one might expect, all these terms have different connotations; but they are all at times used interchangeably with the term folk art, for which a satisfactory definition has proven hard to come by.

Folk art expresses cultural identity by conveying shared community values and aesthetics. It encompasses a range of utilitarian and decorative media, including cloth, wood, paper, clay, metal and more. If traditional materials are inaccessible, new materials are often substituted, resulting in contemporary expressions of traditional folk art forms. Folk art reflects traditional art forms of diverse community groups — ethnic, tribal, religious, occupational, geographical, age-or gender-based — who identify with each other and society at large. Folk artists traditionally learn skills and techniques through apprenticeships in informal community settings, though they may also be formally educated.

Rural Areas Benefit From Recreation and Tourism Development

Beautiful scenery—lakes, mountains, forests—attracts people to rural resort areas in the United States. Rural recreation areas have grown rapidly in recent years, and recreation and tourism development has become a popular vehicle for rural economic development. Recreation development involves more than just tourist-related businesses, such as hotels and restaurants; it encompasses all economic growth that results from people moving into the community to take advantage of its recreational amenities. This kind of development has the potential to dramatically transform a stagnant rural community into a thriving community by attracting retirees, entrepreneurs, and young workers, diversifying the economy, and improving the quality of life with a broader array of goods and services.

But recreation development comes with potential problems. Some problems are growth-related—such as congested roads, crowded schools, environmental strains, housing shortages, despoiled scenic views, and conflicts over land use and public policies. Other problems are specific to the tourism industry's workers (unskilled or foreign), many of whom earn relatively little and have few fringe benefits. And another downside: Criminals may be particularly attracted to some recreation areas.

Is recreation and tourism development a viable economic option for rural areas? ERS examined some key questions about the socioeconomic effects of rural recreation development. The answers are generally favorable, with improved employment conditions, earnings, and incomes; lower poverty rates; and healthier and better educated populations. However, conditions vary by type of recreation area, and higher housing costs and crime rates can accompany the more favorable outcomes.

More Work, Higher Earnings

Definitions and Methodology

The word "recreation" is used in this article to refer to the leisure activities of tourists as well as seasonal and permanent residents. However, when discussing recreation's estimated impact on various socioeconomic indicators, the term 'recreation development' usually refers to the extent to which a county depends on recreation development for employment, income, and housing.

ERS used the 2002 version of its *recreation county typology* developed by Ken Johnson and Calvin Beale to analyze rural recreation areas nationwide. The number of recreation counties studied was 311, including 11 types varying by geographic location, natural amenities, and form of recreation.

ERS examined selected indicators of socioeconomic well-being in rural recreation areas nationwide, using county-level data from the 2000 Census and other Federal data sources. First, socioeconomic conditions and trends in rural recreation counties were compared with those in other nonmetro counties (excluding metro areas). Socioeconomic conditions and trends were also compared across various types of rural recreation counties. Next, multiple regression analysis was conducted to estimate the impact of recreation-dependency on socioeconomic conditions and trends in the 311 rural recreation counties.

Because of rapid employment growth in rural recreation areas and a potentially broader array of jobs, including more seasonal and part-time positions that appeal to residents unable to work full-time, year-round jobs, employment options would likely be enhanced by recreation development. However, it may not be easier for residents to find jobs due to competition with other workers who have recently moved to the area.

ERS researchers found that recreation development, measured by the extent to which a county's employment, income, and housing depend on recreation and tourism, is linked to a higher percentage of the working-age population having jobs. This percentage-employed measure encompasses discouraged workers who had dropped out of the labor force, making it a more comprehensive and meaningful measure of employment conditions. Moreover, recreation development led to an increase in this employment measure during the 1990s for all age groups, except the population ages 65 and older.

Jobs that are usually associated with recreation development, such as those in hotels and restaurants, are assumed to be low paying with few fringe benefits. Some related service jobs, such as those in retail businesses, may also pay low wages. However, low-wage workers in recreation areas may have access to more opportunities to work part-time and seasonal jobs to supplement their incomes, and some service and construction jobs associated with recreation development pay quite well. Recreation development appears to have increased the growth in earnings per job during the 1990s. But average earnings per job in 2000 were not significantly higher in rural recreation areas. To better measure what residents earn from employment, ERS looked at total earnings per resident worker, which includes earnings from second jobs (part-time and seasonal). Second jobs are expected to be more readily available in recreation counties than elsewhere. Total earnings per resident were substantially higher ($2,000 more per worker) in recreation counties than in other rural counties. Contrary to conventional wisdom, recreation development seems to have increased residents' earnings.

Cost of Living Higher, Better Education and Health

Anecdotal evidence suggests that housing costs have risen rapidly in some of the most well-known recreation areas, becoming so high that many workers can no longer afford to live in the area, sometimes requiring long commutes. In addition, higher housing costs may prevent the children and grandchildren of some long-term residents from finding housing in their home towns. While this may be true in some recreation areas, it is not known how widespread this higher cost of living is. However, median rent for housing (an important component in cost of living) in recreation counties is 23 percent higher than in other nonmetropolitan (nonmetro) counties, reducing some of the economic advantages for recreation county residents, but only partially. Median household incomes are $3,185 higher in recreation counties than in other counties, while median annual rent is only $1,080 higher in recreation counties. This implies that the higher rent offsets about a third of the recreation county income advantage.

Recreational development might attract migrants who tend to have higher levels of education than nonmigrants. As expected, ERS research found that recreational development leads to a more educated population, particularly when education is measured by the share of adults with college degrees.

Recreation development is also associated with good health (measured by age-adjusted death rates), as might be expected from the higher number of physicians (per 100,000 residents) in recreation counties than in other rural counties. The availability of physicians, however, was not responsible for the good health of residents. Other factors, such as greater opportunities for physical exercise, may explain the health advantages associated with recreation development. In addition, the pristine environments of many recreation counties, with clean air and water, might lead to better overall health.

More Crime, Other Social Problems

When recreation development is unplanned or occurs too rapidly, it can lead to congested roads and can strain the capacity of public services. Recreation areas have significantly higher rates of population growth than other rural areas, suggesting that some growth-related social problems, such as school crowding, housing shortages, pollution, and loss of identification with the community, may be present. ERS researchers examined road congestion by looking at commute times and found that recreation development was not linked to the commute time to work in 2000. If anything, recreation development appears to have helped keep down commute times in recent years because recreation counties had smaller increases in average commute times during the 1990s than other rural counties.

Recreation development can also result in higher poverty rates if significant numbers of low-wage, low-skilled workers arrive to work in tourist-related service establishments. However, ERS research indicates that recreation development results in significantly lower levels of poverty in rural recreation areas. In addition, recreation and tourism development appears to have contributed to declines in local poverty rates during the 1990s.

Another possible disadvantage is higher crime rates: Criminals may be drawn to recreation communities to prey on tourists, or certain types of recreation, such as casino gambling, could attract illicit activity. Crime rates (for serious crimes) are higher in recreation counties than in other rural counties. However, the way crime rates are calculated may be biased inherently against recreation areas. Crimes against tourists and seasonal residents are counted in the crime statistics, but tourists and seasonal residents are not counted as part of the population base upon which the crime rates are calculated. Thus, even if people in recreation areas do not have a higher chance of becoming victims of crimes, the crime rates for these areas will appear higher than elsewhere because of this bias. Nevertheless, one could still argue that recreation-related crime adds to the local cost of policing and incarcerating criminals, just like recreation-related traffic adds to the cost of maintaining roads.

Conditions Vary From Place to Place

The benefits of recreation development for rural areas appear to be generally positive. This finding, along with the finding that socioeconomic effects vary significantly from one place to another, will inform policymakers seeking to achieve meaningful development through this strategy.

Agri-tourism: Innovative Income Generating Activity for Enterprising Farmers

Agriculture is backbone of Indian Economy. 85 percent of the population is directly or indirectly dependent on Agriculture where as 26 percent of GDP comes from Agriculture. 110 million farmers are dwelling in 6.25 lakh villages producing more than 200 MT of food grains feeding the country. More than profession, business, agriculture is culture. Hence, adding additional income generating activities to existing Agriculture would certainly increase contribution of Agriculture to national GDP. Serious efforts need to be made in this direction. Agri-Tourism is one such activity.

Tourism is termed as instrument for employment generation, poverty alleviation and sustainable human development. During 1999-2000, direct employment created by tourism is 15.5 millions. Besides, tourism also promotes national integration, international understanding and supports local handicrafts and cultural activities. During 2000, number of foreign tourists visited India is 26.41 lakhs. India's share in world tour market is just 0.38 percent. With this meager share, foreign exchange earned is Rs.14,475 crores. Turnover in domestic tourism is much more than this. To promote domestic tourism, thrust areas identified by Government of India are development of infrastructure, product development and diversification, development of eco-adventure sports, cultural presentations, providing inexpensive accommodation, streamlining facilitation procedures at airports, human resource development, creating awareness and public participation and facilitation of private sector participation. In this process, important stakeholders are state and central department of tourism, Indian Institute of Tourism and Travel Management, Tourism Development Corporations, foreign embassies, Travel Agents Association of India (TAAI), Indian Association of Tour Operators (IATO), Tourists, Transport Operators Association, Indian convention promotion bureau and Pacific Asia Travel Association (PATA).

Promotion of Agri-tourism involves some more important stakeholders namely Ministry of Agriculture and line departments at state and central governments and farmers. Promotion of Agri-Tourism needs conceptual convergence with Rural Tourism, Eco-Tourism, Health Tourism, Adventure Tourism and culinary adventures. Greatest advantage of Agri-Tourism are:

1). It brings major primary sector Agriculture closer to major service sector tourism. This convergence is expected to create win-win situation for both the sectors.

2). Tourism sector has potential to enlarge.

3). Agriculture sector has the capacity to absorb expansion in Tourism Sector.

Scope for Agri-Tourism:-Agri-Tourism has great scope in the present context for the following reasons.

(1). An inexpensive gateway:-The cost of food, accommodation, recreation and travel is minimum in Agri-Tourism. This widens the tourist base. Present concept of travel and tourism is limited to urban and rich class which constitute only small portion of the population. However, the concept of Agri-tourism takes travel and tourism to the larger population, widening the scope of tourism due to its cost effectiveness.

(2). Curiosity about the farming industry and life style:-The urban population basically which has roots in villages always has curiosity about sources of food, plants, animals, raw materials like wood, handicrafts, languages, culture, tradition, dresses and lifestyle. Agri-tourism which revolves around the farmers, villages and agriculture has the capacity to satisfy the curiosity of this segment of population. Agri-tourism provides scope for re-discoursing the rural life which is rich in diversity.

(3). Strong demand for wholesome family oriented recreational activities villages provide recreational opportunities to all age groups i.e. children young, middle and old age, male, female, in total to the whole family at cheaper cost. Rural games, festivals, food, dress and the nature provides variety of entertainment to the whole family.

(4). Health consciousness of urban population and finding solace with nature friendly means Modern lifestyle has made the life stressful and average life span has comedown. Hence, people are in constant search of pro-nature means to make life more peaceful. Ayerveda which is pro-nature medical approach has roots in villages. Indigenous medical knowledge of villagers is respected. Organic foods are in greater demand in urban areas and foreign countries. In total, health conscious urban population is looking towards pro-nature villages for solutions.

(5). Desire for peace and tranquility:-Modern life is the product of diversified thinking and diversified activities. Every individual attempts to work more, in different directions to earn more money to enjoy modern comforts. Hence, peace is always out of his system. Tourism is the means for searching peaceful location. Peace and tranquility are inbuilt in Agri-tourism as it is away from urban areas and close to nature.

(6). Interest in natural environment-Busy urban population is leaning towards nature. Because, natural environment is always away from busy life. Birds, animals, crops, mountains, water bodies, villages provide totally different atmosphere to urban population in which they can forget their busy urban life.

(7). Disillusionment with over crowded resorts and cities- In resorts and cities, over crowded peace seekers disturb each others peace. Hence, peace is beyond cities and resorts. Even though efforts are made to create village atmosphere in the sub urban areas through resorts, farm houses, it looks like a donkey painted with tiger colour. Artificiality is highlighted and not satisfying.

(8). Nostalgia for their roots on the farm Cities are growing at the cost of villages. Villagers are migrating to cities in search of jobs and seeking comforts of modern life. Hence, yesterdays villagers are todays urbanites. Deep in the heart of urbanites lies the love and respect for their ancestors and villages. Hence, visit to villages satisfies their desire. This is also expressed through the hatredness of urbanites to flat culture and love for farmhouses located in the outskirts of cities. Any opportunity to visit villages and spend time with family is dream of any urbanite. But, minimum decent facilities are always problem. Agri-tourism attempts to overcome this problem.

(9). Rural recreation -Villages provide varieties of recreation to urbanites through festivals and handicrafts. Villagers (farmers) lifestyle, dress, languages, culture/traditions which always add value to the entertainment. Agriculture environment around farmers and the entire production process could create curiosity among urban taught. Places of agriculture importance like highest crop yielding farm, highest animal yielding farm, processing units, farms where innovations tried add attraction to the tourists. Agriculture products like farm gate fresh market, processed foods, organic food could lure the urban tourists. As result of this Agri-atmosphere in the villages, there is scope to develop Agri-tourism products like Agri-shopping, culinary tourism, pick and own your tree/plot, bed and breakfast, pick and pay, bullock cart riding, camel riding, boating, fishing, herbal walk, rural games and health (Ayurvedic) tourism.

(10). Educational value of Agri-Tourism:-Agri-tourism could create awareness about rural life and knowledge about agriculture science among urban school childrens. It provides a best alternative for school picnics which are urban based. It provides opportunity for hands on experience for urban college students in Agriculture. It is a means for providing training to future farmers. It would be effectively used as educational and training tool to train agriculture and line department officers. This provides unique opportunity for education through recreation where learning is fun effective and easy. Seeing is believing, doing is learning and most importantly experiences are USP of Agri-tourism.

Basic principles of Agri-Tourism : Agri-tourism should ensure the following three basic principles.

1. Have something for visitors to see:-Animals, birds, farms and nature are the few things which Agri-tourism could offer to the tourist to see. Apart from these, culture, dress, festivals and rural games could create enough interest among forest in Agri-tourism.
2. Have something for visitors to do:-Participating in agricultural operations and swimming, bullock cart riding, camel riding, buffalo riding, cooking and participating in the rural games are the few activities to quote in which tourist can take part and enjoy.
3. Have something for visitors to buy:-Rural crafts, dress materials, farm gate fresh agriculture products, processed foods are the few items which tourist can buy as memento for remembrance.

Three important factors which contribute to the success of Agri-Tourism

1. Farmer: Majority of the cases, farmer is less educated, less exposed and innocent. For farmer, any outsider is a guest and treated wholeheartedly without any commercial motive. Treating guest is pleasure for them than pain. He entertains the guest while entertaining himself in the process. He is not like an exploitative natured businessman which itself facilitate a clean tourism atmosphere
2. Village : Village, which is located far from the city lacks urban facilities, but blessed with natural resources. The investment is made by nature in the form of water

bodies, fields, forest, mountains, deserts and islands. Community is more homogenous and treating a guest is part of their culture rather than a profession leading to natural environment required for urban tourist.

3. Agriculture : Rich resources in agriculture namely land, water and plants are unique from place to place bringing diversity and creating curiosity. Each field is unique which adds to the attraction of tourists. The way of cultivation and the products are great attraction to the urban population. Indigenous knowledge of rural people is a wealth, which adds to novelty and curiosity of urban population.

Combination of farmer, village and agriculture create a wonderful situation which provides unlimited satisfaction to the tourist specially from urban areas.

Bibliography

Ali, Asghar : *Mandal Commission Controversy*, Delhi, Ajanta Publications, 1991.

Allen, John C. and Dillman, Don : *Against All Odds: Rural Community in the Information Age*, Boulder: Westview Press, 1994.

Benjamin, Joseph: *Scheduled Castes in Indian Politics and Society*, New Delhi, Ess Ess Publications, 1989.

Botkin, Daniel, Harmonies, B. Discordant : *A New Ecology for the 21st Century*, Oxford and New York: Oxford University Press.

Chauhan, M.S. and K.L. Dangi : *Handbook of Rural Sociology*, Agrotech, Delhi, 2010.

Coppack, P. M.: *Entrepreneurial and Sustainable Rural Communities*, Mt. Allison University Press 1990.

Damon, William : *Social and Personality Development, Infancy through Adolescence,* New York: Norton, 1983.

Diwan, Jagmohan : *Fundamentals of Rural Sociology*, Cyber Tech Pub, Delhi, 2009.

Doshi, S.L. & Jain, P.C. : *Rural Sociology*, Rawat, Delhi, 1999.

Durkheim, Emile: *The Division of Labor in Society*, New York: Free Press, 1964 .

Gies, Frances : *Women in the Middle Ages*. New Jersey: Barnes and Noble, 1978.

Gorhe, Neelam: *Social Development and Dalit Women*, Gyan Pub. House, New Delhi, 1995.

Gurukal, Rajan: *The Formation of Caste Society in Kerala*, Rawat Publications, New Delhi, 1994.

Helen E. Longino : *Feminism and Science*, Oxford and New York, Oxford University Press, 1996.

Jayapalan, N. : *Rural Sociology*, Atlantic Pub, Delhi, 2002.

Jeff Hass: *Economic Sociology: An Introduction*, Manohar, Delhi, 2008.

John, D. Kasarda: *Contemporary Urban Ecology*, New York: Macmillan, 1977.

Khan, Masood Ali : *Cultural Sociology of India*, Arise Pub, Delhi, 2006.

King, Margaret L.: *Women of the Renaissance*. Chicago: University of Chicago Press, 1991.

Kukreja, Sunil : *Case Studies in Political Sociology*, Serials Pub, Delhi, 2006.

Kumar, Arvind : *Fundamentals of Rural Sociology*, Cyber Tech Pub, Delhi, 2009.

Louis, Prakash : *The Political Sociology of Dalit Assertion*, Gyan, Delhi, 2003.

MacDonald, S.: *Evolutionary Perspectives on Human Development,* Thousand Oaks, CA: Sage Publications, 2004.

Pandey, R K : *Urban Sociology : Planning, Administration and Management*, Sarup and Sons, Delhi, 2006.

Ramesh, G S : *Philosophy of Indian Sociology*, Global Vision, Delhi, 2005.

Reddy, L. Venkateswara, Narayana, M. Lakshmi : *Methods of Teaching Rural Sociology*, Discovery, Delhi, 2004.

Ruhela, S.P. : *Research Tools in Sociology of Education*, Indian, Delhi, 2001.

Satyamurthy, T.V.: *Region, Religion, Caste, Gender and Culture in Contemporary India*, Delhi, OUP, 1996.

Silverberg, James: *Social Mobility in the Caste System in India*, Mouton Publishers, The Hague, 1968.

Singh, Balveer : *Medical Sociology of Tribal Community*, Himanshu, Delhi, 1992.

Singh, Yogendra : *Ideology and Theory in Indian Sociology*, Rawat, Delhi, 2004.

Young, Jora : *The Ecology of Hope*, New Haven: New Society Publishers, 1997.

Index